The Law and Parliament

Edited by

Dawn Oliver
Professor of Constitutional Law, University of London

and

Gavin Drewry
Professor of Public Administration and Director of the Centre for Political
Studies, Royal Holloway College, University of London

for the Study of Parliament Group

Butterworths
London, Edinburgh, Dublin
1998

United Kingdom	Butterworths, a Division of Reed Elsevier (UK) Ltd, Halsbury House, 35 Chancery Lane, LONDON WC2A 1EL and 4 Hill Street, EDINBURGH EH2 3JZ
Australia	Butterworths, a Division of Reed International Books Australia Pty Ltd, CHATSWOOD, New South Wales
Canada	Butterworths Canada Ltd, MARKHAM, Ontario
Hong Kong	Butterworths Asia (Hong Kong), HONG KONG
India	Butterworths India, NEW DELHI
Ireland	Butterworth (Ireland) Ltd, DUBLIN
Malaysia	Malayan Law Journal Sdn Bhd, KUALA LUMPUR
New Zealand	Butterworths of New Zealand Ltd, WELLINGTON
Singapore	Butterworths Asia, SINGAPORE
South Africa	Butterworths Publishers (Pty) Ltd, DURBAN
USA	Lexis Law Publishing, CHARLOTTESVILLE, Virginia

A CIP Catalogue record for this book is available from the British Library.

ISBN 0 406 98092 6

Typeset by Doyle & Co, Colchester
Printed and bound in Great Britain by William Clowes Limited, Beccles and London

Visit us at our website: http://www.butterworths.co.uk

Contributors

Dr Nicholas Baldwin is Director of Wroxton College of Fairleigh Dickinson University near Banbury in Oxfordshire, and is also lecturer and tutor in British Government at the College.

Professor Robert Blackburn is Professor of Constitutional Law at King's College London.

Professor Gavin Drewry is Professor of Public Administration in the Department of Social and Political Science and Director of the Centre for Political Studies at Royal Holloway College, University of London.

Dr Philip Giddings is a Senior Lecturer in the Department of Politics at the University of Reading.

Patricia Leopold is a Senior Lecturer in the Department of Law at the University of Reading.

Geoffrey Lock was Head of Research in the House of Commons Library from 1977 to 1991.

Dr Geoffrey Marshall is Provost of the Queen's College Oxford, author of several works in the field of British Constitutional Law and Politics.

John McEldowney is a Reader in Law at the University of Warwick.

Professor Dawn Oliver is Professor of Constitutional Law at the University of London.

Professor Michael Rush is Professor of Politics in the Department of Politics at the University of Exeter.

Barry Winetrobe is a Senior Research Clerk in the Home Affairs Section of the Research Service of the House of Commons Library.

Preface

The Study of Parliament Group was founded in 1964 as a forum in which parliamentary scholars and officers of the two Houses of Parliament could meet to discuss, under Chatham House Rules of confidentiality, issues of mutual interest to do with the working and reform of Parliament. It includes among its current elected membership academics – mainly political scientists and public lawyers – and clerks, library officials and other officers of the House of Lords and the House of Commons. Over the years its members have, under the auspices of the Group, produced many major books[1] and articles on the workings of Parliament and its academic members have also regularly given evidence to major select committee inquiries into parliamentary procedure and related matters.

The Group's preferred mode of working has been through specialised study groups, typically consisting of about a dozen members, drawn from both the academic and the official sides, with a particular shared interest in the subject concerned. This book is the product of a study group on Law and Parliament, which was established in 1995. The study group met regularly over a two-and-a-half year period to discuss aspects of the project, often with fascinating contributions from outside speakers. We would like to thank the busy people who took the trouble to come to talk to us, and the Nuffield Foundation, whose award of a small grant supported our travel and other incidental expenses. In its later stages, the study group benefited from some shared activities and membership with another, more recently established, study group on parliamentary standards and conduct, convened by Professor Michael Lee. In the summer of 1997, the contributors participated in a one-day workshop, held in the Faculty of Laws at University College London, to discuss the early drafts of chapters.

The academic membership of the study group was a mixture of political scientists and lawyers, reinforced by one present and one former member of the House of

---

1 Recent examples include: Gavin Drewry (ed) *The New Select Committees: A Study of the 1979 Reforms* (2nd edn, 1989) Clarendon Press; Charles Carstairs and Richard Ware (eds) *Parliament and International Relations* (1991) Open University Press; Mark Franklin and Philip Norton (eds) *Parliamentary Questions* (1993) Clarendon Press; Donald Shell and David Beamish *The House of Lords at Work* (1993) Clarendon Press; Philip Giddings (ed) *Parliamentary Accountability: A Study of Parliament and Executive Agencies* (1995) Macmillan; Philip Giddings and Gavin Drewry (eds) *Westminster and Europe: The Impact of the European Union on the Westminster Parliament* (1996) Macmillan.

Commons Library (the scholarship of whose staff is more than a match for that of many academics). These different academic perspectives, and the complementarity of 'insider' and 'outsider' perspectives, worked strongly to the study group's benefit, and has, we believe, also enhanced the breadth and the balance of this book. Many of the issues discussed – devolution, the incorporation of the European Convention on Human Rights, wider issues of accountability, the decision to change the law to allow MPs to waive privilege in defamation actions – are of equal interest to political scientists and public lawyers, and to parliamentarians. We hope that our readers, probably coming from a similarly broad range of backgrounds, will find them as fascinating as we have done.

At the time of completing this book the Human Rights Bill was completing its passage through Parliament. It was not clear whether it would receive the royal assent. We decided to assume that it would be an Act by or shortly after publication and have referred to it as an Act throughout, using section numbers as at 3 July 1998.

Finally, we should explain one omission from this book. It will be noticed that it contains only occasional references to, and no separate chapter on, the European Union. This is not because of any Eurosceptical bias on the part of the editors or the contributors but because another study group has recently produced a book on *Westminster and Europe* – about to be revised – which we commend to our readers.

Gavin Drewry
Dawn Oliver
July 1998

Contents

Table of statutes

List of cases

Chapter I

The law and Parliament

Dawn Oliver and Gavin Drewry

Introduction

Each of the chapters in this collection considers various ways in which the law impacts on the Parliament of the United Kingdom. This is a subject that has many aspects, and one that is fraught with complications and pitfalls, not least because an important part of Parliament's role is as a legislature – a law-making body. This means that Parliament operates in a complex legal environment, to which the exercise of its own legislative function contributes. Moreover, it has other functions that are of a judicial character, most obviously seen in the role of the Appellate Committee of the House of Lords and in the powers of the two Houses to enforce their privileges. A number of preliminary points should be made to set the subject in context.

The Westminster Parliament was brought about as a result of the union of the Parliaments of Scotland and England and Wales under the Acts and Treaty of Union between England and Scotland of 1707 and the Union with Ireland Act 1800. Until recently, the constitution of the United Kingdom has been regarded as unitary,[1] a somewhat imprecise term used by political scientists in contradistinction to 'federal' – though in practice, both federal and unitary systems come in many shapes and forms, and the demarcation line between them is far from clear cut. In the United Kingdom context, usage of the term focuses on the centralisation of power in the United Kingdom Parliament and in government in Whitehall. However, it is probably more accurate in the light of recent and continuing changes in sub-national government to think of the United Kingdom as a union than as a unitary state.[2] This will be increasingly a more appropriate way of looking at it as the plans for the decentralisation of power to Scotland,[3] Wales,[4] London,[5] English regions[6] and to Northern Ireland, take effect and the centralisation of power in the Westminster Parliament and the

1 See eg A W Bradley and K D Ewing *Constitutional and Administrative Law* (12th edn, 1997) at p 45.
2 See S Rokkan and D Urwin *Economy, Territory, Identity. Politics of West European Peripheries* (1982); *Strategies for Self-Government: The Campaigns for a Scottish Parliament* (1996).
3 See Scotland Bill, House of Commons, 1997; and the White Paper *Scotland's Parliament*, 1997 (Cm 3658); and see ch XII below.
4 See Government of Wales Bill, House of Commons, 1997; and the White Paper *A Voice for Wales*, 1997 (Cm 3718).
5 See White Paper *New Leadership for London*, 1997 (Cm 3724).
6 See Constitution Unit *Regional Government in England* (1996).

Whitehall government is consequently reduced, probably asymmetrically, in favour of other centres in the Kingdom.

The plans for decentralisation will involve devolving extensive legislative power to a new Scottish Parliament,[7] retaining only specified powers at Westminster (as was the arrangement with the Northern Ireland Parliament under the Government of Ireland Act 1920). While the Scotland Act cannot prevent the Westminster Parliament from legislating for Scotland in the future in areas devolved to the Scottish Parliament, the political reality is likely to be that such power will not be exercised. Much more limited powers, to make subordinate legislation, will be devolved to the Welsh Assembly. The Westminster Parliament – the 'sovereign' law-making institution in the United Kingdom – will therefore be profoundly affected by these changes. The moves towards decentralisation, and the likelihood that political control of the sub-national bodies will be in the hands of different parties from those constituting the national government in London, will inevitably lead from time to time to boundary disputes between Westminster and the devolved bodies, which will in turn – unless political relationships break down completely – lead to the evolution of compacts and understanding between the tiers as to the proper use of legislative powers at each level.

It is worth noting, too, that there are to this day three different legal systems in the United Kingdom, those of England and Wales, of Scotland and of Northern Ireland. Each of the three jurisdictions has its own civil law (contract, tort and property law), criminal law and family law, and special Acts are passed for England and Wales, and Scotland on these matters. Since the prorogation of the Northern Ireland Parliament in 1972, and its abolition in 1973, legislation for Northern Ireland has been enacted by Order in Council.[8] The court systems (and the legal professions) of England and Wales, Scotland and Northern Ireland are also distinct from one another – but the House of Lords, the most obvious surviving vestige of the historic High Court of Parliament, is the final court of appeal for all three jurisdictions[9] and thus exercises a limited unifying function.

Constitutional territory

One theme that draws together the chapters in this volume is that of constitutional territory, both in a functional sense and a spatial and geographical sense. So far as functional territory is concerned, the story is of two institutional branches of government, performing complementary functions, but independent of one another, facing one another across a constitutional divide, and each jealously guarding its boundaries against unwarranted intrusion by the other. Thus, Parliament is precluded from criticising individual judges, other than on a formal motion for their removal from office; the sub judice rule limits parliamentary discussion of current or pending cases in the courts. For their part, the courts must defer to the legislative sovereignty of Parliament – as explained below. This bears some resemblances to the US

---

7   See ch XII below.
8   Northern Ireland Act 1974, Sch 1, para 1.
9   Though appeals from Scotland in criminal matters cannot be taken to the House of Lords.

constitutional doctrines of separation of powers and checks and balances, though not of course, in the United Kingdom, specified in a written constitution. Some of the authors of chapters in this volume have positioned their chapters on one side of the divide, others on the opposite side; all of us have tried to identify the many bridges that cross the chasm.

The significance of the geographical sense of territorial subdivision has already been noted in our introductory remarks about relations between the nations and regions of the United Kingdom and the existence of three legal systems. The history of the United Kingdom Parliament – the product of successive unions – carries into the present different theories about parliamentary power. Before the union between the Parliaments of Scotland and England, a quality of limited power inhered in the Scottish Parliament.[10] By contrast, the English Parliament had acquired unlimited sovereignty from the Crown in 1688 as a result of the Glorious Revolution of that year: the English Parliament could pass legislation on any matter, regardless of whether it was contrary to international obligations, morality, or reason.[11] The courts in the three jurisdictions and the Appellate Committee of the House of Lords, the highest United Kingdom court, have adopted the view that the United Kingdom Parliament has not inherited the Scottish doctrine of limited power, but possesses legislative supremacy: 'What Parliament enacts is the highest form of law'.[12] This doctrine is not, however, universally accepted in Scotland.[13]

The supreme law-making power exercised by the sovereign Parliament of the United Kingdom ostensibly relegates the courts to a passive, even submissive, role in applying and interpreting legislation. Recently, however, a number of extra-judicial observations have raised the possibility that the courts could refuse to give effect to a statutory provision that was in some respects profoundly undemocratic. For instance, Sir John Laws[14] and Lord Woolf of Barnes[15] have both made this point. There are also academic arguments in favour of such a position.[16] However, Lord Irvine of Lairg (when he was Shadow Lord Chancellor) has rejected this possibility.[17] So this particular boundary between the respective territories of courts and Parliament, and the claim that the courts may have to depart from the strict doctrine of parliamentary sovereignty in the face of perceived threats to fundamental democratic principles, are the subjects of continuing debate.[18]

10 See J Mitchell *Strategies for Self-Government: The Campaigns for a Scottish Parliament* (1996) and *Constitutional Law* (2nd edn, 1968) ch 5 and pp 92-98. But cf *McCormick v Lord Advocate* 1953 SC 396. Lord President Cooper observed (at 412) that he found in the Union legislation no provision that the Parliament of Great Britain should be 'absolutely sovereign' in the sense that the Parliament should be free to alter the treaty at will.

11 *Cheney v Conn* [1968] 1 All ER 779 at 782. This view of the law was at that time of relatively recent development. See *R v Hampden, Ship Money Case* (1637) 3 State Tr 826. See generally A W Bradley 'The sovereignty of Parliament – In perpetuity?' in J L Jowell and D Oliver (eds) *The Changing Constitution* (3rd edn, 1994).

12 *Cheney v Conn* [1968] 1 All ER 779.

13 *McCormick v Lord Advocate* 1953 SC 396.

14 Sir John Laws 'Law and Democracy' [1995] PL 72.

15 Lord Woolf 'Droit Public – English Style' [1995] PL 57.

16 See eg T R S Allen *Law, Liberty and Justice* (1993) p 282.

17 See Lord Irvine of Lairg QC 'Judges and Decision-Makers: The Theory and Practice of *Wednesbury* Review' [1996] PL 59.

18 See also A W Bradley 'The sovereignty of Parliament – In Perpetuity?' in J L Jowell and D Oliver (eds) *The Changing Constitution* (3rd edn, 1994).

were to pursue this position, they would undoubtedly bring themselves ~~not~~ only with the Executive – which is not unusual – but also with men... ~~the~~ two Houses of Parliament. The Human Rights Act 1998[19] represents a recent and firm decision by the Executive, which has been endorsed by Parliament, that the courts should *not* have power to strike down or disapply primary legislation which they find to be incompatible with the provisions of the European Convention on Human Rights. But they will have power to make a declaration of incompatibility. The Lord Chancellor has explained this approach as follows:

> This innovative technique will provide the right balance between the judiciary and Parliament. Parliament is the democratically elected representative of the people and must remain sovereign. The judiciary will be able to exercise to the full the power to scrutinise legislation rigorously against the fundamental freedoms guaranteed by the Convention but without becoming politicised. The ultimate decision to amend legislation to bring it into line with the Convention, however, will rest with Parliament. The ultimate responsibility for compliance with the Convention must be Parliament's alone.[20]

The view is sometimes taken that the sovereignty of Parliament also means that the courts should not go behind the legislative texts before them and concern themselves with the procedures and processes of Parliament. From this the argument may be put that it would be a denial of sovereignty if legislation were to purport to bind the two Houses to follow particular procedures, such as two-thirds majorities in each House, if they wished to amend legislation.

The question whether what is at issue here is really sovereignty deserves to be explored. It is indeed currently the position that the courts will not inquire into parliamentary procedure with a view to determining whether an Act was properly passed in the two Houses. According to *Edinburgh and Dalkeith Railway v Wauchope*,[1] all that a court can do is to look at the Parliament roll. If from that it appears that an Act was duly passed, the courts will not intervene. This rule was applied in the more recent case of *British Railways Board v Pickin*,[2] in which the House of Lords held (reversing the decision of the Court of Appeal) that the courts could not consider allegations that the British Railways Board had fraudulently concealed certain material facts from Parliament in order to secure the enactment of a section of the British Railways Act 1968. This is an aspect of the common law of parliamentary privilege which holds that the Houses are solely responsible for their own proceedings. It is reinforced by art 9 of the Bill of Rights 1688, which provides that the freedom of speech and debates and proceedings in Parliament are not to be impeached or questioned in any court or place outside of Parliament.[3]

It does not follow from this, however, that for Parliament to be bound to follow a certain procedure before amending legislation, and for the courts to have jurisdiction to hold Parliament to that procedure, would be a denial of its sovereignty. In the Privy

---

19 See ch XI below.
20 Lord Irvine of Lairg, Lord Chancellor in 'The Development of Human Rights in Britain under an Incorporated Convention on Human Rights' [1998] PL 221 at 225-226.
 1 (1842) 8 Cl & Fin 710 at 723, HL.
 2 [1974] AC 765, HL.
 3 See further ch IV below.

Council case of *Bribery Comrs of Ceylon v Ranasinghe*[4] Lord Pearce was of the view that a Parliament is no less sovereign if it is compelled to follow certain procedures in making legislation. This would seem to make sense, as most legislatures of sovereign states are bound by their written constitutions to follow prescribed procedures before amending their constitutions or passing legislation that conflicts with provisions of the constitution. It would be surprising if the position in English law was that only Parliaments that are free to legislate on any subject matter by simple majority of those voting are truly sovereign, and all others, including the legislatures of, for instance, the United States of America, France and India are not. Unless, of course, the concept of sovereignty is to be given a very rigid and narrow definition.

The implication of this line of argument is that it would be possible for the United Kingdom Parliament to legislate to change the common law rules of parliamentary privilege and to amend art 9 of the Bill of Rights so as to give the courts jurisdiction to inquire into the procedure followed in Parliament in the course of producing an Act, and to strike down an Act if the prescribed procedure had not been followed. Clearly, if this were done it would raise the possibility of conflict between the courts and Parliament and it is no doubt partly because such conflicts are seen to pose threats both to the authority and independence of the judiciary and to the authority and reputation of Parliament that no such legislation has ever been seriously suggested.

The legislative omnicompetence of the United Kingdom Parliament has been affected substantially by the United Kingdom's membership of the European Community – yet another example of the pervasiveness of territorial considerations in the subject of the law and Parliament. By s 2 of the European Communities Act 1972, which came into effect in January 1973:

> All . . . rights, powers, liabilities, obligations and restrictions from time to time created or arising by or under the Treaties, and all such remedies and procedures from time to time provided for by or under the Treaties, as in accordance with the Treaties are without further enactment to be given legal effect . . . shall be recognised and available in law, and be enforced . . . and the expression 'enforceable Community rights' and similar expressions shall be read as referring to one to which this section applies.

In other words, the courts in the United Kingdom must give effect to European law.

In the early days of the Community, before the United Kingdom became a member, the European Court of Justice developed the doctrine of primacy of European law over the law of member states.[5] In the eyes of the Community – now the Union – and its courts even the laws of the constitutions of the member states must yield to provisions of European law.[6] The courts of the United Kingdom accepted the ruling of the European Court of Justice in Luxembourg in the *Factortame* case[7] that an Act of the United Kingdom Parliament that is incompatible with the legal obligations contained in the European Treaties should be disapplied. Hence, the legislative

---

4   [1965] AC 172, PC.
5   See eg *Costa v ENEL* Case 6/64 [1964] ECR 585.
6   *Internationale Handelsgesellschaft mbH v Einfuhr und Vorratstelle fur Getreide und Futtermittel* Case 11/70 [1970] ECR 1125.
7   *R v Secretary of State for Transport, ex p Factortame (No 2)* [1991] 1 AC 603, HL. See also *R v Secretary of State for Employment, ex p Equal Opportunities Commission* [1995] 1 AC 1, HL.

supremacy of the United Kingdom Parliament is now subject to an important exception, where European Community law issues arise.

Alongside the law of the European Community (and in some contexts interacting with it) is the human rights agenda of the Council of Europe, embodied in the European Convention on Human Rights, of which Britain was an original signatory and which it played an important part in drafting. The Human Rights Act 1998 incorporates parts of the European Convention of Human Rights into United Kingdom law. But in doing so it maintains the sovereignty of the United Kingdom Parliament. It provides that '. . . if the court is satisfied that the provision [in primary legislation] is incompatible with one or more of the Convention rights, it may make a declaration of that incompatibility'. So the United Kingdom courts will not be able to disapply or strike down provisions in Acts of Parliament. They will be able only to declare the position. At this point, however, it is worth noting that a form of variable territorial geometry is evolving in the United Kingdom. The Scottish Parliament and the Welsh Assembly will be vulnerable to having their measures struck down as invalid on the ground of incompatibility with the Human Rights Act, while the United Kingdom Parliament will be immune from such challenges to its Acts.

The variable geometry of our legal system is also illustrated by the fact that, where a point of European law arises, our courts and tribunals are obliged by art F(2) of the Treaty on European Union to take account of the provisions of the European Convention on Human Rights,[8] and this might lead a court to disapply a United Kingdom measure, whereas where no point of European law arises, the convention obligations as incorporated in the Human Rights Act yield to provisions in United Kingdom statutes and, often, statutory instruments.[9]

The comments above highlight the fact that the United Kingdom consists of and relates to a number of constitutional territories (or in legal parlance, jurisdictions), both beyond our boundaries (ie in the European Community) and within the country. But this collection of essays is also about another kind of constitutional territory, based on concepts such as the separation of powers, judicial independence, and parliamentary privilege.

Winetrobe[10] discusses the separation of powers issues related to the lack of autonomy of the two Houses of Parliament from the government, noting the ways in which ministers can take advantage of parliamentary privilege and other facilities deriving from the fact that they are members of one or other House for their own, rather than Parliament's advantage. In effect, there is no separation of powers here, and Parliament is prevented from acting autonomously from government in many of the fields in which, according to our theory of ministerial responsibility to Parliament, it ought to be independent. The fusion extends even to matters of domestic and administrative management in the House of Commons. This fusing of the two institutions extends into many areas which are not generally appreciated – matters relating to parliamentary papers, for instance. But on matters of the regulation of standards of conduct, the House of Commons has been concerned to protect itself

---

8   See eg *Maurissen and the European Public Service Union v Court of Auditors*: C-193, 194/87 [1990] ECR I-95; *R v Human Fertilisation and Embryology Authority, ex p Blood* [1997] 2 All ER 687, CA.
9   Section 3.
10   See ch II below.

against interventions either by government or by the courts, as their handling of the allegations of sleaze in the 1990s shows.[11]

Although in many ways the respective roles of Parliament and the courts are complementary (eg Parliament legislates and the courts interpret and apply Parliament's legislation), there is a frontier between the two which is jealously guarded. Some quotations seem apposite here. Prime Minister James (now Lord) Callaghan once told the House of Commons that:

> We should beware of trying to embroil the judiciary in our affairs, with corresponding caveat that the judiciary should be very careful about embroiling itself in the legislature.[12]

In 1986 the Justice Committee on The Administration of the Courts considered the objections that might be raised to extending the powers of the Parliamentary Commissioner for Administration (PCA) to include investigations of judicial behaviour, a change favoured by some members of the committee. One objection, it said, 'is that, as the Ombudsman reports to the House of Commons, this would *encourage MPs to pry into the affairs of the judiciary*'. But this objection was then rejected on the grounds that the PCA is an independent officer who 'would only investigate a complaint if he was satisfied that it was serious', and, the report continued, 'if a serious complaint is made, it would seem better that it should be investigated by an independent person of the standing of the Ombudsman *than for it to become the subject of ill-informed speculation in Parliament*'.[13] (So much for parliamentary accountability for the administration of justice – the subject of our own chapter in this collection, though the PCA has since acquired the power to examine alleged maladministration by court officials.)

Matters like the sub judice[14] rules, Parliament's exclusive jurisdiction with regard to its own privileges,[15] the understanding that the Law Lords should steer clear of party political controversy – though this does not prevent them from contributing on legal points during the passage of Bills that have controversial aspects[16] – and the bar on parliamentary criticism of judges other than on a motion for removal, are also pertinent here. But the established stand-off between the courts and Parliament is being eroded, both by Parliament, as with the amendment by the Defamation Act 1996 of the Bill of Rights 1688, which enables a member of Parliament to waive privilege in defamation actions[17] and by the courts in their willingness to consult Hansard for guidance in statutory interpretation.[18]

The subject 'the law and Parliament' embraces both the law relating to the legislative capacity of Parliament – broadly, issues to do with the sovereignty of Parliament which have been noted above – and Parliament's own law about its own operations, often referred to as 'the law and custom of Parliament',[19] enshrined in the

11 See chs II and VII below.
12 HC Deb, 15 December 1977, col 909.
13 JUSTICE *The Administration of the Courts* (1986) para 4.6 (our emphasis). See ch III below.
14 See chs IV and V below.
15 See ch IV below.
16 See ch X below.
17 See ch V below.
18 See ch IX below.
19 See ch IV below.

cumbrous and cumbrously titled volume, *Erskine May's Treatise on The Law, Privileges, Proceedings and Usage of Parliament*, the twenty-second edition of which was published while this book was nearing completion.[20]

As *Erskine May* puts it:

> The 'law of Parliament' includes those aspects of Parliamentary activity that depend for their effectiveness on recognition by the courts, and such law – although it may be unwritten – is changed only by way of statute. But most parliamentary procedure and usage derives from the admitted right of each House to regulate its own proceedings, a right which led a former clerk of the Commons to observe, 'What does it signify about precedents? The House can do what it likes. Who can stop it?' [per John Ley, Clerk 1820-1850][1]

Parliamentary law thus includes the standing orders of the two Houses, which set out the nuts and bolts of legislative process, including the requirement that each Bill should be 'read' three times in each House and that the two Houses should agree on the terms of the Bill before royal assent is given. (The Parliament Acts provide for a Bill to receive the royal assent without the consent of the Lords in limited circumstances.[2]) It should be borne in mind, however, that the standing orders of the two Houses do not provide an exhaustive statement of the procedures of Parliament and many matters are governed by practice and previous decisions of the two Houses. For instance, nothing is said in the standing orders about decisions being taken by simple majority of those present and voting. It does not need to be; it is part of the customary law of Parliament, and everyone involved knows by inherited memory that it is so. The custodians of parliamentary law include officers of the two Houses, notably the Clerks, and much of the function of providing legal advice to Parliament is connected with issues arising from this body of law.[3]

Given that the procedures followed in the two Houses are not generally justiciable in the courts (see above), can the rules that regulate procedure be said to be law at all? This raises difficult issues about the nature of law which there is not the space to explore here. The traditional but not very convincing answer is that the two Houses of Parliament are, or were historically, courts of record and in this respect are in the same position as the ordinary courts, having the right to regulate their own procedure, if necessary resorting to coercion to enforce their own rules.[4] Contempt of court is undoubtedly part of the law of England and contempt of Parliament may also be said to be part of that law. However (apart from the appellate functions of the House of Lords), it is no longer the case that the two Houses act as courts save in exceptional circumstances – private Bill procedure resembles judicial procedure – and it would be more realistic to recognise that the 'law' of Parliament is in practice a set of rules that are treated as binding in the two Houses and are enforced by them with the acquiescence of the courts, and that to this extent they may be treated as laws.

In addition to the law and custom of Parliament, which is not normally justiciable in the courts, there is a whole body of parliamentary law which is within the

---

20 Erskine May *Parliamentary Practice* (22nd edn, 1997).
 1 Ibid, p 3.
 2 See Parliament Acts 1911 and 1949; *Erskine May*, pp 569-570.
 3 See ch VI below.
 4 See ch IV below.

jurisdiction of the courts – or may be within their jurisdiction.[5] The *Stockdale v Hansard* saga of the late 1830s illustrates the potential for conflict between parliamentary law and the law enforced in the courts. *Pepper v Hart* is another example.[6] Further, there are delicate questions about the applicability of ordinary law – ordinary statutes, European Union law, for instance – to Parliament.[7]

It is not universally recognised that Parliament's sovereignty would be undermined by a recognition that the two houses might be subject to law enforced by the courts. Examples are to be found in Winetrobe's and Lock's chapters[8] in this volume: arguments have been put to the effect that the two Houses should be entirely self-regulating on matters of conduct, and are rightfully to be exempted from duties to comply with health and safety and employment legislation on the grounds that for Parliament to be bound by such rules would represent a denial of its sovereignty.[9] The parallel being drawn here is with a different notion of sovereignty, closer to sovereign immunity than to sovereignty as such.[10] In the United Kingdom the sovereign in person and her diplomatic representatives abroad enjoy sovereign immunity but not legislative supremacy – the two do not necessarily go hand in hand.

Leopold[11] examines another set of boundaries, those between Parliament and the courts, with reference to the extent of civil and criminal liability of members of Parliament. This raises issues of the extent of application of art 9 of the Bill of Rights 1689, which prohibits the impeaching or calling in question of freedom of speech or debates or proceedings in Parliament in any court or place outside Parliament. It is often not obvious whether acts have taken place in or outside Parliament or whether reliance on something said or done in Parliament amounts to a challenge to the freedom of speech or debates or proceedings in Parliament. Criminal liability for bribery of MPs has been a particular problem in recent years.[12]

The subject 'the law and Parliament' embraces the role of lawyers *in* Parliament, and Parliament's own access to legal advice and information. Since legislation passed by – or in the case of statutory instruments, through – Parliament is supposed to be a central protection against poor and despotic government, what legal advice is available to the two Houses when performing their legislative functions? And what advice do they have on the legal aspects of their domestic affairs – their dealings with their own staff, with the media, security arrangements, copyright, and so on? In practice, although there is a large number of lawyers among the body of MPs and peers themselves,[13] the availability of such advice is limited.[14] The issue of legal advice to Parliament raises interesting separation of powers, constitutional territory issues – for instance concerning the role of the Attorney General in advising

---

5   See ch IV below.
6   [1993] AC 593. See ch IX below.
7   See chs IV and VI below.
8   Chapters II and IV below.
9   It is worth noting that it is not intended that the Scottish Parliament or the Welsh Assembly should enjoy such immunities.
10 See ch II below.
11 Chapter V below.
12 See chs V and VII below.
13 See ch X below.
14 See ch VI below.

Parliament and the government, possibly at the same time, as in *Pepper v Hart*,[15] and of the Treasury Solicitor in advising the House of Commons during the 1997 dissolution.[16] These examples – and more could be given – illustrate the pervasiveness of territorial problems in Parliament's relationship with the law.

Lawyer-MPs have been influential throughout the history of the House of Commons and lawyers have – partly by virtue of the House's appellate function – also played a key role in the Lords. Indeed the Lords' possession of a particularly strong body of legal expertise – crucial to its role as a revising chamber – is sometimes invoked in resistance to arguments for its reform or abolition. The Labour Government of Prime Minister Blair – himself a barrister, though in common with practically all busy lawyer-politicians these days, not a practising one – seems to be dominated by them. They tend to have above average membership of standing committees and select committees, for instance, and in the Lords they participate more than non-lawyers.[17] Their contributions often reflect their legal interests. Hence, lawyers and the discipline of law colonise – to pursue the territorial metaphor – much of the activity of Parliament.

Accountability

A second theme (the first is Constitutional territory) in this volume is accountability. This term is often confused or conflated with responsibility.[18] Generally, accountability involves the idea that a person or body should give an account or explanation and justification for its acts and should put things right, if it is in its power to do so, when mistakes have been made. But accountability does not entail that the person giving the account necessarily had it as part of his or her job to perform the acts of which an account is being given, nor does it involve the idea that the person giving the account is to blame if something has gone wrong. Responsibility, by contrast, does involve the idea that a body has a job to do and must take the blame if the job is not well done. In the context of British government, accountability does not necessarily mean that the responsible person must explain how the job is being done – indeed, civil servants are prevented from giving explanations to Parliament except on behalf of their minister; nor does it entail that the responsible person is under an obligation to put matters right – he or she may often not be in a position to do so; again, civil servants are cases in point.[19]

For present purposes, the concepts of accountability and responsibility are relevant because they involve the idea that Parliament and its committees can and should hold ministers and others who spend public money to account for their policies and general conduct of public affairs, and that the House of Commons collectively, and individual members, are accountable and responsible for their own conduct.[20] Particular problems over accountability of and to Parliament and its members arise under the topic of the

15   [1993] AC 593. See chs VI and IX below.
16   See ch VI below.
17   See figures given by M Rush and N Baldwin, in ch X below.
18   On this see P Giddings (ed) *Parliamentary Accountability: A Study of Parliament and Executive Agencies* (1995).
19   See D Oliver and G Drewry *Public Service Reforms. Issues of Accountability and Public Law* (1996) ch 1.
20   See ch VII below.

law and Parliament. First, there is an ingrained fear that the integrity and independence of the courts might be compromised if they were accountable to Parliament. There has been a process of accommodation between the House of Commons, the Lord Chancellor's Department and the courts in the last 15 years or so which has increased the accountability to Parliament of the courts, without posing any credible threat to judicial independence.[1] Secondly, there is a strongly held view that the most appropriate way in which the rights of citizens can be protected is via the accountability and responsibility of ministers to Parliament, coupled with a fear of the implications of increased judicial involvement in setting and policing standards of good administration. Professor Fred Ridley observed, in 1984, that –

> the idea of 'political' rather than 'legal' protection of citizens against administration is deeply embedded in British political traditions and has imprinted itself on British ways of thought.[2]

This contrasts, he pointed out, with the much stronger administrative law traditions that are found throughout the rest of Western Europe.

However, over the last 30 years or so, political responsibility for the relations between citizens and the state has been complemented by increasing forms of legal or legally regulated accountability. The jurisdiction of the courts in judicial review has developed quite dramatically in this period (though that is not a subject for this volume, being concerned with the relations between the courts and the Executive rather than the relationship between the courts and Parliament). But the development of judicial review has meant that there are other channels through which citizens may be able to obtain redress of their grievances, and to some extent this may have lessened the importance of Parliament's role in holding ministers to account. On the other hand, judicial review suffers from the disadvantage that it is expensive, complicated and slow, so quick, cheap, effective methods continue to be attractive.[3]

A third concern has been with standards of conduct in Parliament itself.[4] Here, the accountability issue is that members of the House of Commons are supposed to be primarily accountable to their constituents, to their parliamentary party, and to the public interest generally. If MPs accept payments from or enter pecuniary relationships with outside bodies, the position is likely to be that they create an accountability and responsibility relationship with those outside bodies that will subvert their duties and accountability to their constituents, parties and the public interest. The 'Nolan' reforms to the House of Commons, including the adoption of a code of conduct that sets out the duties and accountability criteria for MPs, are designed to protect these traditional lines of accountability – and to restore the reputation of Parliament as a whole in the country.

One sub-theme within accountability is the changing relationship between traditional parliamentary accountability and other devices – including ombudsmen (grafted onto

---

1   See chs III, IV, V and VII below.
2   'British approaches to the redress of grievances' (1984) 37 Parliamentary Affairs 1 at 3. See ch VIII below on this point.
3   See ch VIII below.
4   See ch VII below.

the traditional parliamentary system),[5] which might be seen as part of this trend to displace ministerial accountability to Parliament as the principal means for the redress of grievances, as we move towards a minimalist contract state in which more and more public functions are hived off and contracted out. It is possible to read into developments such as these an implicit recognition that Parliament is not capable of protecting citizens adequately against the administration.

With the enactment of the Human Rights Act, the United Kingdom is about to move towards greater legal, rather than political, protection of the citizen against the state.[6] Public bodies, especially ministers and their departments, will be increasingly accountable to the courts for their acts which impinge on fundamental rights and freedoms recognised in the Act. The principal differences between accountability to the courts (legal accountability) and accountability to Parliament (political accountability) are that the criteria for legal accountability are defined by law rather than by the feeling of the House at the time; that judgments about conduct and decisions made in court follow an open hearing at which evidence is called and tested by cross-examination, whereas in Parliament no such procedure may be available; and judges seek to make their decisions on the basis of the evidence as they evaluate it and the legal argument, and they give reasoned decisions, whereas in Parliament, 'judgment' is the outcome of ministerial writhing at the dispatch box or in a select committee. The opinion formed by Parliament is not necessarily based in evidence and reason, it is the upshot of the reactions of a collection of political individuals, it is likely to be – and entitled to be – influenced by considerations of political expediency, and it is not reasoned.

The passage of the Human Rights Act is bound to result in a much more rights-based legal and political culture than we have had hitherto. Although, as we have seen, the Act preserves the legislative sovereignty or supremacy of the United Kingdom Parliament, the passage of the Act will no doubt affect the nature of the grievance-chasing functions of MPs and of the Parliamentary Commissioner for Administration.[7] Aggrieved citizens may be able to bring many of their grievances within the provisions of the Act and the convention which it incorporates into United Kingdom law rather than, for instance, expecting their MP or the minister to deal with it on an informal basis. The Act requires, for instance, by art 8 of the convention which it incorporates, that public bodies respect a person's private and family life, home and correspondence. Article 6 requires that citizens have a fair and public hearing by an independent and impartial tribunal in the determination of their civil rights (a point here is whether civil rights include rights in public law – it is suggested that they do), and requires a fair trial for those charged with criminal offences. Article 14 forbids irrational discrimination in the enjoyment of the rights under the convention. These are all rights that are commonly interfered with by public bodies, especially the police – though often such interferences will be justified by the exceptions in favour of acts that are necessary in the public interest which the convention sets out. Article 8 (privacy), for instance, permits of such exceptions. But it seems likely that complaints of breaches of these provisions will join complaints of other forms of maladministration in the surgeries and postbags of MPs and the caseloads of the PCA. Thus, the

5   See ch VIII below.
6   See ch XI below.
7   See ch VIII below.

accountability of government and other public bodies will be extended and measured against the new standards and criteria set out in the Human Rights Act, and their accountability will be to Parliament, to the PCA and, increasingly, to the courts.

Then there are the issues of: (a) how far and by what means the administration of justice and the operation of the courts themselves – increasingly seen in new public management terms – should be subject to parliamentary accountability;[8] and (b) how far and by what means the activities of parliamentarians should be subject to independent scrutiny, especially where standards of conduct are in issue.[9] It is coming to be increasingly recognised that accountees, as much as accountants, need to be accountable in our system. In effect, we are developing a network of accountability systems, each designed in its own way to secure that parliamentary, governmental and judicial activities are open, accounted for, subject to scrutiny and remediable when things go wrong. The reliance on accountability mechanisms is typical of the liberal assumptions underlying our constitutional arrangements, which do not assume that any particular body or person is infallible and strive to keep open the channels for protecting the public against the fallibility of those in power.

To draw the threads together, then, the questions that this volume will seek to explore are the nature and extent of the constitutional territories – spatial and conceptual – that both link and divide Parliament and the law; how they impact on its effectiveness; and how appropriate and how effective the mechanisms of public accountability involving Parliament really are. One lesson, above others, emerges clearly from this exercise. Although the essays in this volume confirm that the metaphor of constitutional territoriality is highly apposite, they also make clear that the boundaries between the law and Parliament are far more permeable than might at first sight be supposed; that, necessarily, Parliament and the courts must, while separate, work in harmony through a mixture of overt co-operation and through more subtle processes of interaction by way of mutually supportive osmosis.

---

8   See ch III below.
9   See ch VII below.

Chapter II

The autonomy of Parliament

Barry K Winetrobe

Autonomy: constitutional, legal, political and practical

Any discussion of the role and function of Parliament, as with any political/
constitutional topic, is made complex by the intricate web of contexts involved, from
the 'high ground' of constitutional theory to the everyday world of politics. A country
with no written constitution relies to a very large degree on the operation of a mixture
of principles, doctrines and conventions to flesh out such 'constitutional law' as exists
in statute and case law. The closer one approaches the apex of the British political
system, the more strict law tends to give way to 'non-legal' forms. Much exists almost
despite express law (Parliament, the Crown, the Cabinet and Prime Minister, for
example), the law simply recognising their existence and regulating certain aspects
of their operation. Even those governmental areas created in their modern form by
strict law, especially statute – such as the judiciary or local government – owe much
of their mode and style of operation to pre-existing custom and practice. Thus, the
reality of the British constitution can be even further at variance with its theoretical
'constitutional' position than is the case in a state with a written constitution. A
description of the constitution in terms of the Crown, in the personal rather than the
political sense, would not accord with modern circumstances. It would be simple, but
not entirely inaccurate, to describe the development of British constitutional history
as a transfer of executive power from the personal Sovereign to the political,
ministerial government, with Parliament in a permanently[1] subservient position to
the Executive, fighting to maintain some form of control over it.

As Parliament does not itself govern, its modern role seems to be to balance the two
functions of an 'executive legislature', processing and passing the legislation desired
by government, and a democratic counterweight to the potentially absolute power of
the Executive.[2] These two functions have opposite impacts on the relationship of
Parliament to the Executive. As a legislature, it is obviously convenient (though not,
in theory, essential) for the Executive to be represented within Parliament to ensure
the smooth and successful passage of its business. On the other hand, when
Parliament is seeking to 'hold the government to account' and to scrutinise its

1 Other than perhaps crucial, revolutionary periods as in the seventeenth century.
2 Much prerogative power is still largely outwith parliamentary and, until very recently, judicial
control. See *R v Criminal Injuries Compensation Board, ex p Lain* [1967] 2 QB 864; *Council of Civil
Service Unions v Minister for the Civil Service* [1985] AC 374, HL.

activities, propriety and practicality would seem to require the maximum degree of separation between the supervisor and the supervised. This potential and actual contradiction is at the heart of Parliament's dilemma as to its proper role and function, and how it can give effect to it. Can Parliament maintain, and be seen to maintain, a proper degree of autonomy while operating within a 'Westminster model' of governmental membership in, and practical control of, Parliament? Bagehot described the Cabinet as a committee of the legislature.[3] Perhaps it would be more accurate nowadays, in some respects, to describe Parliament as a committee of the government.

Because of Parliament's historical battle with the Crown (in the shape of the monarch or of ministers) of whatever complexion, it has evolved over time a thick constitutional layer of protection. This is a mixture of, for example, statute, such as the Bill of Rights; a legal jurisdiction, deriving in part from its status as the 'high court of Parliament',[4] and political levers such as the concept of 'confidence'[5] and formal financial powers. Some of this protection is aimed, not directly at the Executive, but at the judiciary, although in reality the beneficiary of much of this protection may not be Parliament as such but the Executive itself.

If one wishes to give this issue a conventional constitutional term, it would be 'separation of powers', a notion of some degree of separation or otherwise between the three main organs of government, and a degree of autonomy for each. As with many constitutional concepts, its use may serve to conceal or confuse as much as it reveals or explains. There is a common danger in a UK-type situation in seeking to derive continuity and causation where little or none may exist.[6] Nevertheless, at the risk of perpetuating existing constitutional myths, it can be useful to apply a 'separation of powers' analysis to the position of Parliament in the political system for two reasons. First, so much of the existing discussion – academic, political and, especially, judicial – tends to adopt this approach, for whatever reason. Secondly, a 'separation of powers' approach does provide a convenient analytical framework within which to consider the pivotal and multi-layered constitutional position of Parliament.

Separation of powers in the United Kingdom constitution

The doctrine of the separation of powers is one of those central concepts of the present United Kingdom constitution, which, like the rule of law and the sovereignty of Parliament, is always quoted as some form of constitutional incantation.[7] How far do those politicians, academics and others who chant this mantra seriously consider the content and meaning of the concept of the 'separation of powers'? Do they

---

3   W Bagehot *The English Constitution* (1993) p 70.
4   See chs IV and V.
5   See J Seaton and B Winetrobe 'Confidence motions in the UK Parliament' (1995) 64 Table 34.
6   The theory and practice of individual ministerial responsibility is a classic example of this.
7   See eg the Lord Chancellor, Lord Irvine of Lairg, in his keynote address to a conference at University College London on 4 July 1997 on a UK Bill of Rights, and the incorporation of the European Convention on Human Rights: 'The British Constitution is firmly based on the separation of powers. It is essential that incorporation is achieved in a way which does nothing to disturb that balance. It is for Parliament to pass laws, not the judges' (transcript, p 4).

recognise the distinction between a system, such as that in the United States, where the concept is deliberately incorporated into the very fabric of the constitutional structure, and one, such as that in the United Kingdom, where it is not? Those who give the matter some thought realise that it is our system's deviation from, rather than adherence to, the 'pure' form of the doctrine that is a vital element in a clear understanding of the United Kingdom constitution. The most obvious example is probably the multiple role of the Lord Chancellor, being head of the English judiciary,[8] 'Speaker' of the House of Lords and a senior Cabinet minister. Yet some of these deviations are so entrenched in our thinking that sometimes we almost assume them to be akin to constitutional 'laws of nature', that, far from being constitutionally dangerous, are either neutral or even positive elements in our system of government.

Perhaps the most obvious example of this ambiguity of thinking is the link between Executive and Legislature, demonstrated by the presence of virtually the whole government in the two Houses of Parliament (primarily the Commons).[9] This is often seen as the foundation of the 'Westminster model' of parliamentary government, embracing Bagehot's 'efficient secret of the English Constitution . . . of the close union, the near complete fusion, of the executive and legislative powers'.[10] It is, perhaps, along with the legislative supremacy of Parliament, the defining concept in the United Kingdom constitution, regarded at one at the same time both as the glory of our parliamentary system and its greatest practical problem or obstacle.

It is not always appreciated that the Executive's membership of Parliament allows ministers, qua ministers, to have virtually all the financial and other benefits, privileges and facilities[11] of Parliament which are open to MPs or peers, in addition to such benefits, privileges and facilities as they have as ministers of the Crown. The privileges of Parliament, especially that of freedom of speech, are also available to the government itself through its ministers, in terms of speeches and reports. For example, ministers may make use of the unopposed return procedure (as in the 1996 Scott Report on the 'arms to Iraq' affair) to invest controversial and potentially libellous reports they have commissioned with privilege under the Parliamentary Papers Act 1840. As Leopold has noted, the actual decision to publish a report in this way is taken by the minister, although the formal, legal decision is made by the House, 'which will not have the opportunity to see the report before it takes the decision to order its publication'.[12] It 'gives the misleading impression of parliamentary approval

---

8   Who, in addition, can and sometimes will participate in cases before the final domestic court of appeal, even those involving the government itself in its various manifestations.

9   The appointment of many members of the Upper House directly by the Executive, is another obvious example. The particular example of members of the Executive with parliamentary functions, such as the Leaders of the two Houses, is considered further below.

10   *The English Constitution* (1993) p 67. J A G Griffith and M Ryle *Parliament: functions, practice and procedures* (1989) calls this a 'constitutional requirement' (p 3) which may perhaps be an overstatement for what is a constitutional *fact*.

11   This is not universally so. The House of Commons Library, for example, will generally not provide substantive assistance to ministers in their ministerial capacity. Ministers will also not use the traditional forms of parliamentary activity such as question or debate. They will be subject qua members to the same duties and obligations as other members.

12   P Leopold 'The publication of controversial Parliamentary papers' (1993) 56 MLR 690, 692. And see ch V below.

for the publication of possibly defamatory comments'.[13] Government can use Parliament and its procedures, even those where parliamentarians have virtually no opportunity of debate on or opposition to the action being taken in its name. How well do those involved in the subject matter of any report published in this way, as well as the media and the public generally, understand the actual extent of parliamentary involvement in the publication and even the content of such a report? In such cases, parliamentary privilege, albeit granted by statute, could be described as executive or governmental privilege by another name.

This duality of jurisdiction – parliamentary and ministerial – can cause difficulties, especially in the oversight of ethical conduct of ministers. This issue has become more transparent as the various codes of conduct have either become publicly available,[14] or have been enacted in the aftermath of the 1995 Nolan Report, with the creation of the Commons Standards and Privileges Committee and the office of Parliamentary Commissioner for Standards, and the tighter rules on members' interests. In the early days of these innovations, the jurisdictional boundary between conduct as a minister and as a member of Parliament has not always been clear. The complex issue of political finance, for example, spills over not only into the parliamentary and executive arena, but also into the formally 'private' world of political parties themselves. We have even seen the actual or requested involvement of the Standards Commissioner (at present, Sir Gordon Downey) or the chair of the government-appointed Committee on Standards in Public Life (formerly Lord Nolan, now Lord Neill of Bladen) in difficult matters such as potential conflicts of interests arising from private donations to political parties.[15] The distinctiveness of Parliament's legal and constitutional place in the British political system may not survive these growing interrelationships of judicial and quasi-judicial jurisdictions unscathed.

Constitutional reform has enjoyed a strong revival in recent years, with proposals ranging from ad hoc changes proposed to the House of Lords or the voting system, to root and branch comprehensive reform including a written constitution. Yet structural change cannot be successfully proposed or considered in the absence of a genuine understanding of the operative constitutional concepts in our present arrangements, and the relationship between the theory and the reality of these concepts. If 'separation of powers' is an empty or misleading concept in our constitutional thought, then, in the absence of some other theory which more accurately describes present reality, we cannot understand properly how Parliament, in particular, operates in the British political and governmental system.

Parliament has been rightly jealous of its independence, fought for over the centuries in the face of hostile executives, both monarchs and ministers. Through the operation of privilege, it maintains formal internal autonomy from external forces

---

13 Ibid at 693.

14 Such as *Questions of Procedure for Ministers* (from July 1997, the *Ministerial Code*), first officially published in 1992.

15 Lord Neill has even been reported as having been approached by the Conservative Party over the various allegations of breaches of electoral law in the close-run Welsh devolution referendum in September 1997. The media's (and perhaps the public's) confusion over the proliferation of such offices is illustrated by the description of each of them from time to time as the 'Parliamentary watchdog' or even more confusingly as the 'Parliamentary Ombudsman'.

such as the public ('strangers'), the government and the courts. No matter how apparently trivial an alleged interference with this autonomy may appear to a modern eye, Parliament can wheel out a formidable array of weapons, including art 9 of the Bill of Rights to defend its privileges.[16] Yet, in the apparently routine operational areas of its activity, such as the printing of its papers, the recruitment of its staff and other similar services, Parliament often resorts, of necessity or otherwise, to the use of external providers in the public and private sector. Parliament is, of course, a part of the 'public sector' in the widest sense of that term, but it is not a part of the governmental sphere of that 'public service'. For various practical and financial reasons, Parliament has recently been developing in-house services in a number of areas, but these changes have not generally been motivated by questions of constitutional principle and propriety.

Parliament is at a distinct disadvantage when seeking to assert its position vis-à-vis the Executive and the judiciary. When there is a situation where constitutional theory and political/governmental realities are out of sync, opportunities can arise for 'creative' activism by organs of government. In this case, Parliament, unlike the courts and the Executive, rarely has the opportunity to exercise the sort of autonomous initiative that, for example, enables the judiciary to develop the theory and practice of judicial review, and governments to act in ways that test existing constitutional limits. The legislative process which led to the enactment of what became s 13 of the Defamation Act 1996[17] was initially at the behest of a member of Parliament whose particular case had highlighted the grievance which the provision sought to remedy, and was introduced by a cross-bench peer. However, that legislative process appeared to have at least the necessary, if formally tacit, support of ministers in both Houses, which helped to ensure its successful passage, notwithstanding its controversial nature on a matter fundamental to Parliament itself. Again, ministers took the lead, at the prompting of the Nolan Committee, on the possible reform of the application of the criminal law to the bribery of parliamentarians, involving consideration of the relationship between parliamentary privilege and the ordinary law.[18]

---

16 In practice, the House of Commons has imposed, in recent years, a variety of self-denying ordinances in the operation of its privilege powers to avoid bringing itself into ridicule and disrepute.

17 This provided for waiver of privilege by members whose defamation actions could otherwise be halted by the operation of art 9 of the Bill of Rights 1689. See ch V below.

18 See the Home Office discussion paper, *Clarification of the law relating to the bribery of Members of Parliament*, December 1996. In it, ministers stated that this issue was, at least initially, 'a matter of policy for *the Government and* Parliament rather than a question of law for the Law Commission' (para 3) (emphasis added). See further the follow-up Home Office paper published in June 1997, *The prevention of corruption*. When giving evidence to the Joint Committee on Parliamentary Privilege on the concurrent departmental review of corruption law and Parliamentary review of privilege, the Home Secretary, Jack Straw, said: 'I accept it is to some extent a chicken and egg situation but I respectfully say that it would be I think very difficult for any ministers of the Crown to go before Parliament with proposals for extending or creating offences of bribery of or corruption by Members of Parliament without the benefit of advice from this Committee because the first question would be put: "Well this is a matter first and foremost for Parliament rather than for ministers"' (minutes of evidence, 20.1.98, HC 401-iii, 1997-98, Q106).

Internal autonomy

Parliament does not govern. This is such an obvious statement that it should require no elaboration or explanation. The term 'parliamentary government' means 'not government by Parliament, but government through Parliament'.[19] Conventional wisdom takes it for granted that a significant executive role for Parliament is constitutionally undesirable and probably, in practical terms, impossible to operate. Visions of parliamentary committees *actually running things* – the Health Committee, chaired by the Health Secretary, administering the Health Department for example – would, no doubt, horrify many people.[20] Yet our constitutional language, especially in the courts, regards Parliament as a legal being when legislating, and even an autonomous legal personality in this capacity when making choices and deciding the form and content of legislation. It is common and well-understood shorthand to refer to inanimate bodies or buildings when meaning their occupants: 'Downing Street' and 'Buckingham Palace' are particularly familiar instances. But the courts' constitutional use of 'Parliament' is more than that, because 'Parliament' is being used by them to support a legal argument and to justify a particular judicial interpretation of the law. And this is being done in circumstances where the institution of 'Parliament' itself cannot, in any sense other than through the will of the government (private members' proceedings excepted), respond authoritatively to the views the courts have put into its mouth.

Despite its antiquity, it is only in the last 30 years or so that 'Parliament' has acquired some relatively modern administrative machinery with which to run its affairs.[1] These include taking control of the Palace of Westminster itself from the Lord Great Chamberlain in 1965 (although it remains a royal palace), and of part of its own budget (though not in relation to MPs' salaries, allowances and personal staff); the establishment of the Services Committee in the same year; the creation of the House of Commons Commission;[2] the reform of the Commons domestic committees following the 1991 Ibbs Report, and the enactment of the Parliamentary Corporate Bodies Act 1992 allowing property to be held and contracts to be made on behalf of the two Houses by their respective Clerks.[3] The Clerk in each House is also

---

19 *Griffith and Ryle* p 10. See also K Bradshaw and D Pring *Parliament and Congress* (1981) p 9.
20 Such a model could, of course, be as much a scenario for *increased* governmental control of Parliament, as for real parliamentary government itself. A mixed system of this sort in local government is currently under general review.
1 See generally M Lawrence 'The administrative organisation of the House of Commons' (1980) 48 Table 68, and W Proctor 'Implementing Ibbs' (1992) 60 Table 66, 67.
2 Under the House of Commons (Administration) Act 1978. The 1990 Ibbs Report found that, in a survey by MORI that year, 'the majority of Members are ignorant about the Commission. Thirty-seven per cent say that they know nothing about it, including 13 per cent who admit that they have never heard of it'. The latter finding included 7% of those with 11-20 years' experience and 6% with over 20 years' experience. See R Ibbs et al *House of Commons Services: report to the House of Commons Commission* HC 38, 1990-91, Annex B, para 3.
3 The difficulties caused by ad hoc changes of this sort to existing Parliamentary law and practice was illustrated by the then Clerk and Clerk Assistant of the House of Commons, and by the Attorney General in their evidence to the Joint Committee on parliamentary privilege in relation to an action concerning the fenestration contract for the new Parliamentary Building ('Portcullis House'). See HC 401(i) and (ii), and (v) respectively, 1997-98, and the resolution of the House of 12 December 1997 concerning *Harmon (CFEM) Facades (UK) v Corporate Officer of the House of Commons*, HC Deb vol 302, col 1332.

that House's Accounting Officer, which provides a practical link to the analogous role in executive departments and agencies, and the ultimate, if indirect, influence of government on internal finance and administrative practices and policies.[4]

Yet, despite the oft-stated concept of the 'House of Commons matter',[5] it is the numerical majority of the government, and the dominance which it brings, or has been conceded by Parliament, that is the single most important influence on the autonomy or otherwise of Parliament.[6] It could be said that the most important two lines in 'Parliamentary law' are those of Standing Order no. 14(1): 'Save as provided in this order, government business shall have precedence at every sitting.' They set the tone for the overall relationship between government and Parliament.[7] The public, and perhaps many members of the Commons (especially those newly elected), were given a sharp indication of this at the outset of the current Parliament, when, just after the May 1997 general election, the government announced radical changes to the arrangements for Prime Minister's Question Time, when one half-hour Wednesday afternoon session replaced the familiar two 15-minutes sessions on Tuesday and Thursday. Notwithstanding a prolonged period of debate and discussion in the House, a number of Committee reports on the subject, and the apparent centrality of Parliamentary Questions to the House's core function of holding the Executive to account, the episode demonstrated that the means by which that oversight is exercised, even in respect of the most senior minister, rest wholly in the gift of the government itself, rather than under the notional control of the House, through standing orders or resolution.

Griffith and Ryle state at the outset of their study of Parliament:

> One constant has remained since the early eighteenth century: the key to understanding how the constitution works still lies in the relationship between the Government and the House of Commons as the representative body. This relationship is directly and greatly conditioned by the dominant presence in the representative assembly of the Ministers of the Crown.[8]

As Rush and Shaw noted in 1974:

> Even in those cases where free votes have been allowed, the decision to have a free vote has of course been the Government's, and Governments have sometimes rejected the result of such votes.

---

4   As does the 1978 Act's 'broadly in line' principle regarding terms and conditions of the employment of Commons staff (see s 2).

5   Using the Commons for illustrative purposes, and because it is the House most relevant to this argument.

6   Even governments, from time to time, may be hesitant at the extent of their control over Parliament. A cabinet committee of the Coalition Government in the mid 1940s, during consideration of possible changes to post-war Parliamentary procedure, decided it could proceed after it had received a paper from Sir Cecil Carr on 'Changes in Parliamentary procedure since 1880' (MG (43) 6, CAB 87), which had apparently dispelled the Committee's doubts about whether the government rather than Parliament should be taking the initiative on parliamentary reform.

7   Another procedural source of ministerial power in Parliament is in relation to proceedings relating to public money.

8   *Griffith and Ryle* p 5. This is reinforced by ministerial control of financial procedure.

They cited proposals for a new parliamentary building on Bridge Street as an example, and concluded that:

> there is no doubt that in recent years Ministers have become increasingly sensitive to the views of backbenchers on 'parliamentary' matters, including those relating to services and facilities. In the end, however, the government, if it chooses to do so, takes the ultimate decision.[9]

An interesting example of this that they cited was the financing of the House of Commons. The Estimates contained a note stating that remuneration of Officers of the House was exempt from Treasury control and was controlled by the House of Commons Offices Commission, set up by the House of Commons Offices Act 1812.[10] But as the Chancellor of the Exchequer was, with the Speaker, one of the two active Commissioners, 'Treasury influence can therefore be very effectively wielded'. Lock concluded that the note in the Estimates does not accurately reflect the actual situation. The gap between the actual system and the theoretical legal framework is even wider than is customary, as the membership consisted of all Secretaries of State, but not the Leader of the House (as Lord President of the Council at that time) nor Opposition representatives.[11] Government and Parliament, of course, do try to preserve, where they can, at least the veneer of respect for the separation of powers. For example, the government's forward expenditure plans, published each year, include, in the section on the House of Commons, the following: 'The application of performance indicators to the Legislative Assembly and its membership is inappropriate unless the Assembly decides otherwise.'[12]

Governmental dominance can extend to internal parliamentary matters through its party's majority not only in the House itself, but also on its committees. It can manifest itself, for example, over the structure and membership of the departmental select committees. Ministers and whips are well represented on the statutory and domestic committees that administer the House of Commons, for example. The House of Commons (Administration) Act 1978 expressly provides for the membership of the Leader of the House of Commons on the House of Commons Commission.[13] The Leader of the House is also a member of the important Finance and Services Committee, and Whips (of both sides of the House) are members of the various domestic committees. The government's influence over the two Houses, in the sense discussed here,[14] is exercised primarily by the Leader of the House. A brief examination of the history of the office, especially in the Commons, reveals the extent to which it developed as a means of executive (initially monarchical) control and

---

9   M Rush and M Shaw (eds) *The House of Commons: services and facilities* (1974) pp 43, 44.
10 Discussed below. For a characteristic example of the relationship in the days before the House of Commons (Administration) Act 1978 see R Crossman *The diaries of a cabinet minister* (1976) vol II, pp 739-740.
11 In *Rush and Shaw* pp 29, 30.
12 Eg March 1996 (Cm 3220) p 105, para 7.
13 See s 1, which also provides that, in addition to the Leader of the House, the Speaker and a member nominated by the Leader of the Opposition, the Commission is composed of three other members, *none of whom shall be a Minister of the Crown* (emphasis added).
14 The Whips are, of course, the main means of control over the actions of members in relation to parliamentary proceedings.

management of the House, which became of growing importance as the House gained independent influence vis-à-vis monarchs and their ministers, ultimately through the rise of party.[15] The post was often described in this period as 'minister for the House of Commons', 'minister for the House of Commons in the Closet' and 'minister for the King in the House of Commons'.[16] It was the practice until the last war (with the exception of Lloyd George's premiership) that the Prime Minister, when in the Commons, was also Leader of the House, but the increasing complexity of parliamentary management led to the clear division of responsibilities which we see now started when Attlee appointed Herbert Morrison as Leader of the House in 1945.[17]

The office has two broad and distinct functions: managing the House on behalf of the government (especially in the management of the legislative programme); and representing the House as a whole where appropriate.[18] Indeed, Morrison recognised the complexity inherent in this dual role when he listed five responsibilities of a Leader: '. . . to the Government, to the government's own supporters on the back-benches, to the Opposition, to the House as a whole, and to the individual Minister in charge.'[19] Holders of the office often recognised the non-partisan nature of the parliamentary function, but in modern times it is perhaps inevitable that the partisan ministerial function not only is the primary role, but is perceived virtually universally as such. This makes it more difficult for the non-partisan nature of the parliamentary role to be fully accepted and exercised.

A recent and interesting example of this arose during the November 1997 debate in the House of Commons on the Standards and Privileges Committee reports on the 'cash-for-questions'/Neil Hamilton affair. A senior member of the Nolan Committee on Standards in Public Life, Tom King, regretted that the Leader of the House was not a member of the Standards and Privileges Committee. He said:

> A unique feature of the job of Leader of the House is that it is not a party political appointment. The Leader is the one member of the Government who must speak for the whole of Parliament. It is important that we have someone in that position on the Committee.[20]

Winding up the debate, the Leader of the House, Ann Taylor, said that:

15   This was of particular importance when the Prime Minister was a peer.
16   See eg J B Owen *The rise of the Pelhams* (1957) p 283, on the role of Henry Pelham.
17   During the war, Attlee, Cripps and Eden acted as Churchill's Leaders of the House.
18   See J Biffen (a former holder of the office) *Inside Westminster* (1996) pp 100-102. A recent example of the dual role could be seen in a written answer by the Leader of the House, Ann Taylor, to a question addressed to the member representing the House of Commons Commission, on the application of Crown immunity to the Palace of Westminster: 'Legislation affecting Crown immunity in the Palace of Westminster is a matter for HM Government. However, it is the policy of the Commission, notwithstanding immunities and exemptions provided for in legislation, to apply relevant statutory provisions throughout the parliamentary estate . . .' (HC Deb vol 297, 30 June 1997, written answers, col 45w).
19   Lord Morrison of Lambeth *Government and Parliament* (3rd edn, 1964) p 131. For an example of the potential difficulties caused by the dual role, see the exchange between Tam Dalyell and the Leader of the House, Tony Newton, during business questions on 23 January 1997, on a demand for action on allegations made on television by Mohamed Al-Fayed (HC Deb vol 288, col 1082).
20   HC Deb vol 301, 17 November 1997, col 97.

although I think it is possible to wear two hats – as Leader of the House and as a member of the Government – it was extremely important that the Committee should be seen to be free from political interference.[1]

Governments do not always get their way over 'House of Commons matters', such as on MPs' pay and allowances or on the implementation of the 1995 Nolan Report on MPs' standards and interests.[2] But this does not disguise the extent to which Parliament itself generally acquiesces in ceding initiative and control of its internal affairs to the wishes of government,[3] from 'privilege' issues, to creation of scrutiny mechanisms such as departmental select committees,[4] to 'housekeeping' matters, including legislation relating to the administration of Parliament itself.[5]

A recent instance is the publication of a consultation paper by the Home Office on the possible application of the bribery and corruption laws to members of Parliament,[6] which, while it was described as being intended 'for consideration by the Select Committee on Standards and Privileges',[7] was apparently also published at large. The Nolan Committee had recommended that 'the Government should now take steps to clarify' the relevant law.[8] The first report of the Select Committee on Standards in Public Life (the Commons committee appointed to advise on the implementation of Nolan) said that 'the Government should ask the Law Commission to undertake an immediate review' of the relevant law.[9] In the consultation paper the government set out why, while agreeing on the need for clarification, 'it felt that this was a matter of policy for the Government and Parliament rather than a question of law for the Law Commission', though it did not rule out their possible later involvement.[10] It may be

---

1 Ibid, col 119.
2 See the revolt on pay on July 1983, and decisions on 6 November 1995 on the Nolan resolutions.
3 Lawrence has described how the Compton Inquiry in the early 1970s came about at the initiative of ministers rather than members themselves ((1992) 60 Table 66, 70). The Ibbs Inquiry in 1990, on the other hand, was proposed, at least formally, by the House of Commons Commission, and it made its report to the Commission.
4 Griffith and Ryle commented in 1989 that 'the need to obtain Government approval for physical changes intended to be of benefit to members or staff of the two Houses restricts the independence of the legislature. This has somewhat limited the development of services needed by the Commons for the scrutiny of the executive' *Griffith and Ryle* p 133.
5 The National Audit Act 1983 (which began life as the Parliamentary Control of Expenditure Bill), in so far as it could be said that it relates to parliamentary matters, may be seen as a rare exception, being introduced as a private members' Bill by Norman St John Stevas (himself a former Leader of the House). In 1978 the government of the day did accept a number of back-bench amendments (from both sides of the House) to the House of Commons (Administration) Bill.
6 *Clarification of the law relating to the bribery of Members of Parliament: a discussion paper*, Home Office, December 1996. While the Home Office does have a traditional 'constitutional' remit (including matters, such as election law, which directly affect Parliament), perhaps it could be suggested that, if the initiative of matters of this sort is to come from government rather than from Parliament itself, the Lord Chancellor or one of the Law Officers may be a more appropriate 'author'.
7 Ibid, para 3.
8 1995 (Cm 2850-I) para 2.104.
9 HC 637, 1994-95, para 51. See also the (Salmon) royal commission on standards of conduct in public life, 1976 (Cmnd 6524) ch 4.
10 Ibid, para 3.

noted that the House of Commons had just, a few months previously, approved a Code of Conduct for its members, which expressly included a provision declaring that the acceptance of a bribe in relation to a member's parliamentary conduct 'is contrary to the law of Parliament'.[11]

The direct and close involvement of the government in the administration of Parliament has a long history. The Commission established by the House of Commons Offices Act 1812 consisted of 'the Speaker of the House of Commons for the time being, and the Secretary or Secretaries of State, the Chancellor of the Exchequer, the Master of the Rolls, and the Attorney and Solicitor General for the time being (they and each of them being also Members of the House of Commons)'.[12] Proctor has noted that, although the Speaker was a member, 'the influence he was able to exert on behalf of the House was limited, all the other Commissioners being Government Ministers'.[13] A select committee in 1954, having examined the history and role of the Commissioners, and noting the preponderance of ministers, recommended that the functions should be exercised by a statutory 'House of Commons Commission' comprising the Speaker in the chair, the Leader of the House, the Leader of the Opposition, the Chancellor of the Exchequer, the Minister of Works and 'a suitable number of other Members, not less than nine in number, one of whom should be selected by Mr Speaker as Vice-Chairman'.[14] The Speaker, WS Morrison, agreed with a succinct 'Yes' when asked by a member of the committee if he thought it 'a bit queer . . . that House of Commons business, so far as the Commissioners are concerned, with the exception of yourself, is run by Ministers of the existing Government'.[15]

Sir Edmund Compton, in his review of the administrative services of the House in 1974, noted that 'legally speaking, financial as opposed to functional control over the staffing of the House of Commons services is still vested' in the 1812 Act Commissioners, although in practice financial control had, since they approved a 'Statement of Principles' on 12 February 1970,[16] been delegated to the Clerk of the House as Accounting Officer. Compton concluded that there was a recognition that the functions of the Commissioners –

> appear to be spent, and that the time has come to abolish the Commission on the ground that their responsibilities on behalf of Parliament are fully discharged by two of their number, functioning not as Commissioners but as Speaker and the Chancellor of the Exchequer.

These two public officers would continue to delegate to the Accounting Officer, and receive an annual statement of changes in staff numbers, pay and conditions of service. The residual right to arrange for an independent inquiry on staffing matters which, by para 5 of the 1970 Statement of Principles, vested in the Chancellor acting on behalf of the Commissioners, should vest in the Chancellor '*as Chancellor*'.[17]

11   *The Code of Conduct*, HC 688, 1995-96, p 4, approved 24 July 1996.
12   1812 Act, s 2. Any three, including the Speaker, formed a quorum.
13   'Implementing Ibbs' (1992) 60 Table 66, 67.
14   Report of the Select Committee on House of Commons (Accommodation), HC 184, 1953-54, para 56.
15   Ibid, Q903.
16   Reproduced as annex C to Appendix A of Appendix 20 of the Bottomley Report, *House of Commons (Administration)*, HC 624, 1974-75, pp 103-104.
17   *Review of the administrative services of the House of Commons*, HC 254, 1974, para 6.41.

The Bottomley Report the following year detected 'broad unanimity' among its witnesses that the proposed abolition of the Commissioners 'would detract from the "self-governing" role of the House'. Compton's comment that their function appeared to be spent 'was generally accepted',[18] but the report noted that 'some witnesses . . . thought it would be wrong if this largely defunct power were to be absorbed by the Executive in the person of the Chancellor of the Exchequer'.[19]

The Clerk of the House, for example, said that this:

> would expose the Services of the House to the power of the Chancellor *as Chancellor*, and not as one of the Commissioners; and the Speaker would have no institutional source from which to seek wider support within the House for the House of Commons' view against that of the Treasury.[20]

The Head of the Administration Department asserted that:

> proper staffing of the House, its Committees and its services generally is fundamental to the parliamentary activities of Members . . . If direct control over staff establishment is to pass statutorily out of the hands of the House into those of the Civil Service the Executive is at once placed in a powerful position vis-à-vis the Legislature and all kinds of developments may result.

Such a power was described as a 'hostage to fortune'.[1] Witnesses proposed various forms of reconstituted Commission. One of the Bottomley Committee's criteria for a successful restructuring of the House's administration was that 'overall control over the services of the House must remain with the House and its Members'.[2] It therefore concluded that:

> we do not consider that Sir Edmund's proposal that the Commission under the 1812 Act should be abolished, without alternative provision, would be consistent with the proper degree of control which we consider should be exercised over the services of the House by Members themselves.[3]

It proposed the House of Commons Commission (later created by the House of Commons (Administration) Act 1978), which is the ultimate employer of all House departmental staff. The Committee were 'convinced of the need, in the House of Commons, for an ultimate authority which can express the will of the House in respect of its services, organisation and staff; which can . . . where necessary represent [the interests of Members] to the Executive'.[4] The new Commission would have representation from the official Opposition and from the back-benches. The government would be represented by the Leader of the House, who:

---

18   It met as a body only once in the decade up to 1965: Select Committee on the Palace of Westminster, HC 285, 1964-65, p 56, evidence of Speaker's Secretary.
19   Bottomley Report, para 2.7.
20   Memorandum by the Clerk of the House, Appendix 4, para 45.
1   Memorandum by the Head of the Administration Department, Appendix 11, p 73.
2   Bottomley Report, para 3.1(b). Another was that the House service must remain 'wholly distinct', with a 'quite separate function' from the civil service, 'whose duty it is to serve the Executive': para 3.1(c).
3   Ibid, para 3.3(b).
4   Ibid, para 4.5.

would speak for the Government in the Commission, but he would also be able to speak for the Commission in the Cabinet and answer for the Commission on the floor of the House.[5] But the Chancellor of the Exchequer should not be a member of the Commission; he would find it difficult to combine that function with his responsibilities for examining and approving the House of Commons Vote.[6]

It is interesting that, in the midst of these proposals for the Commons to take more control of its internal administration, the report also suggested that:

> it would be convenient for the Speaker and the Leader of the House to be able to consult the Commission on major decisions currently affecting the House (other than those governed by the procedures and practices of the House) . . . [and] if the Government wished to make changes in the sitting arrangements of the House and its committees.[7]

In the brief debate on the report, the constitutional position received relatively little detailed attention. The Conservative front-bencher, John Peyton, did remind the House that 'Parliament is not a Government Department' and, speaking personally, he thought it:

> already far too much the creature of the Executive . . . I believe that it highly desirable that Parliament should be kept separate from the Executive and free to run its own affairs in its own way, even if that way does not always seem too tidy to those elsewhere.[8]

He hoped that the report:

> will do something to help preserve Parliament from being sucked into the maw of Whitehall for no better reason than that the Executive today is achieving increasing dominance over our affairs. I believe that the independence of Parliament is something that we must guard as being of particular importance at a time when personal liberties are very much under threat.[9]

For the government, the Minister of State at the Privy Council Office, Gerry Fowler, said that:

> this is where we see Parliament at its best – when its interests are at stake . . . I agree that we do not want Whitehall spreading its tentacles into the House. Whoever is in Government will, I am sure, take the same view.[10]

---

5   The Leader of the House would also chair the Services Committee because 'his Ministerial position adds great weight to the Committee's conclusions; and his membership of both the Commission and the Services Committee would provide a link between the two bodies . . .': para 4.21.

6   Ibid, para 4.7.

7   Ibid, para 4.13.

8   HC Deb vol 901, 4 December 1975, col 1973.

9   Ibid, col 1974.

10   Ibid, col 1978.

Nolan, 'sleaze' and parliamentary self-regulation

The ethics debate of recent years, for which the term 'Nolan' is a convenient shorthand, has highlighted the whole autonomy (or 'self-regulation' issue), and the Nolan Committee's first report, published in May 1995, was the most considered review of parliamentary self-regulation for some time.[11] The twin pillars of the Nolan approach for the public service were that 'internal systems for maintaining standards should be supported by independent scrutiny'.[12] The report, stating that the House of Commons 'is at the heart of our democracy' and that members' standards 'are crucially important to the political well-being of the nation', asserted that 'those standards have always been self-imposed and self-regulated because Parliament is our supreme institution'.[13]

The report set out what is, in effect, the case against complete self-regulation. It noted the protracted history of the Register of Members' Interests and concluded that 'the overall picture is not one of an institution whose Members have been quick to recognise or respond to public concern'.[14] 'On the other hand', the report continued, 'we do not believe that the position is so grave that it has to be addressed outside the framework of the House's own rules'. Having set out what it required in principle to deal with these problems, it continued:

> We believe that the House can do this itself, and that the package which we set out below will help it to do so. It is a powerful and flexible mixture of disclosure and enforcement which will serve the public interest better than the inflexibility of statutory procedures.[15]

It accepted that 'parliamentary privilege' 'is designed to ensure the proper working of Parliament, and is an essential constitutional safeguard',[16] and one of the consequences of privilege is 'that the House of Commons regulates the activities of its Members itself'. The report declared that 'because parliamentary privilege is important for reasons entirely unconnected with the standards of conduct of individual Members of Parliament, we believe that it would be highly desirable for self-regulation to continue'.[17] But for self-regulation to continue successfully, 'it is essential that Resolutions of the House – in effect the legal framework which the House imposes on its own operations – should be regarded as binding on all Members, and should be firmly, promptly and fairly enforced'.[18] It believed that there was a perception within the House that standards resolutions do not have the same impact as laws or regulations, 'even though they are the law of Parliament'. This was due in part to the reluctance of the House (and its relevant staff) to sit in judgment on fellow members unless the matter was very serious.[19] They regarded this attitude as

---

11 *Standards in public life* (Cm 2850) (2 vols). See further ch VII below.
12 Ibid, summary, para 7.
13 Ibid, para 2.1.
14 Ibid, para 2.58.
15 Ibid, para 2.59.
16 Ibid, para 2.91.
17 Ibid, para 2.92.
18 Ibid, para 2.93.
19 Ibid, para 2.96.

entirely understandable but wrong, and emphasised the need for the development in the House of a culture of adherence to standards resolutions.

This analysis led the committee to its central proposal in this respect, that *'this can best be taken forward by combining a significant independent element with a system which remains essentially self-regulating'*,[20] through the proposed Parliamentary Commissioner for Standards who would, inter alia, play an independent role in the enforcement of the House's standards rules. The committee believed this approach 'should be sufficient to achieve the necessary detachment without recourse to the courts or indeed any surrender of privilege. The recommendations . . . should enable Members to secure a fair, thorough and expeditious hearing without removing the jurisdiction of the House of Commons'. The report noted the suggestion by some witnesses that such procedures should be put on a statutory basis.

The House of Commons debated the first Nolan report, one week after its publication,[1] when members explored various aspects of the self-regulation issue, and the Nolan proposal for a Parliamentary Commissioner for Standards in particular.[2] Jeff Rooker, winding up for the Opposition, claimed that:

> by and large we have proved ourselves incapable of putting our own house in order. That is the ultimate proof that self-regulation can be self-delusion . . . I would argue that we are the highest court in the land, but we should not be a law unto ourselves because we are the law makers. That is the distinction I draw. I do not understand why some hon. Members find the House under threat if we look for something other than complete self-regulation.[3]

A clear exposition of the opposite approach came from Sir Dudley Smith, who said that 'Parliament's sovereignty is being undermined'. The standards commissioner 'will be a veritable gauleiter' and the parliamentary committee to which the commissioner will report 'will be his poodle'. He believed that:

> for good or ill, Parliament must police itself. The public decide whether they like us and, if they do not, they throw us out . . . Parliament is the highest court in the land and cannot be ruled by a High Court judge, however eminent, or by a registrar, however qualified or respectable . . . Parliament must safeguard its sovereignty and deal with the situation circumspectly.[4]

Several members considered the notion of statutory regulation.[5]   Nicholas Budgen, for example, emphasised that, as Nolan was proposing material changes and restrictions in members' terms of employment, they would have to be set out in statute. Edward Leigh supported the statutory approach, not only for certainty, but also because of the principle of a separation of the Executive and the Legislature:

---

20 Ibid, para 2.99 (emphasis added).

1 Interestingly, the government, in its response, said that the recommendations affecting MPs 'are a matter for the House of Commons to decide, and they are not addressed in this response': 1995 (Cm 2931) p 2.

2 HC Deb vol 260, 18 May 1995, cols 481-570.

3 Ibid, cols 560-561.

4 Ibid, col 545.

5 Ibid, cols 482, 486, 488.

If the House is to be regulated in this tight way – which may or may not be the right thing to do – it should be by statute. Hon. Members should know exactly where they stand, and should not be bound by a commissioner effectively appointed by the Executive to oversee independent Members of Parliament.[6]

Tristan Garel-Jones pointed out that 'if we were to have a statute, would we not be handing over the scrutiny of this House to the judges and to legal interpretation?'[7] David Hunt, opening the debate for the government, said that a statutory route:

would be a fundamental constitutional change because the conduct of the House is not a matter of statute, and if the terms upon which hon. Members serve were to be encompassed in statute, it would be a fundamental constitutional change.[8]

Ann Taylor, then Shadow Leader of the House, responding to an intervention by Mr Budgen on the need for statute for major changes in members' terms and conditions, thought that 'a bogus point that should not delay us'.[9]

Some members suggested that, if there were to be an 'ethics commissioner', it should be the Speaker, or at least her appointee and based in the Speaker's Office. Sir Archie Hamilton said that 'that would remove many of our fears about an independent commissioner over whom, once we had appointed him or her, we would have no control at all'.[10] Iain Duncan Smith said that if there had to be a commissioner 'such an appointee must come solely from [Madam Speaker's] office. There is no way that I will vote for somebody from outside this place, who does not know of the pressures and the work of the House, to sit in judgment on Members'.[11] John Garrett said that he had long argued for a 'new and independent role for the Speaker', and if this included the supervision of parliamentary standards, 'that would mean that we would have constant access to the guardian of our standards'.[12]

The Nolan/sleaze episode in recent years was a rare example of the House debating whether to permit 'external' controls (in the form of the Parliamentary Commissioner for Standards) on its internal affairs.[13] The question of continued parliamentary self-regulation was much considered, and there was some disquiet that a government-appointed committee was examining such issues. Tony Benn thought that the Nolan Committee was a 'permanent royal commission . . . clean contrary to article 9 of the Bill of Rights, which stipulates that no one from outside may presume to regulate what we do',[14] and the Conservative, Iain Duncan Smith declared that 'my views on the

---

6 Ibid, col 487.
7 Ibid, col 487.
8 Ibid, col 482.
9 Ibid, col 499.
10 Ibid, col 532.
11 Ibid, col 554.
12 Ibid, col 546.
13 A peer, the Liberal Democrat, Earl Russell, has contributed in the press to the debate on these issues, warning of the danger of self-regulation, especially if it means internal disciplinary processes, where 'internal values' may conflict with the more general issues of criminal guilt or innocence and due process. He queried, for example, whether government backbenchers would be willing to suspend or expel 'offenders' from their own side in a situation of small or no government majority in the Commons: 'Insider trade-off' Guardian, 11 November 1996.
14 HC Deb vol 260, 18 May 1995, col 532. See further ch V below.

position of Parliament mean that I should like to have had some say in deciding what would be set up'.[15]

The House returned to many of these issues when debating the Standards and Privileges reports on the Neil Hamilton case in November 1997. This highlighted the potential conflict between the principle of self-regulation (within an essentially party political forum) and the conventional requirements of due process and natural justice, and the Nolan solution of a select committee, buttressed by an independent investigatory mechanism in the shape of an Officer of the House, the Parliamentary Commissioner for Standards.[16] Tony Benn repeated his arguments against self-regulation of the Nolan form:

> Self-regulation means, in effect, that we decide on an arbitrary basis instead of laying down the law as to what should or should not be acceptable and leaving judges to determine it. If Parliament passes a law saying what is and is not acceptable, that is self-regulation, but the determination falls to the judges, not to the House.[17]

Conclusion

Constitutional lawyers, being lawyers, abhor a system without rules. That is one reason why *the* constitutional rule, the sovereignty of Parliament, is so often protected and cherished. It is not to be surrendered, either at all, or at least not unless and until it can be traded in for a full package of rules in a written constitution or bill of rights. It also means that humble political practices and habits of action are often sanctified into quasi-rule status as 'constitutional conventions', complete with the precedents, interpretations, breaches and exceptions just as real rules have. In our unwritten constitution system, conventions apparently are what give life to our political system.

Yet that must be an incomplete description, for it is the interrelationship of these rules and conventions with the *political culture* that truly makes our system what it is. So in the area of the relationship between Parliament and the other two governmental organs, notably the executive, notions of separation of powers are not in themselves sufficient descriptions, without recognising the *culture of acquiescence* that pervades Parliament's approach to the government of the day. As Barker and Rush have correctly noted:

> Any discussion of the role of the Member of Parliament is complicated by the fact that there is a degree of conflict between theory and practice in that the work of the Parliament in general and the House of Commons in particular is carried on in an atmosphere of lip-service to a number of constitutional norms . . . all of which are in practice subordinated to the political realities of Cabinet government whereby the government of the day normally controls the House of Commons rather the House of Commons controlling the government.[18]

15   Ibid, col 552.
16   HC Deb vol 301, 17 November 1997, cols 81-120. The Nolan recommendations were defended in the debate by one of its members, Tom King: col 96.
17   Ibid, col 93.
18   A Barker and M Rush *The Member of Parliament and his information* (1970) p 21.

There is no doubt that Parliament, and, in particular, the House of Commons, has (or at least had[19]) some form of collective ethos, fostered and protected to some extent by its unique legal position. Members of both Houses jealously guard their autonomy and the self-regulation of Parliament, and this can be deployed in situations, such as Nolan, when it is perceived to be under threat.[20] Such episodes, and the reforms of the 1960s and 1970s which gave Parliament, and the Commons in particular, more formal and practical autonomy, demonstrate that, when Parliament is required to think about the issue as one that is more than mere constitutional theory, separation of powers arguments are, consciously or otherwise, asserted in defence of parliamentary self-regulation. But most of the time the relationship between Parliament and the Executive develops ad hoc, when inertia or convenience may have more impact than awareness or protection of the constitutional niceties.

It can be argued, with some justice, that the development of a more contractual customer/supplier relationship between Parliament and various governmental bodies (and often through them to private contractors) has not only regularised the financial and accounting relationship, but has given Parliament more practical autonomy in its administration. While, in theory, Parliament could become an almost totally self-sufficient 'state within a state', that clearly is not a totally practical option. Information technology and other developments may make many 'in-House' services, such as printing, more feasible, but the vast majority of its daily necessities will continue to depend to some degree on external supply. An organisation does not, per se, lose significant autonomy simply by the fact of its dealings with the external world. That depends on the degree of its genuine negotiating, financial and other strength vis-à-vis that outside world. Parliament will have to deal with both the public and private sector. It may deal with one through the other. It may delegate these functions to outside agents. None of these relationships necessarily of itself attacks whatever one views as the proper degree of parliamentary autonomy.

Introducing the Lords second reading of the Parliamentary Corporate Bodies Bill in March 1992, the Lord Privy Seal, Lord Waddington, said that the situation led Parliament into deep legal waters:

> and the fact of the matter is that neither House constitutes a legal persona, able to do the sort of things one inevitably has to do as the owner of the property. It is not an entirely new problem and I have to concede that up to now we have managed to muddle through. Clerks of Parliaments have for instance entered into contracts making themselves personally liable, which has been very brave of them.[1]

---

19 See eg Butt's description of the eighteenth-century Commons' corporate spirit and manners, due to the social cohesion of its membership and the small, enclosed political society of the age, as demonstrated in its hostile attitude to the intrusion of the outside world's attempts to report its proceedings: R Butt *The power of Parliament* (2nd edn, 1969) pp 53-54.
20 Criticisms of the procedures adopted by the post-Nolan standards machinery (the Parliamentary Commissioner and the Standards and Privileges Committee) in the recent Neil Hamilton case has prompted the committee to review its own role in relation to inquiries conducted by the Commissioner (Eighth report of 1997-98, HC 261, para 11). This has involved, inter alia, consideration of an appropriate 'appeal' body, and the committee has borne in mind the impact on Parliamentary self-regulation of resort to an external body, perhaps on the model of election courts.
1 HL Deb vol 536, 6 March 1992, col 1110.

'Muddling through' seems to sum up both Parliament's theory and practice on its constitutional relationship with the Executive generally and its legal and practical relations in particular.

Chapter III

Parliamentary accountability for the administration of justice

Gavin Drewry and Dawn Oliver

Introduction

The purpose of this chapter is to examine some of the issues and tensions surrounding the accountability to Parliament of those responsible for the administration of justice. Some of those issues are endemic to British public administration and include the familiar gap between the theory and the reality of ministerial responsibility in an age of 'big government', in which ministers know about, still less control, only a small fraction of what is done in their name by the civil servants employed in large and often physically dispersed departmental empires. A currently much-discussed variant of this is the elusive and often-shifting location of the demarcation line between 'policy' and 'operational' matters, particularly in the context of 'Next Steps' executive agencies (of which the departments concerned with the administration of justice have at least their fair share[1]). The 'big government' problem is compounded by the failure of Parliament itself to modernise its practices and procedures for scrutinising the Executive – with the honourable, though qualified, exception of the introduction of specialised departmentally related select committees in 1979.[2]

On top of these generic accountability issues there is another factor which raises sensitivities that are peculiar to the administration of justice. That factor is judicial independence, a constitutional principle of universally acknowledged importance, though discussion of its practical implications is often clouded by mythology and muddled thinking.[3] Some of the people responsible for the delivery of justice functions – in particular, for the day-to-day running of the courts – are civil servants, answerable in the last resort to ministers, who in turn are answerable (subject to the caveats already noted) to Parliament for the acts and defaults of those civil servants.

The principal minister referred to here is the Lord Chancellor. He has many peculiar constitutional characteristics. For one thing, he sits in the House of Lords rather than in the elected House of Commons. For another, his position – at the

---

1 See below for examples.
2 A select committee on the modernisation of the House of Commons is sitting at the time of writing.
3 See G Drewry 'Judicial Independence in Britain: challenges real and threats imagined' in R Blackburn (ed) *Constitutional Studies: Contemporary Issues and Controversies* (1992).

interface between the Executive and the judiciary – makes him in many respects ministerially sui generis. However, as we shall see, the balance of the office's functions has changed greatly over the years – driven by the restructuring of the administration of the courts instituted by the Courts Act 1971, and more recently by the 'public management' revolution – so that it is now much more akin to a conventional ministry, perhaps even (save that some legal functions still reside in the Home Office and with the Law Officers) a ministry of justice.

But in any case, the primary 'administrators' (or 'deliverers') of justice are not ministers or civil servants but the judges themselves, resistant to any ministerial instruction, and whose independence from executive and parliamentary interference is protected by well-established constitutional rules and conventions. These include (so far as the higher judiciary is concerned) ones dating back to the Act of Settlement 1701 that make their salaries a permanent charge on the Consolidated Fund and their tenure subject to termination only on an address to Her Majesty by both Houses of Parliament. So far as day-to-day oversight of the judiciary by Parliament itself is concerned, discussion of current or impending proceedings in the courts (particularly the criminal courts) is restricted by the operation of a sub judice rule. An extension of the latter was seen when the Maxwell brothers, through counsel, refused to give evidence to the Social Services Committee in its inquiry into Pension Funds, on the grounds that their doing so might prejudice their position in the context of a prospective prosecution for fraud.[4]

Even the court officials, already mentioned, may sometimes find themselves caught between their status and obligations as civil servants and their duty to the judges who dispose of the business of the courts over which they preside. This, as we shall see, was for a while the basis of a dispute about whether the remit of the Parliamentary Commissioner extended to allegations of maladministration against court officials, subject to the instructions of judges – a dispute statutorily resolved in the Courts and Legal Services Act 1990.

At one level, this issue encapsulates the tension between the 'professional' and the 'political'. Similar tensions are to be found throughout the public sector: another familiar example is to be seen in the debates about whether the professional judgments of NHS doctors can and should be liable to be countermanded by hospital managers, on budgetary and other grounds. There is certainly an element of this professional territoriality in the matters considered here, particularly given that 'justice', alongside 'health' and 'education', has become caught up in the managerial revolution that has been so prominent a feature of the political agenda since the early 1980s, and swept along by the preoccupations, so prominent in the Thatcher years, with efficiency, effectiveness and economy. Indeed, the senior judiciary has itself, in some cases reluctantly, in others less so, come to recognise the inevitability of this tendency – as recent debates about the funding of legal aid, and the Woolf Report on the Administration of Civil Justice, bear eloquent witness. But the constitutional undercurrents – aspects of which are apparent in most of the chapters in this book – make the issue of parliamentary accountability for courts and the judicial process

---

4   Social Security Committee, First Special Report, 1991-92, *The Conduct of Mr Ian Maxwell and Mr Kevin Maxwell*, HC 353.

particularly problematical, and interesting. An extreme, and democratically uncomfortable, formulation of the core question might be – can an institution that is constitutionally 'independent' logically be 'accountable' to *anyone*, apart from itself?

The interest is all the greater given that the courts and their decisions have become more and more politically salient, through the growth of judicial review and the impact of decisions both of the European Court of Justice and the European Court of Human Rights. The incorporation of the European Convention on Human Rights into United Kingdom domestic law holds out the prospect of a further raising of the political profile of the judiciary.

Some parliamentarians may feel uncomfortable with the prospect of the traditional emphasis in Britain upon political rather than legal methods of accountability and redress of grievances being displaced by mechanisms of administrative and constitutional law, and with the fact that judges are beginning to intrude onto some hitherto inviolate parliamentary turf. Some of these concerns surfaced in the debates in both Houses on the Scott Report, and have surfaced again in the Blair government's proposals – in the aftermath of various 'sleaze' scandals, and the Nolan Report – for making corrupt MPs liable to prosecution in the courts.[5]

In summary, the continuing managerial reforms of the administration of justice, combined with the increasing political impact of judicial decisions and the higher political profile of the judiciary, have combined to challenge the continued sustainability of practices and conventions that have traditionally shielded the courts from parliamentary scrutiny. There have already been important developments in this area, and some of them are discussed below. There are bound to be more – a prospect that we will return to in our concluding section.

The administration of justice: a 'special' public service?

In many respects, the administration of justice closely resembles many other public services, not least in terms of its claims upon public expenditure and manpower. In 1997-98, the planned expenditure of the Lord Chancellor's Department (LCD) – the United Kingdom's nearest approximation to a Ministry of Justice – was £2,424m (nearly two-thirds of which is attributable to legal aid), on top of which the Northern Ireland Courts Service added another £829m.[6] The Lord Chancellor's Department employs about 11,000 civil servants (most of whom now work in the Courts Service Executive Agency) – which makes it bigger than many other major Whitehall departments, such as the Ministry of Agriculture Fisheries and Food

---

5   In December 1996 the Home Office published a document entitled *Clarification of the Law Relating to the Bribery of Members of Parliament*, which was addressed to the Commons Select Committee on Standards and Privileges. After the 1997 general election the subject was taken up by the Joint Committee on Standards and Privileges. Because of these reviews by Parliament itself and by the Home Office, the Law Commission decided to omit any consideration of the law relating to bribery of MPs and ministers from its report on *Legislating the Criminal Code: Corruption* (Law Com no 248) HC 525, 1997-98, see paras 1.21-1.22.

6   *Departmental Report of the Lord Chancellor's and Law Officers' Departments: The Government's Expenditure Plans, 1995-96 to 1997-98*, 1995 (Cm 2809). The figures cited do not include the Lord Chancellor's responsibilities for the Public Record Office.

(MAFF), the Department for Education and Employment (DfEE) and the Foreign and Commonwealth Office (FCO).

The costs of the Law Officers' Departments (Attorney General's Department and the Scottish Crown Office and Lord Advocate's Department) added another £368m (of which 81% was to fund the Crown Prosecution Service). A broader definition of 'justice' would require us to add the cost of some Home Office functions: in particular, police (£3,813m), prisons (£1,499m), probation and criminal policy (£506m) and criminal injuries compensation (£261m). This chapter is mainly concerned with matters of parliamentary accountability in relation to courts and the judiciary, most of which fall within the remit of the Lord Chancellor's Department; but the somewhat unclear boundaries between these and other aspects of the administration of justice form part of the background and the substance of the discussion, as will become apparent later.

As has already been noted, the new public management revolution has begun to have a significant impact on the administration of justice. A lot of justice functions – including some of the ones within the purview of the Lord Chancellor and the Law Officers – are delivered by Next Steps agencies, notably the Courts Service and the Land Registry. The Treasury Solicitor's Department, responsible for giving legal advice to many central departments, and for much government litigation, is an agency. Most of the government's conveyancing needs are met by another agency, the Government Property Lawyers, based in Taunton. Some in-house government legal services (but not core legal advice to ministers) have been market tested and/ or contracted out. There is a Courts Charter and a Legal Services Ombudsman. The movement towards greater transparency in the public administration of legal services has brought a lot of documentation – framework agreements, annual reports, business plans, even a published summary of the procedures for making judicial appointments – into the public domain, providing (in theory at least) a promising basis for enhanced public accountability.

The Lord Chancellor's Department: from museum to ministry

As already noted, the member of the cabinet with core responsibility for the administration of justice is the Lord Chancellor, among whose interesting characteristics is the fact that – unlike his ministerial colleagues, whose main qualification for advancement is their political track record and high standing in their party – he is required to be an expert in the main subject of his department's business. A Lord Chancellor often (though by no means always) has a limited party political background and little if any parliamentary experience. Students of the British constitution have long invoked the Lord Chancellor as living proof that separation of powers is a myth. Certainly, his multiple role in superintending/ appointing the judiciary, safeguarding its independence from Executive interference, sitting from time to time as an appellate judge, and answering to Parliament for matters pertaining to the machinery of justice, requires some very nimble footwork and an ability to wear several hats at the same time without looking uncomfortable. Increasingly, in modern times, the Lord Chancellor has become pre-eminently a departmental minister – or perhaps even, given Lord Irvine's special responsibility for overseeing the Labour government's big agenda of constitutional reform, an inter-departmental minister.

A Lord Chancellor's Office – the modern Lord Chancellor's Department in embryo – was set up in 1885. It was originally, and long remained, very small, being concerned almost entirely with ecclesiastical and judicial patronage. The late R M Jackson observed that, in 1912, when Viscount Haldane first became Lord Chancellor (after serving for several years as Secretary of State for War), 'he doubtless felt that his new department needed some attention, for it was then not far removed from being an interesting little museum'.[7] A few years later, the Report of the Committee on the Machinery of Government,[8] chaired by Haldane, recommended the transformation of the Home Office into a Ministry of Justice, with the Lord Chancellor retaining his responsibilities for judicial appointments and presiding over a new Imperial Court of Appeal. In the 80 years since then, there has been an episodic, but often heated, debate about the desirability or otherwise of establishing a Ministry of Justice in some form or another, a debate often characterised by a surprising amount of emotion (much of it to do with perceived threats to judicial independence from making judges accountable to a political minister in the Commons) and a lot of semantic confusion.[9] In the mid-1980s Lord Chancellor Hailsham (while having claimed, himself, in a rare appearance before a Commons Select Committee, to be a Minister of Justice[10]) said of the Alliance Parties' proposal for a new Department of Justice that such a move would be 'constitutionally very dangerous' and a menace to the independence of the judiciary.[11]

Some variants upon the 'Ministry of Justice' theme have impinged on the political agendas of the 1990s, but circumstances have radically changed since 1918. Haldane's vision of an Imperial Court of Appeal never came to pass.[12] Since the 1940s, changes in the arrangements for judicial business in the House of Lords have made it much harder for Lord Chancellors to find time to sit judicially. And since the early 1970s, following the Courts Act 1971 which led, inter alia, to the County Courts Service being brought under the wing of a radically enlarged and reconstituted Lord Chancellor's Department, that department has grown from a tiny museum-like 'Office', into a major spending 'Department'.

The democratic imperative of judicial independence has had to try to learn to coexist with another democratic imperative – that of public accountability. The sheer size and costliness of the services administered and delivered by the Lord Chancellor's Department require commensurately bigger and more robust mechanisms of public accountability than might have sufficed, or have been thought to suffice, in the era of the old Lord Chancellor's Office. But in considering this we have also to note the impact of the New Public Management revolution and the cult of efficiency,

---

7 R M Jackson *The Machinery of Justice in England* (7th edn, 1977) p 583.

8 1918 (Cd 9230) ch X.

9 See G Drewry 'Lord Haldane's Ministry of Justice – Stillborn or Strangled at Birth?' (1983) PA 61 396-414; G Drewry 'The Debate about a Ministry of Justice – A Joad's Eye View' [1987] PL 502-509.

10 Fourth Report from the Home Affairs Committee, 1980-81, *The Prison Service*, HC 412, Evidence, QQ 995-996.

11 (1986) *Guardian*, 26 May.

12 See R Stevens *The Independence of the Judiciary* (1993) pp 68-69.

effectiveness and economy that has been such a feature of the Thatcher and Major years and looks like remaining so under Mr Blair's New Labour. The Lord Chancellor's Department, like every other department in Whitehall, has become subject to the new disciplines of efficiency reviews, the Financial Management Initiative (FMI), Next Steps, the Citizen's Charter, market testing, etc. The Civil Justice Review (initiated in the 1980s by Lord Hailsham), the notorious Green Papers that followed the Review, the more recent Woolf Report on Civil Justice, the re-structuring of legal aid, and pressure on the professions to alter their arrangements for charging for work done – for instance, on a conditional fee or contractual basis – are all products or by-products of the new hegemony of performance-driven public management.

In a public lecture delivered in 1987[13] (around the time that Lord Mackay succeeded Lord Hailsham as Lord Chancellor), Sir Nicolas (now Lord) Browne-Wilkinson, then Vice-Chancellor of the Supreme Court, identified several developments in the last 30 years or so that, in his view, posed a threat to the continuing independence of the administration of justice. He noted, for instance, the post-1971 shift in the administrative control of the courts from judges to civil servants in an expanded Lord Chancellor's Department. Acknowledging that the theoretical distinction between administrative and judicial functions is not so easy to maintain in practice as some might like to pretend, he suggested that this shift has 'given rise to stresses between the judiciary and the administrators as to their different functions'.[14] The administrative listing of cases for trial is a notoriously vexed illustration of this. The controversy over the former exclusion of the Parliamentary Commissioner from reviewing alleged maladministration on the part of court staff, discussed below, is another. Lord Browne-Wilkinson pointed to worrying deficiencies in the command structure, in that there is no machinery for resolving disputes between judges and administrators, short of the Lord Chancellor himself.[15]

The point on which he laid greatest stress concerned the recent development of Financial Management and Value for Money disciplines relating to public expenditure, and their application to the Lord Chancellor's Department:

> the requirements of judicial independence make the Lord Chancellor's Department wholly different from any other department of state. It is not for the executive alone to determine what should be the policy objectives of the courts. It is not for the executive alone to determine whether or not a particular judicial procedure provides 'value for money'. Justice is not capable of being measured out by an accountant's computer . . . [U]nder our constitution it is for the judge to determine what is just, and what is not just, subject always to legislation passed by Parliament. As a result of such policy being applied to the Lord Chancellor's Department, that department is being required to formulate policy and to make determinations as to 'value for money' according to financial yardsticks and without, for the most part, even consulting the judges.[16]

Thus, he went on:

13   Sir Nicolas Brown-Wilkinson 'The Independence of the Judiciary in the 1980s' [1988] PL 44-57.
14   Ibid at p 46.
15   Ibid at p 47.
16   Ibid at pp 48-49.

The Lord Chancellor's own position, representing as he does simultaneously both the independent judiciary and the interests of government, is becoming more and more difficult, since the price to be paid for obtaining funds for the administration of justice is dependent on satisfying the Treasury that any particular course represents, in their terms, value for money.[17]

His Department is forced by the demands for financial economy to move more and more into areas which the judges have traditionally considered to be their exclusive preserve.

While conceding that 'there is no justification for a claim that the legal system has a greater right to public funds than, for example, the National Health Service or education',[18] he argued that, while the fixing of the total budget must be a political act, judges must, in the interests of judicial independence, be involved – through the creation of a new 'collegiate body of judges', funded by and answerable to the Lord Chancellor – in the preparation of the estimates and in the allocation of the budget once it has been voted by Parliament.[19]

Even if we accept Lord Browne-Wilkinson's diagnosis, it is hard to see how the latter proposal could be made to work in practice. A few years later, in another public lecture,[20] Lord Chancellor Mackay himself seemed implicitly to reject this plea for direct judicial involvement, certainly in respect of funding matters, while at the same time defending his own position as a minister in the House of Lords:

The House of Commons is not itself a policy-making body. In such a system, the judicature needs a minister to act as its friend at court, who can compete on equal terms – so far as differences in size permit – with other spending departments for a share of the public money. The intensity of political conflict in the House of Commons also makes it desirable, in our system, that the judiciary should not become directly involved in the politically-charged process of obtaining resources. The Lord Chancellor serves to insulate them from that process.

The present writers' view is that the Browne-Wilkinson thesis about the Lord Chancellor's Department being 'wholly different' from other ministries is overstated. In the 1980s, and even more so in the 1990s, the department has come to look increasingly like other spending departments, deeply imbued with the culture of New Public Management – a culture which is unlikely to change under Tony Blair and Lord Irvine. By the same token, Lord Mackay's characterisation of the Lord Chancellor's role as one of 'insulating' judges from the political rough and tumble of resource allocation perpetuates the conventional wisdom of a different era.

There is indeed some irony in Lord Mackay's use of this metaphor given that his tenure as Lord Chancellor marked a sharp change of style from that of his predecessor, Lord Hailsham, a traditionalist High Tory English barrister, who had been fiercely protective of the judiciary against any whiff of political or parliamentary interference –

---

17 Ibid at p 50.
18 Ibid at pp 53-54.
19 Ibid at p 56.
20 Lord Mackay of Clashfern 'The Role of the Lord Chancellor in the Administration of Justice' Earl Grey Lecture, University of Newcastle, 24 February 1990.

witness his objections to scrutiny of his department by the Home Affairs Committee or the ombudsman, as discussed below. Lord Mackay, a Scots Law Lord by background, was not a member of the English legal establishment and he did not allow his own talk of 'insulation' to get in the way of his evident determination that the administration of justice should deliver efficiency, effectiveness and economy, and a good service to the public. His approach sometimes brought him into conflict with the bar and the judiciary, most notably in the furore inside and outside Parliament generated by his three Green Papers on aspects of legal services and the legal professions, published in January 1988. Indeed, his 'ministerial' concern about public finance manifested itself in his dissenting judgment in *Pepper v Hart*.[1] Some of the insulation may have melted in the heat of controversy, but the Mackay years did see some significant developments in the mechanisms for parliamentary scrutiny of the administration of justice – as discussed below.

Lord Mackay's Labour successor, Lord Irvine, is another Scot, though a member of the English Bar. He has shown no signs at all of seeking to reinstate the Hailsham ethos. But in the Autumn of 1997 he did backtrack on an earlier commitment to appoint a committee to advise on judicial appointments – in circumstances outlined later in this chapter.

The Lord Chancellor's accountability to Parliament

In January 1992, Lord Mackay appeared before the Commons Home Affairs Committee for the first time since the Committee's remit had been extended to include the Lord Chancellor's Department.[2] He told the Committee that:

> I think it is extremely important for the working of our democratic institutions that there should be in the Cabinet a person who represents in a particular way the system of justice. I think it is also very helpful that there should be, at the head of the judiciary, someone who can be accountable to Parliament and can hold office in such a way that if Parliament is dissatisfied with the way in which its responsibilities are being discharged he could be relieved of his office without the necessity which protects all holders of permanent judicial office.[3]

So far as parliamentary accountability is concerned, there have been two main criticisms. First, it has long been a matter for adverse comment that the Lord Chancellor does not sit in the Commons; until quite recently the Attorney General (who has no power to instruct the officials of the Lord Chancellor's Department, and has a job that is quite different from that of the Lord Chancellor) deputised for him, acting 'as a courier between the Commons and the Lord Chancellor – and indeed as a courier who rarely brings any reply'.[4] The position was improved in April 1992,

---

1   [1993] AC 593, discussed in ch IX; see D Oliver '*Pepper v Hart*: a suitable case for reference to *Hansard*?' [1993] PL 5.
2   See below.
3   Transcript, 29 January 1992, Q 1.
4   R Brazier 'Government and the Law: Ministerial Responsibility for Legal Affairs' [1989] PL 64-94 at 68.

following the transfer to the Lord Chancellor's Department of Home Office responsibilities for the administration of magistrates' courts, when the Lord Chancellor was given the support of a parliamentary under secretary. The latter regularly answers parliamentary questions, makes statements and takes part in legislative and other debates on matters relating to the Lord Chancellor's responsibilities, in the Commons. The Blair government has retained this office, held at the time of writing by Geoff Hoon, MP.

Secondly, his relations with the judiciary are highly secretive, and the manner in which his powers of discipline, patronage and promotion are exercised has given rise to intermittent concern. Robert Stevens has culled some lurid episodes that bear upon this from his trawl of the files of the Lord Chancellor's Department.[5] So far as judicial appointments are concerned, there is now a published document on the Lord Chancellor's policies and procedures, the first version of which appeared in 1986 (when Lord Hailsham still held the office), and the subject has – as we shall see – been examined by the Home Affairs Committee.[6] Despite this modest movement towards greater transparency and public debate, and recent further statements on the subject by Lord Irvine,[7] many aspects of the relationship between the Lord Chancellor and the judiciary are still shrouded in mystery, based on the mythology of judicial independence, which tends to undermine public confidence and inhibit parliamentary scrutiny.

Let us consider just one aspect of this: the removal of members of the higher judiciary on a formal address – something that has not actually happened since 1830.[8] Paterson and Bates have pointed out that no Scottish or English judge has ever actually been removed in modern times. Not, they rather cryptically suggest, 'because there have not been any unfit or incapable judges during that time', but because:

> The perceived importance of the separation of powers and the independence of the judiciary is such that successive Lord Chancellors and Lord Presidents have preferred to put pressure – sometimes very strong pressure – on judges to resign rather than to invoke more formal measures. Since 1890 there have been at least 15 instances where judges of the superior courts in the United Kingdom have been the subject of strong pressures or inducements to resign, ostensibly on the grounds of ill-health which they were reluctant to face up to or incapable of recognising.[9]

And, they go on:

> The problem with such an approach is not just the secrecy with which it is pursued but that it provides no overt support for the democratic principle that public officials who are entrusted with considerable powers should be held accountable for the exercise of these powers.

There is a third area of difficulty, perhaps the most sensitive. A JUSTICE Committee, chaired by John Macdonald QC, was appointed in 1985 to examine the Administration

---

5   R Stevens *The Independence of the Judiciary: The View from the Lord Chancellor's Office* (1993).
6   Third Report, 1995-96, *Judicial Appointments Procedures*, HC 52.
7   See below.
8   S Shetreet *Judges on Trial* (1976) pp 143-144.
9   A Paterson and St J Bates *The Legal System of Scotland* (2nd edn, 1986) p 172.

of the Courts. It looked at, among other things, the problem of how best to handle public complaints against judges. Its report said that some members of the committee believed that the increasing tendency for public authorities to be involved in litigation would make it 'increasingly difficult for the public to accept that judges are independent when the head of the judiciary, who is responsible for their behaviour, is also a leading member of the government'. One solution, they suggested, would be to restrict the role of the Lord Chancellor to being head of the judiciary and Speaker of the House of Lords – which 'would be a logical solution if as some have suggested, a Ministry of Justice is set up, with its departmental Minister in the House of Commons'.

Since then, a lot of changes have occurred. There is now a Courts Charter, an extended role for the ombudsman to investigate complaints against courts administrators, a junior Lord Chancellor's Department minister in the House of Commons – and an apparently greater willingness on the part of Lord Chancellors than in the past to take tough action in the case of public concern about the professional performance of senior judges.[10] These are important and useful developments, but they only scratch the surface of accountability. The Blair government was initially committed to the establishment of a Judicial Appointments and Training Commission, which would be subject to scrutiny by a new Departmental Select Committee on Legal Affairs. The latter, which would have operated alongside the Home Affairs Committee, would potentially have been an important addition to the armoury of House of Commons scrutiny of the administration of justice. However, at the time of writing, these ideas seem to have been shelved.

The role of select committees

Opening the Commons debate in July 1979 on motions to establish a new system of departmentally-related select committees, Norman St John Stevas rejected a proposal by the Procedure Committee[11] that the Home Affairs Committee should undertake scrutiny of both the Lord Chancellor's Department and the Law Officers' Department. In his speech (prompted, as it has since been made clear, by Lord Hailsham) St John Stevas spoke of the threat to the independence of the judiciary that might arise –

> if a select committee were to investigate such matters as the appointment and conduct of the judiciary and its part in legal administration, or matters such as confidential communications between the judiciary and the Lord Chancellor and the responsibility of the Law Officers with regard to prosecutions and civil proceedings.[12]

He added that the Lord Chancellor's functions are all 'deeply interwoven with judicial matters'. But, as several members pointed out, it simply is not true to suggest that judicial independence is threatened by committee investigations into the administration of, for instance, legal aid (or for that matter the Public Record Office).

10 Eg the resignation, early in 1998, of Harman J, following an interview with the Lord Chancellor about strong criticisms by the Court of Appeal of the time it had taken him to issue a judgment.
11 First Report, HC 588, 1977-78, para 5.24.
12 HC Debs, 25 June 1979, cols 35ff.

It seems clear, in any case, that the Procedure Committee never envisaged the Home Affairs Committee looking at judicial activity as such.

Both the Home Affairs Committee and the Liaison Committee subsequently pressed the government to change its mind, without success. Meanwhile, Lord Hailsham voluntarily gave evidence to the Home Affairs Committee, both in its Prisons inquiry and its Remands in Custody inquiry, without any visible harm befalling the British constitution, or for that matter, Lord Hailsham. It may be noted also that the Lord Chancellor's Department has, in any case, always been answerable to the Public Accounts Committee – which has, potentially, an important role to play in the scrutiny of policy effectiveness via the National Audit Office's extended responsibilities for the conduct of Value for Money Audits.

Ten years later, the Procedure Committee, in its inquiry into the Working of the Select Committee System,[13] reopened the matter. Lord St John of Fawsey told the Committee that the exclusion had been at the strong insistence of the then Lord Chancellor, Lord Hailsham, to whose views he had deferred on 'tactical' grounds, so as not to jeopardise the entire package of proposals for committee reform.[14] The Committee recommended that the order of reference of the Home Affairs Committee should be extended to cover matters within the responsibilities of the Lord Chancellor's Department and the Law Officers' Department, excluding consideration of the merits of individual cases.

This time the Government (Lord Hailsham now having retired to the back-benches) accepted it.[15] A Commons motion, implementing this along with many other of the Procedure Committee's recommendations, was debated and carried on 18 July 1991.[16] The standing order setting out the terms of reference of the Home Affairs Committee was amended to empower the committee to examine the 'policy, administration and expenditure of the Lord Chancellor's Department (including the work of staff provided for the administrative work of courts and tribunals, but excluding consideration of individual cases and appointments)'. A similar change was made to the terms of reference of the Scottish Affairs Committee with respect to scrutiny of the Lord Advocate's functions.

However, six years later, the Conservative Chairman of the Home Affairs Committee opined that 'the Lord Chancellor's and Law Officers' Departments have been inadequately scrutinised' and mooted the possibility of establishing a separate select committee to cover these areas.[17]

With reference to the exclusion of individual judicial appointments from the terms of reference of the select committees, the Leader of the House observed that the Committees would 'be free to examine the appointments system as a whole'. The Home Affairs Committee was soon to take advantage of this new freedom.

---

13 Second Report, 1989-90, HC 19-I.
14 Evidence to Select Committee on Procedure *The Working of the Select Committee System* HC 19-II, 1989-90, para 742.
15 Government response 1991 (Cm 1532).
16 HC Debs, 18 July 1991, cols 579-608.
17 Liaison Committee *The Work of Select Committees* HC 323-I, 1996-97, p 46.

Work of the Home Affairs Committee: judicial appointments

In 1995 the Home Affairs Committee embarked on an inquiry into the subject of judicial appointments procedures. Its two-volume report was published in the summer of 1996.[18] Like so many select committee reports, this one is an invaluable resource for anyone interested in the subject under investigation. But, for the purposes of this chapter, the importance of the exercise lies in the fact that it happened at all. A select committee inquiry into something that has hitherto been such a closeted area of government marks a welcome progression from the dark ages of almost total lack of public information and accountability on the subject. The substantive value of the exercise lies almost entirely in the voluminous oral and written evidence, from an impressive array of official, professional and academic witnesses, rather than in the committee's own conclusions which, in this case, are generally bland and uncritical.

The section of the report dealing with Proposals for a Judicial Appointments Commission are a case in point. The committee received a considerable body of evidence from JUSTICE, NACRO, the Howard League for Penal Reform and the Law Society, arguing for some variant of a Commission. It noted the Labour Party's consultation paper on 'Access to Justice', which had recently floated a similar proposal. The proposal for a Commission was strongly opposed by the Lord Chancellor and by the Lord Chief Justice, appearing in his capacity as Chairman of the Judges' Council. In the end, the committee, 'while not discounting its merits', concluded that 'the value of a consultations network might be diminished if a Judicial Appointments Commission were to play a part in selecting judges'.[19] This is not a particularly convincing argument, given that it is the 'network', and the secrecy associated with its operation, that has given rise to particular concern.

The committee seemed to attach very little weight to the argument that the *appearance* of fairness and neutrality in the judicial appointments process matters every bit as much as the reality when it comes to maintaining public confidence in the judiciary, and although the arguments for an Appointments Commission are by no means all one way, its dogged endorsement of the status quo paid scant regard to an impressive weight of contrary evidence.

On 23 June 1997, seven weeks after the general election, the Lord Chancellor announced the government's intention to consult on the merits of establishing a Judicial Appointments Commission.[20] However, four months later, on 9 October 1997, he further announced that his 'very heavy workload' had led him to decide to put the issue on the back burner.[1] However, he did go on to announce some improvements on existing practice relating to judicial appointments, most importantly, that High Court appointments would, in future, be advertised. There was also to be an important innovation in respect of parliamentary scrutiny: as recommended by the Home Affairs Committee, in future the Lord Chancellor would report annually to Parliament on the operation of the judicial appointments system, the first such report to cover the period 1998-99.

18 *Judicial Appointments Procedures* HC 52, 1995-96.
19 Ibid para 142.
20 HL Debs, 23 June 1997, col WA 145.
 1 Lord Chancellor's Department Press Notice 220/97; HL Debs, 15 October 1997, cols WA 193-194.

The statement also indicated that there were to be longer-term reviews of the possibility of establishing an ombudsman to examine complaints of unfair treatment in the judicial appointments process.

The role of the Parliamentary Commissioner for Administration

The JUSTICE Committee mentioned above looked at the machinery for dealing with public complaints about the administration of the courts. The inquiry excluded consideration of complaints about the merits of courts' decisions (in respect of which there is often a right of appeal) and, time and time again, the report comes back to the need to preserve judicial independence by separating administrative' matters from 'judicial' ones – a distinction which is far from watertight in practice. Lord Mackay told the Home Affairs Committee that, so far as administration of the courts is concerned, it was important 'that judges be involved and direct the administrator as to what is to be done', and said that the relationship between judges and administrators 'is based on a partnership'.[2]

Thus, the report discusses the role of the Parliamentary Commissioner for Administration, who in 1984 reached a 'concordat' with the Lord Chancellor's Department about the location of the boundary line between 'administrative' and 'judicial' (a matter best left, the JUSTICE committee argued, in another part of the report, to the 'common sense' of experienced Lord Chancellor's Department officials), since when 'the number of complaints involving the Department has risen'. The 1984 agreement subsequently broke down following the Lord Chancellor's Department's obtaining counsel's opinion to the effect that court staff supplied by the department but working under the instructions of judges did not come within the purview of the Parliamentary Commissioner Act 1967: and the select committee on the PCA took evidence on the subject both from Lord Hailsham and Lord Mackay, though in separate sessions.[3] Lord Mackay subsequently agreed to bring his department within the purview of the PCA by way of a new clause in the Courts and Legal Services Bill, and this was done. The impact of this extension of the ombudsman's remit is considered below.

Meanwhile, the JUSTICE Committee also noted the rather startling fact that, in dealing with complaints by disgruntled litigants, the Lord Chancellor's Department's refusal to accept responsibility for administrative actions carried out on the instructions of a judge meant that only 5% of complaints are accepted for consideration. It said, with some understatement, that it is not surprising if such a low take-up rate gives rise to 'some lack of confidence' in the system.[4]

In fact, the committee – in common with so many other people – became preoccupied with the issue of judicial independence, to a point where it virtually lost sight of any legitimate claims of public accountability. At one point it considered the objections that might be raised to extending the powers of the PCA to include investigations of judicial behaviour, a change favoured by some members of the

---

2   Transcript of evidence, 11 March 1992, Q 111.
3   Evidence of Lord Hailsham, 31 March 1987, 1986-87, HC 284-ii; evidence of Lord Mackay, 26 January 1989, 1988-89, HC 159.
4   JUSTICE Report, para 3.7.

Committee. One objection, it said, 'is that, as the Ombudsman reports to the House of Commons, this would encourage MPs to pry into the affairs of the judiciary'. But this objection was then promptly rejected on the grounds that the PCA is an independent officer who 'would only investigate a complaint if he were satisfied that it was serious', and, the report continues, 'if a serious complaint is made, it would seem better that it should be investigated by an independent person of the standing of the Ombudsman than for it to become the subject of ill-informed speculation in Parliament'.[5]

Since the jurisdiction was extended, there has been a steady trickle of PCA cases on matters to do with the administration of justice. In the five-year period 1992-96, the ombudsman received 190 complaints against the Lord Chancellor's Department, mostly concerning the Courts Service (which became an executive agency in 1995). This represents just 2.8% of the 6,704 cases received by the PCA during this period. Of the 190 complaints, 32 (16.8%) were upheld wholly or in part. We must also take account of the complaints against Lord Chancellor Department agencies – the Land Registry (47 complaints, three upheld wholly or in part) and the Northern Ireland Courts Service (six complaints, one upheld); and against the Scottish Courts Administration, which is an agency operating under the Scottish Courts Service in the Scottish Office (four complaints, none upheld). But even when we do this, the aggregate figures do not at first sight suggest that the ombudsman is making a huge impact as a channel of accountability and redress in this context.

A look at the cases themselves confirms that – as with the PCA's caseload as a whole – most of the cases upheld concern those minor but infuriating inefficiencies that can so often afflict the public's dealings with officialdom. The great majority have been to do with the loss or misfiling of legal documents by court staff. Thus, in 1994,[6] the PCA reported on five cases, four of which had to do with the shortcomings of county court staff – two of the cases involving the same court. In one of the latter cases, the staff mislaid files, and this led to the complainant being wrongly listed as a defendant in a trial rather than an arbitration. The error was later compounded when judgment was wrongly entered in the Register of County Court Judgments. The ombudsman criticised the Lord Chancellor's Department for the delay in deleting the erroneous entry and for poor handling of the complaint. The complainant received reimbursement of his legal fees, with interest.

Although it is probably quite correct to say that the ombudsman has not revolutionised accountability for the administration of justice, three points should be borne in mind. First, what looks like a small case to the world at large may be of immense importance to the individual: the loss of court papers and/or the misrecording of a judgment can be both very damaging and very costly. Secondly, the general lessons learned from individual cases can have a beneficial knock-on effect on the quality of administration: ombudsman reports are full of references to departments promising to tighten up their procedures in response to adverse findings. Thirdly, and most important, the symbolism of admitting the PCA onto hitherto sacred turf, and so successfully confronting an ancient and largely irrational taboo about judicial independence cannot be overestimated. The extension of the ombudsman's jurisdiction

5   Ibid para 4.14.
6   *Annual Report of the Parliamentary Commissioner for Administration* HC 307, 1994-95.

is one of several manifestations of the 'normalisation' of the administration of justice as a public service, like any other.

Conclusion

Much anxiety has been expressed over the years about the need to maintain the territorial boundary line between Parliament and the courts in the interests of preserving judicial independence from the threat of contamination by parliamentary scrutiny. The reference by the JUSTICE Committee to the dreadful prospect of Parliament being allowed 'to pry into the affairs of judiciary' is a particularly vivid, and paranoid, illustration of this. But, perhaps inevitably, many of the old taboos have faded away in recent years. As the 'administration of justice' has become the 'public management' of justice, with the Lord Chancellor's Department playing an ever-growing part in the drive for more cost-effective and consumer-sensitive legal services, so it has come to be accepted that these services – and their public finances – should be subject, in the usual way, to parliamentary scrutiny. The growth of judicial review – and the prospective effects of incorporation of the European Convention on Human Rights – have made it harder to resist the claims of parliamentarians to look, from time to time, at activities of courts that have obvious political implications.

It is usually the case that, when light is shone into a hitherto locked and darkened room, fears that bogeymen are lurking in the corners prove to be groundless. There are many faults and flaws in the administration of justice, including sometimes the conduct of judges, but greater transparency reveals this to be the exception rather than the rule. And it encourages improvement when improvement is shown to be needed. There has not been a revolution in the arrangements for parliamentary scrutiny, but there has been a significant accumulation of important incremental changes. Above all, there has been a change in culture, consequent largely, we believe, on the diminution of the Lord Chancellor's former role in insulating the judges from any kind of outside comment that could, however fancifully, be thought 'political'. The judges nowadays – released in the late 1980s from the Kilmuir Rules, which had barred them from talking to the media – often speak up for themselves, in public, on matters of policy. A lot of them seem to enjoy doing so. There is no sign that this in any way compromises their political neutrality. And the relationship between the courts and Parliament has, by and large, become – and is likely to become increasingly so in the future – a more open and healthy one.

Chapter IV

Statute law and case law applicable to Parliament

Geoffrey Lock

Introduction

This chapter deals with some of the statute law and case law relating to Parliament. The phrase 'the law of Parliament' is sometimes used to cover the body of rules – mostly non-statutory – regulating the activities, privileges and immunities of the Houses: resolutions, standing orders and conventions. For example, the phrase is used in this sense in several paragraphs of the first Report of the Nolan Committee.[1] The body of domestic rules is sometimes called 'the common law of Parliament' and sometimes 'the law and custom of Parliament' (*lex et consuetudo parliamenti*). Much of the law of Parliament in this sense 'lies outside the scope of the *ordinary* law of the land',[2] and is beyond the purview of the courts. However, this chapter is mainly concerned with areas of parliamentary law which are *within* the jurisdiction of the courts.

Inflexibility or elasticity?

There is a divergence of view on the attributes that should characterise a desirable code of parliamentary law. On the one hand are ranged most parliamentarians who rate highly the qualities of elasticity and flexibility and warn against 'unduly detailed and prescriptive rules'.[3] The opposite camp consists of critics who deplore uncertainty, unpredictability, imprecision and arbitrariness.

There is a well-argued statement of the first point of view in the 1939 Report of the Select Committee on the Official Secrets Act:

> The privileges of Parliament, like many other institutions of the British constitution, are indefinite in their nature and stated in general and sometimes vague terms. The elasticity thus secured has made it possible to apply existing privileges in new circumstances from time to time. Any attempt to translate them into precise rules must deprive them of the very quality which renders them adaptable to new and varying conditions, and new or unusual

---

1   *Standards in Public Life* First Report of the Committee, Chairman Lord Nolan, 1995 (Cm 2850-1) ch 2.
2   S de Smith and R Brazier, *Constitutional and Administrative Law* (7th edn, 1994) p 25.
3   Nolan Report, ch 2, para 87.

combinations of circumstances, and indeed, might have the effect of restricting rather than safe-guarding Members' privileges . . .[4]

An ill-disposed observer might conclude that all this was akin to making up the rules as one went along and moving the goal-posts while the game was in progress. In any case, commending what purports to be a body of law for its vagueness does appear somewhat odd.

The Nolan Committee contrasts the flexibility of the House's own rules with 'the inflexibility of statutory procedures' and expresses its strong preference for the former, while mentioning that some witnesses, including a former Leader of the House (Mr Biffen) would have preferred statutory provision.[5] However, the Committee concluded 'that Resolutions of the House in matters of conduct are not perceived by all Members as having the same impact as laws or regulations, even though they are the law of Parliament', and that the House needs to develop a culture in which resolutions are regarded as binding.[6] Thus, the two sets of rules – statutory and domestic – are currently *not* regarded by everybody as of equal status.

The Nolan comparison between the two types with regard to flexibility is also questionable; statutes can also be uncertain, and therefore flexible. For example, the following is an extract from a memorandum submitted by the Bar Council to the 1967 Select Committee on Parliamentary Privilege:

> The uncertainty which affects the law of Parliamentary Privilege comes from the dearth of ordinary case law, a paucity of statutes and a large number of Parliamentary precedents of doubtful relevance to the present day. The uncertainty arises in two main ways:
>
> (i) in determining whether an alleged privilege exists . . .
>
> (ii) in the application and enforcement of a particular privilege . . . Within the accepted head of Freedom of Speech, for instance, there are many areas of uncertainty, e.g. the meaning of a 'proceeding in Parliament' within Article 9 of the Bill of Rights . . . There is no doubt that the uncertainty can sometimes give an impression of arbitrariness.[7]

The example given by the Bar Council relates to a key piece of parliamentary statute law – so statutes are *not* necessarily detailed and clear, as opposed to broad-brush, flexible domestic rules.

The Bar Council's 1967 memorandum was wide-ranging and contained a number of trenchant criticisms. The Law Society submitted a much briefer paper to the same select committee, obsequious in tone and confined to two points: the need for a definition of 'proceedings in Parliament' and the desirability of a procedure whereby a solicitor could obtain an advance ruling on whether a contemplated action would be regarded as a breach of privilege.

---

4   Report from the Select Committee on the Official Secrets Act (1938-39; HC 101) p xiv.
5   Nolan Report, ch 2, paras 59 and 102. In debate three MPs, Mr Benn, Mr Leigh and Mr Budgen, supported the view that the rules should be made statutory.
6   Nolan Report, ch 2, paras 96 and 98.
7   Report from the Select Committee on Parliamentary Privilege (1967-68; HC 34) pp 171-172.

Little change resulted from the 1967 Select Committee Report or from the Report of the Privileges Committee ten years later.[8] Some procedural recommendations were approved, but nothing was implemented that would have involved legislation.[9]

Antiquity and obscurity

As mentioned in the last section, some of the difficulties over parliamentary law stem from its antiquity and obscurity, and some examples are briefly listed here. Some are discussed in more detail later in the chapter.

Twice during the 1950s the House of Commons consulted the Judicial Committee of the Privy Council on points of law: in 1950 on whether a clergyman of the Church of Ireland was disqualified from membership of the House of Commons,[10] and in 1957 on the meaning of the Parliamentary Privilege Act 1770.[11] To turn to another matter, in 1984 there was a divergence of view on whether a mad peer could be compulsorily detained in a mental hospital, or whether this infringed privilege of peerage. Three Law Lords took one view, and the Attorney General and the Lord Advocate (both of whom subsequently became Lord Chancellor) took another.[12] The question was left unresolved. There are also doubts about the Parliamentary Papers Act 1840 – for example, whether the Act applies to Command Papers;[13] and, until recently, broadcasting staff responsible for parliamentary television and radio broadcasts were not protected by parliamentary privilege against actions for defamation over the content of broadcasts, whereas the MPs and peers whose utterances are transmitted *are* fully protected.[14] Broadcasting staff are now (it is thought) protected against defamation actions under the Defamation Act 1996, but they still have no protection against possible prosecutions for obscenity, blasphemy and criminal contempt of court. The most important piece of parliamentary statute law is undoubtedly

---

8   HC 417, 1976-77.
9   See G Marshall in M Ryle and P G Richards (eds) *The Commons under Scrutiny* (1988) pp 219-221, and in S A Walkland (ed) *The House of Commons in the Twentieth Century* (1979) pp 245-246.
10   The MacManaway case; the Judicial Committee reported that such a person was disqualified (Cmd 8067).
11   *Re Parliamentary Privilege Act 1770* [1958] AC 331 (also printed as Cmnd 431). See: G F Lock 'Parliamentary Privilege and the Courts: the Avoidance of Conflict' [1985] PL 67-68. The Judicial Committee confined itself to dealing with the narrow issue which had been referred to it, and made little use of the opportunity to comment on the Act more generally. The report from the Judicial Committee was one stage of the Strauss case of 1957-8, in which a clash between the House of Commons and the courts was narrowly avoided. Briefly, the London Electricity Board threatened to sue Mr Strauss, MP, for some remarks in a letter to a minister which it considered defamatory, and the matter was referred to the Committee of Privileges. The committee took the view that correspondence between ministers and MPs counted as 'proceedings in Parliament' within the meaning of art 9 of the Bill of Rights, but the House by a narrow majority decided that it did not (HC Deb, 8 July 1958, col 334). The Electricity Board did not persist in its proposed action.
12   Report by the House of Lords Committee for Privileges on Parliamentary Privilege and the Mental Health Legislation (HL 254 of 1983-84). See P M Leopold 'The Compulsory Detention of Peers' [1985] PL 9; G Zellick 'Lords and Lunacy' (1985) 101 LQR 8; G F Lock 'The Application of the General Law to Parliament' [1985] PL 376.
13   P M Leopold 'The Parliamentary Papers Act 1840 and its Application Today' [1990] PL 183-206.
14   P M Leopold 'Parliamentary Privilege and the Broadcasting of Parliament' (1989) 9 LS 53-66.

art 9 of the Bill of Rights 1688,[15] on parliamentary freedom of speech, but its meaning and current application are by no means straightforward.[16] In contrast, similar difficulties seem not to have been encountered over art 25 of the Claim of Right 1689 (c 28), the corresponding Scottish enactment.

The examples given so far are of statute law, but case law can also give rise to problems. In the *Mancroft* case in 1989,[17] there was a possibility that court staff might be called upon to arrest and imprison a peer. They were naturally concerned at the risk that they might be imprisoned in their turn by order of the House of Lords, as the Sheriff of Middlesex was in 1840 by order of the House of Commons.[18] Ancient precedents can still be re-activated, though the social context has changed out of all recognition.

Judicial attitudes

Cases involving Parliament have obliged judges to establish lines of demarcation between the courts and the legislature; they may have to choose between remaining faithful to their judicial principles and precipitating constitutional ferment, though all-out conflicts are fortunately rare. There was a major confrontation between the House of Commons and the Queen's Bench Division of the High Court over the *Stockdale v Hansard*[19] series of cases. In the course of that affair, the House committed officers of the court to prison and some MPs favoured imprisoning the judges for defying the Commons. The court could have riposted by imprisoning parliamentary staff – for example, the Serjeant-at-Arms – but matters did not reach that stage. What was at stake in the conflict was an attempt by the Commons to claim that its resolutions had the force of law;[20] had this claim been admitted,[1] the way would have been open for the Commons to legislate on their own, without the need for the co-operation of the Lords and the monarch. The court did not back down, and implicitly the Commons were forced to recognise that their position was untenable. The true solution to their problems was proper legislation, and the crisis was terminated by the passing of the Parliamentary Papers Act 1840.

Forty-five years later, in *Bradlaugh v Gossett*,[2] Lord Coleridge CJ struck an optimistic note when he remarked of possible conflicts between Parliament and the courts:

> While I do not deny that as a matter of reasoning such things might happen, it is consoling to reflect that they have scarce ever happened in the living centuries of our

15 1 Will & Mary, sess 2, c 2.
16 P M Leopold 'Free Speech in Parliament and the Courts' (1995) 14 LS 204-218; G F Lock 'The 1689 Bill of Rights' (1989) Pol S 552-554.
17 *Barclays Bank plc v Lord Mancroft* and three associated cases (1989, unreported) Wandsworth County Court. See P M Leopold 'The Freedom of Peers from Arrest' [1989] PL 398-399.
18 *Case of the Sheriff of Middlesex* (1840) 11 Ad & El 273.
19 (1839) 9 Ad & El 1; see also *Case of the Sheriff of Middlesex* (n 18 above).
20 Judge Eric Stockdale 'The Unnecessary Crisis: the Background to the Parliamentary Papers Act 1840' [1990] PL 30 at 48-49.
1 *Bowles v Bank of England* [1913] 1 Ch 57.
2 (1884) 12 QBD 271 at 275.

history, and that in the present state of things it is but barely possible that they should ever happen again.

However, his preceding words were less reassuring:

> Cases may be put . . . in which . . . it would be the plain duty of the court at all hazards to declare a resolution illegal and no protection to those who acted under it. Such cases might by possibility occasion unseemly conflicts between the courts and the House.

In the same case, Stephen J drew a distinction between, on the one hand, rights to be exercised within the House such as sitting and voting 'on which the House and the House only could interpret the statute' and, on the other hand, 'rights to be exercised out of and independently of the House on which the statute must be interpreted by the court independently of the House'.[3]

A case 15 years later involved the application of the licensing law to the House of Commons.[4] Although the prosecution of a barman failed on a technicality, the judge, Lord Russell of Killowen CJ, showed by his remarks that, had the technical difficulty been absent, he would not have shied away from the issue because the case involved the House:

> I think it right to say that I am far – very far – from being satisfied that no offence has been committed. I am not at all impressed by the argument that because many of the provisions of the Licensing Acts cannot be worked with reference to the House of Commons, therefore the Acts do not apply.

These examples show that nineteenth-century judges were prepared, when necessary, to adopt a robust approach if they felt that Parliament had overstepped the mark and to express their views forcefully. This attitude was reinforced by academic writers. Sir William Anson, the first edition of whose *Law and Custom of the Constitution*[5] was published in 1886, went so far as to equate parliamentary privilege merely with 'local custom', and said that it seemed –

> now to be clearly settled that the Courts will not be deterred from upholding private rights by the fact that questions of parliamentary privilege are involved in their maintenance; and that except as regards the internal regulation of its proceedings by the House, Courts of Law will not hesitate to inquire into alleged privilege, as they would into local custom, and determine its extent and application.[6]

Sir William Holdsworth, writing in 1924 about the nineteenth-century cases, took a similar view:

> All these cases illustrate the determination of the courts to assert the supremacy of the law over the working of all parts of the constitution. They show that the privileges of each

---

3   Ibid at 282.
4   *Williamson v Norris* [1899] 1 QB 7.
5   Volume 1: Parliament.
6   W Anson *Law and Custom of the Constitution* (5th edn, 1922) p 196.

of the Houses of Parliament are as much subject to the rule of law as the prerogative of the Crown; and that a subject, who complains that he is oppressed by an undue exercise of privilege, has the same right to apply to the courts for redress, as a subject who complains that he is oppressed by an undue exercise of the prerogative. The courts are subject to the enactments passed by King, Lords and Commons, for they are law; but they are subject to no other authority.[7]

The trouble with the Anson-Holdsworth view of the topic is that the two Houses have been reluctant to accept the right of the courts to determine the existence and limits of their privileges. (One particular objection is the possibility that, if an appeal in a case were to be taken up to the highest level, the privileges of the Commons would be determined by the Lords.) As Keir and Lawson put it:

'There may be at any given moment two doctrines of privilege, the one held by the Courts, the other by either House, the one to be found in the Law Reports, the other in Hansard; and there is no way of resolving the real point at issue should the conflict arises.[8]

Among twentieth-century cases, the *Graham-Campbell* case[9] stands out as differing from previous and subsequent cases, and will be discussed below. Judges in other twentieth-century cases, while using less trenchant language than their nineteenth-century predecessors, have tended to emphasise that the privileges of Parliament, while justifiable on grounds of the general good, are offset by a reduction in the rights of litigants, so that what is Parliament's gain is the community's loss. Thus, the Judicial Committee of the Privy Council in 1958 referred to 'the inalienable rights of Her Majesty's subjects to have recourse to her courts of law for the remedy of their wrongs',[10] implying that these rights should be impeded as little as possible by parliamentary privilege. In 1962 Lord Radcliffe mentioned his 'reluctance to treat a Member's privilege as going beyond anything that is essential' and, perhaps with his tongue in his cheek, referred to 'the proper anxiety of the House to confine its own or its Members' privileges to the minimum infringement of the liberties of others'.[11] In 1990 Popplewell J stated that, in his view, a court, 'while giving full attention to the necessity for comity between the courts and Parliament, should not be astute to find a reason for ousting the jurisdiction of the court and for limiting or even defeating a proper claim by a party to litigation before it'. The judge also said:

It was important to realise that there was a no less important principle [than the meaning of certain words in art 9 of the Bill of Rights], that this country's citizens should have free and unrestricted access to the courts of the land and, subject to the rules of the court, be able to present their cases fully and freely.

---

7 Sir W Holdsworth *History of English Law* (1924) vol VI, p 272.
8 Sir D Keir and F H Lawson *Cases in Constitutional Law* (3rd edn, 1948) p 76.
9 *R v Graham-Campbell, ex p Herbert* [1935] 1 KB 594.
10 [1958] AC 331 at 353. See also the abortive note of dissent by Lord Denning MR in which he recommended a course of action under which 'the right of every Englishman to seek redress in the courts of law is preserved inviolate without interference by the House of Commons' [1985] PL 85. Dissents were not disclosed and published until 1966; previously, the fiction had been maintained that the Committee was always unanimous.
11 *A-G of Ceylon v de Livera* [1962] 3 All ER 1066.

And the judge quoted from Magna Carta: 'To no one will we deny or delay right and justice.'[12] However, in 1994, the Judicial Committee of the Privy Council ruled that if there was a conflict between: (a) the need to ensure that the legislature can exercise its powers freely on behalf of its electors; and *either* (b) the need to protect freedom of speech generally; *or* (c) the interests of justice in ensuring that all relevant evidence is available to the courts; then, 'of these three public interests, the first [, (a),] must prevail'.[13]

Two lines of thinking, which are not easy to reconcile, are perceptible in judicial attitudes to these matters: the need to safeguard the interests of litigants, and the desirability of avoiding a conflict between Parliament and the courts. The second aim was formulated in, for example, judgments by the House of Lords in *Pickin*'s case.[14] Lord Reid put the matter thus:

> For a century or more Parliament and the courts have been careful not to act so as to cause conflict between them. Any such investigations as the respondent seeks could easily lead to such a conflict, and I would only support it if compelled to do so by clear authority.

Lord Simon of Glaisdale agreed:

> It is well known that in the past there have been dangerous strains between the law courts and Parliament – dangerous because each institution has its own particular role to play in our constitution, and because collision between the two institutions is likely to impair their power to vouchsafe those constitutional rights for which citizens depend on them. So for many years Parliament and the courts have each been astute to respect the sphere of action and the privileges of the other.

However, deference has its limits and some judges have refused to practise it, notably Hunt J in the Supreme Court of New South Wales in *R v Murphy*,[15] whose judgment was overridden by legislation in the Parliament of the Commonwealth of Australia. Discussed later are the *Mancroft* case,[16] in which the judge declined to follow the decision in *Stourton v Stourton*,[17] and *Bear v State of South Australia*,[18] in which the judge refused to abide by the judgment of Lord Hewart in the *Graham-Campbell* case. To move closer to home, it was suggested in argument before the House of Lords in *Pepper v Hart*[19] that a proposed relaxation of the rule under which courts did not consult Hansard to construe ambiguous statutes would infringe parliamentary privilege, both generally and as formulated in art 9 of the Bill of Rights in particular. This

---

12   *Rost v Edwards* [1990] 2 WLR 1280 at 1293. See P M Leopold 'Proceedings in Parliament: the Grey Area' [1990] PL 475-481.
13   *Prebble v Television New Zealand Ltd* [1995] 1 AC 321, per Lord Browne-Wilkinson at 336. See P Leopold, ch V below.
14   *British Railways Board v Pickin* [1974] AC 765 at 765, 768. See also similar remarks by Lord Donaldson MR in *R v HM Treasury, ex p Smedley* [1985] QB 657 at 666.
15   (1986) 5 NSWLR 18. See Sir Clarrie Harders 'Parliamentary Privilege – Parliament versus the Courts: Cross-Examination of Committee Witnesses' Parliament of Australia, Parliamentary Research Services Background Paper, 8 October 1991.
16   (1989, unreported).
17   [1963] P 302.
18   (1981) 48 SAIR 604.
19   [1993] AC 593, HL. See G Marshall, ch IX below.

argument was firmly rejected by both the minority (Lord Mackay of Clashfern LC)[20] and the majority of the panel of judges. Speaking on behalf of the latter, Lord Browne-Wilkinson said:

> This House and the courts have always been, and I trust will always continue to be, zealous in protecting Parliamentary privileges . . . Although for a considerable time before the resumed hearing it was known that the House was to consider whether to permit Hansard as an aid to construction, there was no suggestion from the Crown or anyone else that such a course might breach Parliamentary privilege until the Attorney-General raised the point at the start of the re-hearing.[1]

The basis of the Attorney General's submissions was a recent letter from the Clerk of the House of Commons. The court was plainly irritated at having the issue sprung on it with little notice, and made it clear that it regarded the point as a red herring. It is obviously important that claims for privilege should be made only when absolutely necessary, or they will become devalued; and the much-prized *cordon sanitaire* between Parliament and the courts might then be at risk.

The *Graham-Campbell* case: Parliament as a statute-free zone

As mentioned above, this case[2] is out of line with the general trend of judicial decisions involving Parliament. Like *Williamson v Norris*,[3] it was concerned with the arrangements for the supply of liquor to the House of Commons and its background is described by the protagonist in his autobiography.[4] The case is important because the judgment in it has formed the basis for some of the corporate immunities of the House since 1935.

The presiding judge was Lord Hewart CJ. Heuston and Brazier consider Hewart to have been the worst Lord Chief Justice since the seventeenth century,[5] ie since Scroggs and Jeffreys. Lord Devlin thought this view to be unfair to Jeffreys, and in his opinion Hewart was 'comparatively speaking . . . the worst chief justice ever', with not 'a grain of judicial sense'.[6] Whatever the merits or demerits of Lord Hewart as a judge, his judgment in the case stands as an authority. Heuston called it 'somewhat unsatisfactory'[7] and de Smith and Brazier said that the court took 'a remarkably generous view of the scope of the internal affairs of the House of Commons'.[8]

Lord Hewart decided that the House was not bound by the law on the permitted hours for the serving of alcoholic drinks, and based his ruling on a quotation from Lord Denman's judgment in *Stockdale v Hansard*.[9] (The quotation was found for him

---

20 At 614.
1 At 645.
2 [1935] 1 KB 594.
3 [1899] 1 QB 7.
4 Sir A P Herbert *Independent Member* (1950) ch 1.
5 R Brazier *Constitutional Practice* (2nd edn, 1994) p 287.
6 Lord Devlin *Easing the Passing – The Trial of John Bodkin Adams* (1985) p 92.
7 R F V Heuston *Essays in Constitutional Law* (2nd edn, 1964) p 94.
8 *de Smith and Brazier* p 351.
9 (1839) 9 Ad & El 1 at 115.

by Avory J, who sat with Hewart.[10]) The relevant passage in Lord Hewart's judgment was as follows:

> The words of Lord Denman CJ in *Stockdale v Hansard* are sufficient for the present purpose. He said: 'The Commons of England are not invested with more of power and dignity by their legislative character than by that which they bear as the grand inquest of the nation. All the privileges that can be required for the energetic discharge of the duties inherent in that high trust are conceded without a murmur or a doubt.' Here, as it seems to me, the magistrate [ie Sir Rollo Graham-Campbell] was entitled to say, on the materials before him, that in the matters complained of the House of Commons was acting collectively in a matter which fell within the area of the internal affairs of the House and, that being so, any tribunal might well feel, on the authorities, an invincible reluctance to interfere.

Lord Hewart's quotation was unrepresentative of Lord Denman's argument, taken as a whole. In the passage from which it was drawn, Lord Denman was giving examples of occasions when the courts would be right to interfere with unreasonable and illegal actions taken by the House of Commons. Denman's judgment continued:

> We freely admit them [the privileges needed by the Commons as the grand inquest] in all their extent and variety; but if, on a resolution of guilt voted by themselves, this grand inquest . . . should mistake their right of initiating a charge for the privilege of passing sentence and awarding execution, will it be denied that their agent would incur the guilt of murder?

Denman was saying that those privileges – and *only* those privileges – needed by the Commons as the grand inquest of the nation were willingly conceded, but these did not include the right to sell parliamentary papers containing defamatory matter to outside customers without incurring the consequences[11] (the point at issue in *Stockdale v Hansard*), so he definitely wished to establish limits on the House's freedom of action. Lord Hewart's judgment, on the other hand, has been interpreted as giving the House *carte blanche* to do what it likes. The 1967 Select Committee on Parliamentary Privilege quoted the ruling as entitling the House '*in a proper case* [to] claim exemption from Acts of Parliament which do not expressly apply to it'.[12] As criteria for what constitutes 'a proper case' have never been determined, in practice the view has been taken that *no* Act applies to Parliament unless it says it does. This view is totally at variance with the opinion expressed by Stephen J in *Bradlaugh* that the Commons 'are bound by the most solemn obligations which can bind men to any course of conduct whatever, to guide their conduct by the law as they understand it'.[13]

Sir Alan Herbert, the instigator of the *Graham-Campbell* case, took a cynical view of its consequences:

> If they can sell liquor without regard to Licensing Acts, they can sell milk or cream without regard to the Sale of Food and Drugs Acts; they can sell bad meat and adulterated

10   R Jackson *The Chief: the Biography of Gordon Hewart* (1959) p 272.
11   (1839) 9 Ad & El 1 at 185.
12   (1967-68; HC 34) p xxxi (emphasis added).
13   (1884) 12 QBD 271 at 286.

bread; they can sell morphine without a certificate and opium without a licence. All these matters might equally be said to 'fall within the scope of the internal affairs of the House.'[14]

The reality has not been far distant from the satire: the sale of bogus 'fine old claret' without regard to the Trade Descriptions Act;[15] the diffusion of blue asbestos fibres by the air-conditioning system and the pollution of a drinking-water tank by a dangerous substance, with no sanctions taken in either case;[16] an outbreak of salmonella in one of the Lords kitchens, with inspectors admitted on a voluntary basis rather than under the Food Safety Act;[17] the disregard of the 50 sq ft per head minimum working space prescribed in the Offices, Shops and Railway Premises Act; non-observance by the Commons' restaurants of the statutory price standstill imposed by the Prices and Incomes Act 1966.

The erosion of the *Graham-Campbell* doctrine

Over the years, the pure doctrine of the *Graham-Campbell* judgment has come to be eroded through a variety of influences.

Voluntary non-observance

As mentioned in chapter VI, members have implemented the Data Protection Act in respect of their own computer databases, although they are under no obligation to do so.

The House authorities voluntarily applied to the staff of the Commons some provisions of the Industrial Relations Act 1971 after Speaker's Counsel had given an opinion that the legislation would not apply – because of *Graham-Campbell*. This action was taken in response to a parliamentary question asked by Mr Grimond.[18] The step was important because it meant that the modern law of unfair dismissal would apply, instead of the draconian procedures of the House of Commons Offices Act 1812[19] (then still in force), which covered the two departments of the House in existence at the date of the Act. A case duly came before an industrial tribunal,[20] with the respondents waiving parliamentary privilege and submitting to the jurisdiction. Following the repeal of the 1971 Act, the 1812 Act came into force again as the undertaking on analogous treatment lapsed.

---

14 *Uncommon Law* (1955 edn) p 412.
15 HC Deb, 21 November 1977, written answers col 1093.
16 HC Deb, 6 June 1985, cols 449-456.
17 E Mitchell et al (1989) BMJ 14 January pp 99-101.
18 HC Deb, 8 July 1971, written answers col 43.
19 52 Geo 3, c 11, repealed 1978.
20 *King v Serjeant at Arms* Industrial Tribunal case No 1719/74. Not reported, but see B Harvey *Industrial Relations and Employment Law* C.1. [1179] and G F Lock 'Labour Law, Parliamentary Staff and Parliamentary Privilege' (1983) 12 ILJ (1983) 28 at 33.

The attitude of the trade unions

The trade unions representing the staff of the House of Commons were most unwilling to be deprived of employee rights enjoyed by other public servants because of arcane arguments about parliamentary privilege, originating in the remote sphere of free speech for members. Pledges about analogous treatment were not regarded as satisfactory, and the answer to the problem appeared to be legislation. The government agreed and provision was made in the Employment Protection Act 1975.[1] This applied to the staff the unfair dismissal provisions of the Trade Union and Labour Relations Act 1974, parts of the Employment Protection Act itself, the Equal Pay Act 1970 and the Sex Discrimination Act 1975.[2] The last was particularly important because of the lamentable record of the House over sex discrimination.[3]

A report compiled in 1945 included a recommendation that 'where suitable, women may be employed with advantage in the grades of Office Clerks', ie the second lowest grade in the hierarchy.[4] This was scarcely a clarion call for total equality of opportunity between the sexes, such as might have been expected from the principal signatory of the report – Frederick Pethick-Lawrence MP, a leading figure in the women's suffrage movement. Ten years later, Dame Irene Ward raised in the House the question of a job advertisement limiting candidates for a vacancy on the staff to males only. In reply, the Prime Minister (Sir Anthony Eden) also deplored the advertisement, but did nothing about it.[5] In 1967 Mr Sydney Silverman attempted to defend another discriminatory advertisement, attacked by Dame Joan Vickers. (The advertisement was based on recruitment regulations signed by the first Labour Speaker, Dr Horace King.[6]) The following year, the then Clerk of the House (Sir Barnett Cocks) evinced a distinctly unenthusiastic attitude to the recruitment of female Clerks, when questioned by a committee about staffing difficulties in his department.[7] It was no wonder that when Sir Edmund Compton, a former ombudsman, came to report in 1975 on the administrative services of the House of Commons, he remarked: 'There is also a need for a recognised code of conditions of service, including the principle of equality of opportunity for men and women.'[8] Churchill, when Prime Minister in 1955, had said that his government favoured the compilation of a code of conditions of service,[9] but nothing had been done. So, when legal compulsion with regard to sex discrimination was finally imposed on the House, it was not before time.

1   Now in the Employment Rights Act 1996, s 195.
2   Part of the Race Relations Act 1976 was added later. On industrial relations law and Commons staff, see G F Lock in M Rush (ed) *The House of Commons: Services and Facilities* Study of Parliament Group, Policy Studies Institute (1983) p 11; Lock (n 20 above); and S Freedman and G Morris *The State as Employer – Labour Law in the Public Services* (1990) pp 73-74.
3   See Lock in Rush (ed) (note 2, above) pp 26-27.
4   Printed in Report from the Select Committee on House of Commons Accommodation, etc (HC 184 of 1953-54) p 135.
5   HC Deb, 30 June 1955, col 503. See also 11 June 1981, col 587 (Mrs Jill Knight).
6   HC Deb, 23 January 1967, col 965.
7   Report from the Select Committee on Science and Technology – Coastal Pollution (HC 421-1 of 1967-68) p 380.
8   Review of the Administrative Services of the House of Commons: Report to Mr Speaker by Sir Edmund Compton (HC 254 of 1974) p 42.
9   HC Deb, 24 March 1955, col 2266.

Other legislation

Besides the labour laws applicable to the staff of the Commons, there has been further legislation to disturb the Hewart ideal of a Parliament untroubled by statute law, in the shape of labour laws applicable to the staff of the House of Lords. (It is also intended eventually to make the Health and Safety at Work Act apply to both Houses on a statutory basis: see below.)

From 1976 to 1993 the staff of the House of Lords were covered by a promise of 'analogous treatment' rather than by the statute law that applied to the staff of the Commons. On 13 April 1976 the House agreed to a Report from the House of Lords Offices Committee that certain Acts should apply by analogy to the staff of the House as if they were Crown employees.[10] The Acts were: Employment Protection Act 1975, Equal Pay Act 1970, Sex Discrimination Act 1975, and, remarkably, the Trade Union and Labour Relations Act 1974 (TULRA). The last item is notable because the authorities in the House of Commons refused to apply TULRA to their staff (except the unfair dismissal provisions), and this refusal was a bone of contention for years (the act applies to civil servants). The Race Relations Act was not applied in the Lords, whereas it was applied (statutorily) in the Commons.

There are two reasons to doubt how effective assurances about analogous treatment would be in a crisis: (a) resolutions of either House have no legal effect and are outside the purview of a court;[11] and (b) if it is one of the privileges of the House that its staff are not statutorily covered by labour laws, then the principle laid down in the *Duke of Newcastle*'s case applies: viz that a privilege can be abrogated only by express words in a statute,[12] so presumably a resolution would not suffice to waive a privilege.

The change from application by analogy to a statutory basis probably stems in part from pressure brought from 1985 onwards by the International Labour Organisation (see below), and was implemented by the Trade Union and Employment Rights Act 1993.[13]

The International Labour Organisation

In the 1980s, the International Labour Organisation (ILO) became involved in certain matters connected with Parliament and the law, and was thus a source of influence at that period.

Most international conventions to which the United Kingdom adheres need to be given legislative effect if they are to be enforced as law by the courts. If conventions have not been incorporated into domestic statute law, courts can take them into account only in so far as they 'adopt a rebuttable presumption that Parliament has not intended to legislate inconsistently' with conventions to which the United Kingdom is a party.[14] ILO conventions are, however, not quite so toothless as this situation

10 HL Deb, 13 April 1976, cols 2034-2036.
11 *Stockdale v Hansard* (1839) 9 Ad & El 1; *Bowles v Bank of England* [1913] 1 Ch 57. Budget resolutions have legal force for a limited period under the Provisional Collection of Taxes Act 1968.
12 *Duke of Newcastle v Morris* (1870) LR 4 HL 661, per Lord Hatherley LC at 668.
13 Section 139A of the Employment Protection (Consolidation) Act 1978, as inserted by para 11 of Sch 7 to the Trade Union Reform and Employment Rights Act 1993; now in the Employment Rights Act 1996, s 194.
14 *de Smith and Brazier* pp 153, 158.

would imply, as their implementation by governments is policed by international committees of experts – groups of eminent jurists drawn from participating countries. Their rulings are, of course, not binding like the judgments of the Luxembourg and Strasbourg courts, but they can be a source of moral pressure. Apart from one United Kingdom representative (at this period a law professor from the University of Sheffield), the panel consists of foreigners unlikely to be greatly impressed by ancient precedents and historic institutions. They are concerned solely with whether participating governments have fulfilled the obligations they incurred when they signed the conventions which the committees oversee.

In March 1980 the United Kingdom ratified the Labour Relations (Public Services) Convention,[15] which came into force for it on 19 March 1981. The 1985 report of the ILO Committee of Experts on this Convention[16] records two complaints from the Trade Union Congress: (a) that House of Lords staff are not covered by any employment legislation; and (b) that House of Commons staff do not receive the same protection under TULRA as that enjoyed by central government employees.

In its reply, the United Kingdom government stated that parliamentary staff were not government employees and therefore were not covered by the legislation, and that legal provisions had to differ because the working of Parliament must not be impeded. The experts commented that the text of the convention provided no basis for the distinction between parliamentary staff and other public servants, and that the restrictions imposed on the former were inconsistent with the principles both of the ILO in general and of Convention 151. (The government had signed the convention very recently, and if it had wanted to exclude parliamentary staff it should have registered a derogation.) The experts called on the government to take measures to correct the position. The dialogue between the ILO and the government rumbled on in the next two annual reports, with the government stalling and the experts reiterating their 1985 views. However, by the 1988 report[17] there was a change in the government's position; they now said that, in the light of a recent High Court decision,[18] House of Commons staff *did* enjoy normal employees' rights, including the parts of TULRA formerly in dispute – on peaceful picketing and trade union immunities. The High Court, in the case cited, thought that crown servants engaged since 1985 might well be employees with a contract of service, rather than being dismissable at will under the prerogative.[19] The line of the government's thinking – this was not spelled out – was presumably that parliamentary staff were employed

15 International Labour Convention No 151, concerning Protection of the Right to Organise and Procedures for determining Conditions of Employment in the Public Service (Cmnd 8252, previously published as Cmnd 7786).
16 ILO Conference, 71st Session 1985. Report III (Part 4A), Report of the Committee of Experts on the Application of Conventions and Recommendations, ILO, Geneva, pp 352-353. For the views of the Staff Side of the House of Commons Whitley Committee, see Appendix 20 to the Second Report from the Employment Committee, 1980-81 (HC 282, pp 342-345).
17 ILO Conference, 75th Session 1968. Report III (Part 4A), p 372.
18 *R v Civil Service Appeal Board, ex p Bruce* [1988] 3 All ER 686. Incomes Data Services, Brief 390 on employment law and practice, February 1989, p 10. The case subsequently went to the Court of Appeal on the question of judicial review: [1989] 2 All ER 907.
19 A position confirmed in *R v Lord Chancellor's Dept, ex p Nangle* [1992] 1 All ER 897. See *de Smith and Brazier*, p 217.

similarly under a contract of service,[20] and therefore enjoyed normal employee rights including all the provisions of TULRA applicable to crown servants.

This new position was, however, not put into statutory form and, since it was based only on the advice of government lawyers and the chain of reasoning was tenuous, it must be regarded as uncertain, and to that extent the outcome of the ILO's intervention was unsatisfactory. No doubt the government, under pressure from the ILO also over the ban on trade unions at GCHQ, wanted to wind the parliamentary staff business up; and in March 1990 the Minister of State at the Department of Employment stated:

> following legal advice, that in the respects in question Parliamentary staff enjoy the full range of normal employees' rights. The Government thus considers that the arrangements for Parliamentary staff are fully in accordance with ILO Convention 151 and that the application of Article 1 of this Convention to Parliamentary staff is no longer at issue.[1]

As mentioned earlier, the other point raised with the ILO – on the lack of statutory cover for House of Lords staff – was dealt with by legislation in 1993.

European Union law

It is of interest to note that the persistence of the ILO caused the government to move from its initial position of a simple rebuff and assertion of the Hewart doctrine to a more accommodating attitude. There may also be lessons to be learnt from this episode over the treatment of European Union law, which cannot simply be ignored.[2] Under s 2 of the European Communities Act 1972, Community (now Union) law prevails over United Kingdom law, presumably including parliamentary law. Examples of subjects covered by laws applying to Parliament based on EU directives are provisions on compensation to employees disadvantaged as a result of health and safety activities[3] and safety signs regulations,[4] and no doubt the purchase of Rosenthal china by the Commons refreshment department stemmed from observance of the rules on competitive tendering that public authorities have to follow. Limitations on the working week of parliamentary staff after signature of the Social Chapter by the United Kingdom will raise more substantial issues; but working patterns have become more civilised since the 'Jopling' reforms,[5] and the 48-hour limit may be defined in such a way that long hours are permitted over short periods. But it would be unwise for the House to assume that it can simply ignore EU law.

---

20 At an earlier date the Department of Employment claimed that parliamentary staff, from cleaners to the Clerk of the Parliaments, were 'office holders', like methodist ministers or golf-club secretaries.
1 Mr Eggar, HC Deb, 15 March 1990, written answers cols 341-342.
2 EU law is also discussed in ch VI below.
3 The Trade Union Reform and Employment Rights Act 1993 gave effect to EC Directive 89/381/ECC.
4 Safety Signs Regulations 1980, SI 1980/1471; Health and Safety Information for Employees Regulations, SI 1989/682.
5 Report from the Select Committee on Sittings of the House HC 20-I and 20-II of 1991-92.

The Health and Safety at Work Act

This Act is not considered to apply to either House with statutory force, this view being based on the judgment in the *Graham-Campbell* case.⁶ Representatives of the Commons staff and members of both Houses have drawn attention to this matter over a considerable period, and have asked that application should be made statutory – for example, the Commons Staff side in a published memorandum of June 1981,⁷ Mr Allen MP, in a question in 1989 to the spokesman for the House of Commons Commission (Mr Beith MP),⁸ and a peer and two peeresses in debate in March 1993.⁹ In response to the last group, Lord Ullswater said that the matter would be dealt with 'in the next appropriate legislation', and Lord Boston of Faversham confirmed on 16 January 1995 that 'the Government are committed to applying the provisions of the Health and Safety at Work Act 1974 to the Palace of Westminster as soon as a suitable legislative opportunity arises'.¹⁰ It is impossible to foresee when this will be. Legislation on insane peers was recommended in 1984 'when cognate legislation is introduced' and is still awaited, so it would not be surprising if further delay were considerable.

Judicial rulings

The *Graham-Campbell* judgment was followed by a lengthy period of judicial quiescence in the field of domestic parliamentary law, but there are now a few signs that some judges are disinclined to accept an invariable obligation to keep their distance from Parliament.

In *Rost v Edwards*,¹¹ Popplewell J ruled that the Register of Members' Interests was not a proceeding in Parliament within the meaning of art 9 of the Bill of Rights, and that evidence about entries in the Register could therefore be given and challenged in court. In *Prebble v Television New Zealand*,¹² Lord Browne-Wilkinson suggested that *Rost v Edwards* had been wrongly decided, but from the context it seems probable that this comment referred only to the judge's ruling on the other, more important, issue before him.¹³ As the main action in *Rost v Edwards* was never tried – it was settled after the judge had ruled on the preliminary issues – there was no opportunity to challenge the ruling on the Register of Interests, and it must therefore be presumed that it stands.

As is mentioned in ch VIII below, the Parliamentary Commissioner for Administration, despite being an Officer of the House of Commons, is subject to the

---

6 HL Deb, 16 January 1995, written answers cols 33-34.
7 See n 16 above.
8 HC Deb, 19 June 1989, col 16.
9 HL Deb, 30 March 1993, cols 875-877.
10 See n 6 above.
11 [1990] 2 QB 460. Under the Defamation Act 1996, s 13(5)(e), 'proceedings in Parliament' are defined as including the Register, but this definition may be confined to the purposes of the Act and may not apply generally.
12 [1995] 1 AC 321 at 337.
13 Namely, that it was possible to proceed by petitioning the House to secure its permission for the calling of evidence on a decision of the Committee of Selection. As this course would undoubtedly result in a violation of art 9, no such procedure would be feasible.

supervision of the courts. In *R v Parliamentary Comr for Administration, ex p Dyer*,[14] Simon Brown LJ 'unhesitatingly rejected the argument' that parliamentary control of the PCA embodied in the Parliamentary Commissioner Act 1967 displaced any supervisory control by the courts: 'I see nothing about the PCA's role or the statutory framework within which he operates so singular as to take him wholly outside the purview of judicial review.' In the *Balchin* case,[15] Sedley J stated that 'the powers and functions of the Commissioner . . . are subject to the supervisory jurisdiction of the court, notwithstanding that the Commissioner, who occupies a unique constitutional place, is answerable to Parliament'; and the judge concluded that, in one respect over the matter before him, the PCA had exercised his discretion incorrectly.

Thus, in the last decade, two types of parliamentary mechanism have come before the courts, which have asserted jurisdiction over them. And, as shown below, judges have adopted modern, common-sense attitudes in two fields, even though this might result in the diminution of privilege by judicial action: the Law Lords on the question of mentally ill peers, and the decision by a county court judge that a peer had to accept disciplines applicable to other citizens. Finally, in Australia, Russell J showed in *Bear v State of South Australia*[16] that, by redefining and narrowing the scope of 'internal affairs', it was possible for the courts to reassert jurisdiction over some domestic parliamentary matters not related to the core functions of Parliament. Thus, over the years, it can be expected that judicial intervention will gradually become more extensive and, if tolerant attitudes are adopted on both sides, equilibrium can be maintained.

To complement the cases to which the last three paragraphs have referred, two recent cases should be mentioned that maintain the traditional demarcation line between Parliament and the courts. The first,[17] in the Belfast High Court, dealt with an application for judicial review of the Speaker's decision that MPs refusing to take the oath or affirm should not be granted access to the facilities available to MPs. The application was refused by Kerr J, who said:

> The Court should be slow to reject a claim by the Speaker that an action taken by her to regulate the availability of facilities and services for MPs is a proceeding in Parliament . . . Were it necessary for me to do so, I would have held that her decision to introduce these restrictions was a proceeding in Parliament – or rather, that her assertion that it was so could not be challenged by way of judicial review.'

As her action was 'squarely within the realm of internal arrangements of the House', it was 'not amenable to judicial review'. The second case[18] was concerned with the Parliamentary Commissioner for Standards and whether it was appropriate for the courts to use supervisory powers over him. The decision of the Court of Appeal (per Lord Woolf MR) was that 'the responsibility for supervising [the Commissioner] was

---

14 [1994] 1 All ER 375.
15 *R v Parliamentary Comr for Administration, ex p Balchin* [1996] NPC 147.
16 (1981) 48 SAIR 604.
17 *R v The Speaker, ex p McGuinness (Application by Martin McGuinness for leave to apply to judicial review)* Northern Ireland High Court, 3 October 1997, QBD.
18 *R v Parliamentary Comr for Standards, ex p Al Fayed* [1998] 1 All ER 93.

placed by Parliament, through its standing orders, on the special standing committee of the House, and it was for that body to perform the supervisory role and not the courts'.

Is there a presumption that statutes do not bind Parliament?

There is a long-standing rule of statutory interpretation that 'an Act of Parliament is presumed not to bind the Crown in the absence of express provision or necessary implication'.[19] In recent years there has been a trend towards the removal of the Crown's privileges and immunities, and examples of statutes that *do* bind the Crown are: the Occupiers' Liability Act 1957; the Road Traffic Act 1960; the Limitation Act 1980; food hygiene laws for National Health Service hospitals;[20] and, in part, the labour laws mentioned above as covering parliamentary staff, in their application to the civil service.[1]

It is sometimes asserted that there is a rule of statutory construction, similar to that applying to the Crown, to the effect that statutes do not bind either House in the absence of express provision. It is submitted that this is incorrect, and that there is no such rule. The dictum of Stephens J in *Bradlaugh v Gossett*[2] is plainly based on the idea that, in general, the law of the land applies to the House of Commons, and Lord Russell of Killowen CJ in *Williamson v Norris*[3] was quite prepared to consider the application of the Licensing Acts to the House, even though the Acts made no express provision. In 1984 the Law Lords on the Committee for Privileges (Lord Diplock, Lord Scarman and Lord Bridge of Harwich), as a piece of statutory interpretation, gave it as their opinion that Pt II of the Mental Health Act 1983 applied to members of the House of Lords, even though the Act is silent on the question.[4]

The doctrine of non-application of statutes to Parliament dates from 1935 and is based on the judgment in the *Graham-Campbell* case. The latter refers to the 'internal affairs' of the House of Commons. Two consequences flow from the way in which the doctrine originated: (1) on the face of the judgment, the House of Lords is not covered; and (2) the phrase 'internal affairs' can be strictly defined by a court, so that (for example) in *Bear v State of South Australia*, an injury to a waitress in a parliamentary restaurant was not regarded as an internal affair; and of course, much earlier, the sale of parliamentary papers to the general public was also not considered to be 'internal'.[5]

Thus the so-called rule is of comparatively recent origin, unlike that applying to the Crown. It is based on case law and could conceivably be reversed by a later judgment. Meanwhile, the safest course is for express provision to be made, so that doubt is removed.

---

19 Sir W Wade and C Forsyth *Administrative Law* (7th edn, 1994) p 839; *Walker and Walker, English Legal System* (7th edn, ed R J Walker and R Ward, 1994) p 46; *de Smith and Brazier* pp 146-147.
20 Though staff of health service bodies are no longer regarded as Crown servants.
1 See p 58 above.
2 See p 56, n 13 above and associated text.
3 See p 52, n 4 above and associated text.
4 See p 50, n 12 above, pp x-xi.
5 *Stockdale v Hansard* (1839) 9 Ad & El 1.

Is Parliament a court?

Parliament is sometimes called the 'High Court of Parliament'. *Hatsell's Precedents* of 1796 refers to 'the Court of Parliament, the first and the highest court in the kingdom',[6] and two centuries later the Nolan Report talks of 'Parliament, the highest court in the land'.[7] However, in modern times Parliament can be regarded as a court in only a limited sense. Stephen J in the *Bradlaugh* case said: 'The House of Commons is not a Court of Justice'[8] and Marshall states that 'in reality Parliament in the twentieth century is not a court'.[9] Impeachment, in which the House of Commons acted as prosecutor before the House of Lords, was last used in 1805 and is now obsolete, as is the procedure for Acts of Attainder, last used in 1798. The handling of divorce proceedings, hitherto dealt with in Private Acts, was transferred from Parliament to the courts in 1857. The right of a member of the House of Lords to be tried by his peers in cases of treason or felony was abolished in 1948. Each House has jurisdiction to regulate its own procedure, but apart from that 'the judicial function of Parliament is now exercised by the House of Lords'.[10] The House of Lords (in practice its appellate committee) acts as the highest court of appeal for England and Wales and for Northern Ireland, and for civil (but not criminal) Scottish cases. Apart from its power to punish contempts, the House of Commons has none of the characteristics of a court, and it is difficult to see how it could function as a judicial body. If the United Kingdom had a written constitution, the House would have to settle for a role solely as a legislative and deliberative assembly and, even in present circumstances, aspirations to a shadowy parallel existence as a court of law are unconvincing. Ritual incantations do nothing to disguise the underlying constitutional realities.

Corporate and personal immunities of Parliament and its members

Other sections of this chapter deal with several of the immunities, and those will not be described again here. There is a full exposition of immunities in general in Mr Abraham's memorandum to the 1967 Select Committee on Parliamentary Privilege,[11] with remarks and recommendations in the report itself. This section will therefore select only a few points rather than attempt comprehensive coverage of the topic.

Some privileges are statutory and some stem from the common law. The most important group is concerned with free speech – immunity from actions for defamation over: (1) matters arising in debate or in 'proceedings in Parliament' (however they may be defined) – art 9 of the Bill of Rights; (2) the content of parliamentary papers – Parliamentary Papers Act 1840; (3) communications in both directions between MPs and the ombudsman – Parliamentary Commissioner Act 1967.

---

6 Hatsell *Precedents of Proceedings in the House of Commons* (1796) vol 1, p 1. See also W Anson *The Law and Custom of the Constitution* (5th edn, 1922, ed M Gwyer) ch 9.

7 Nolan Report, ch 2, para 90.

8 *Bradlaugh v Gossett* (1884) 12 QBD 271 at 285. He added: 'But the effect of its privilege to regulate its own internal concerns practically invests it with a judicial character when it has to apply to particular cases the provisions of Acts of Parliament.'

9 G Marshall in S Walkland (ed) *The House of Commons in the Twentieth Century* (1979) p 205.

10 *Walker and Walker* p 144.

11 (1967-68; HC 34) pp 91-4 and xxii-xxxii respectively.

MPs are exempt from appointment as sheriffs[12] and from jury service (Juries Act 1974). An important category of corporate immunities (barely mentioned by the 1967 Report) was created by the *Graham-Campbell* judgment of 1935, under which the House of Commons was exempted from the operation of much statute law, because it touched its 'internal affairs'. Freedom from arrest in civil suits was formerly important, as readers of Trollope will recall,[13] but lost most of its significance with the abolition in 1870 of imprisonment for debt. There is, of course, no special treatment of members of either House under the criminal law, such as obtains in some countries (where parliamentary immunity must be lifted before legislators can be examined by magistrates or the police).

There are, however, rare occasions on which the possibility of detention may arise. *Stourton v Stourton*[14] involved the application of the Married Women's Property Act 1882. A peer had failed to comply with a court order to restore her furniture to his estranged wife, and she sought a writ of attachment against him for contempt of court. The judge (Scarman J) refused the application, as it would have led to an infringement of the privileges of the Lords. He said he founded his judgment on judicial decisions, not on the practice of the House of Lords, and its basis would have been that it was more important for legislators to be free to attend Parliament than for litigants to enjoy all their private rights.

Some 25 years later, there was another case about a peer who had failed to comply with a court order – the *Mancroft* case[15] before Judge White at Wandsworth County Court. The outcome differed from that in *Stourton v Stourton*, and Lord Mancroft would have been committed to prison if he had not purged his contempt. The judge acknowledged that the dividing line between the two cases was thin, but each had to be decided on its own facts. A distinction had to be drawn between the *coercive* use of the power of committal (from which a peer would be exempt) and the *disciplinary punitive* use (to which he would remain subject), and the judge decided that the case fell into the latter category (though there was of course a coercive aspect). He said:

> If the privilege protects him from the ultimate sanction, then effectively his creditors will be deprived of the important right they would otherwise have had to call for a formal examination; without powers of enforcement and the rights ancillary to them justice is liable to be snuffed out at judgment.

And in later proceedings:

> I ruled that the privilege did not apply – indeed . . . it is unthinkable in modern times that, in circumstances such as they are in this case, it should.

The tone is totally unlike that in *Stourton* – different priorities and less deference to Parliament. Also in the 1980s, the question arose whether a mentally ill peer could lawfully be detained in a mental hospital. There is modern legislation governing MPs

12 In 1904 an MP attempted to waive privilege as he wanted to be a sheriff; Lord Alverstone CJ ruled that he could not: *The Times*, 14 November 1904, p 13.
13 A Trollope *Phineas Finn* (1869) particularly ch 21.
14 [1963] P 302.
15 (1989, unreported).

afflicted by mental illness, but the law on peers is unclear. A case was due to be heard at Preston Crown Court, but lapsed when the peer in question was released from detention. Although the question no longer arose in relation to a current case, it was thought right for the topic to be reviewed generally. The matter was referred to the Lords' Committee for Privileges, who reported in June 1984.[16] The committee stated that it had received two conflicting views in evidence. On the one hand, the three Law Lords on the committee considered further legislation to be unnecessary and that, if the matter ever came before the courts, they would hold that the Mental Health Act 1983 'overrides any previously existing privilege of Parliament or peerage so far as it conflicts with the liability to compulsory detention in hospital under sections 2 to 6'. In the Law Lords' opinion, the phrase 'any patient' in the Act included a peer. On the other hand, the Law Officers advised that it was not possible to predict how the courts would decide; they had considered the Law Lords' opinion and nevertheless concluded that it remained doubtful whether it was lawful to detain a member of the House of Lords without any breach of parliamentary privilege. In his memorandum to the committee, the Attorney General stated: 'It appears from the above that there is no disqualification, either statutory or in common law, to prevent members of the House of Lords who are "mentally disordered" from sitting.' Thus, in his view, there was no change from the situation in 1849 when, maximising their strength in anticipation of a close division, the 'Tory whips pushed past the tellers two quite insane peers rushed from their institutions to the House for the purpose, the keeper of one of them in attendance in the lobby'.[17]

Two points may be made about the Law Lords' opinion. First, they were not in the least concerned that the Mental Health Act contained no express words binding the House of Lords – a feature that the 'authorities' of Parliament have, since 1935, conveniently found to be necessary in order for any Act to bind either House.[18] Secondly, the basis of their interpretation of the statute was, in part, consideration of rational public policy:

> Can Parliament really have considered it to be necessary for the proper functioning of the legislative process in the public interest that mentally disordered peers should be released from detention in a hospital, to which they were confined for their own good, in order to take an active part in making the laws of the land? The only possible answer must be 'No'.[19]

This approach is markedly similar to that of Judge White in the *Mancroft* case – that the social context is taken into account in addition to, and perhaps over-riding, purely legal considerations.

The committee sided with the Law Lords on what the law was, but suggested that legislation should 'on a future occasion' be introduced for the avoidance of doubt. This is still awaited.

---

16   HL 254 of 1983-84.
17   M Bentley *Politics Without Democracy, 1815-1914* (1984) p 137.
18   But it may be that, in strict terms the *Graham-Campbell* judgment does not apply to the House of Lords.
19   HL 254 of 1983-84, p xi.

Bankruptcy law

The law of bankruptcy is referred to at two points in the evidence presented to the inquiry by the Lords' Privileges Committee on mental health law: First, in the opinion of the Law Lords, who explained why they did not regard the topic as relevant; and, secondly, in the memorandum of the Attorney General (Sir Michael Havers), who quoted the bankruptcy legislation as providing a good example of statutory interference with parliamentary privilege. Though in general bankrupts are no longer imprisoned, those who misbehave in certain ways (eg abscond or fail to attend for examination on their affairs) may be arrested by order of the court,[20] and this provision would apply to a peer or MP.

A further reason (not mentioned by Sir Michael) why bankruptcy law is of interest is that, unusually in the field of privilege, there was a case, *Duke of Newcastle v Morris*,[1] decided at the highest level (ie the House of Lords), which is still authoritative on one aspect of privilege in general: viz that a particular privilege can be abrogated only by express words in a statute. The creditor (Morris) started bankruptcy proceedings in June 1869, and the case moved up through the hierarchy of courts, reaching the Lords in July 1870. The dates are mentioned because, while the litigation was in progress, Parliament had passed a new Act, but the case was determined under pre-existing legislation – Acts of 1849 and 1861 taken together. The 1849 Act provided that a bankrupt trader 'having privilege of Parliament . . . may be dealt with under this Act in like manner as any other trader, but such person shall not be subject to be arrested or to be imprisoned during the time of such privilege',[2] unless he committed felonies or misdemeanours connected with bankruptcy. The 1861 Act extended the law to 'all debtors whether traders or not', and the House of Lords[3] decided that 'all debtors' included peers, just as, over a century later, Lord Diplock and his colleagues maintained that 'all patients' included peers. Thus, the Duke lost on the main ground of his appeal: that as a non-trader and a peer he was not subject to the law of bankruptcy. However, the court ruled that he was not subject to imprisonment, even though the 1861 Act was silent on privilege. According to the Lord Chancellor, the fact that the Act contained a clause dealing with all debtors (ie including peers) 'would not lead to the destruction of the privilege unless there was some special clause in the Act striking at and distinctly abolishing it'. With regard to bankrupt peers and MPs:

> . . . it being one consequence of their position, not for their personal benefit at all, but for the good of the state, and resting upon sound grounds of state policy, that they should have a privilege which is secured to them by Common Law . . . that they should be personally free from arrest, that privilege would still follow them.

Lords Westbury and Colonsay agreed.

The new Act passed in 1869 provided that 'if a person having privilege of Parliament commits an act of bankruptcy, he may be dealt with under the Act in like manner as if he had not such privilege'.[4]

---

20 The powers are now in s 364 of the Insolvency Act 1986.
 1 (1870) LR 4 HL 661.
 2 The time of privilege is unlimited in the case of peers.
 3 (1870) LR 4 HL 661, per Lord Hatherley LC at 670-671.
 4 Bankruptcy Act 1869, s 120; re-enacted several times and now appearing as s 427(7) of the Insolvency Act 1986. The 1869 Act came into force on 1 January 1870.

The practical effect of bankruptcy in recent years has been as a disqualification for membership of both Houses. Lloyd's names unable to meet cash calls from their syndicates could have been in grave difficulties, and this could have had serious consequences for the government's survival when its majority was slender during the closing stages of the 1992-97 Parliament.

Attitudes to Parliamentary law

This section surveys examples of the attitudes displayed to parliamentary law by members of both Houses and by governments.

On sex discrimination, the performance of people of left-wing origin (Frederick Pethick-Lawrence, Sydney Silverman, Horace King) was disappointing in comparison with their presumed general principles, and the running was made by Conservative ladies (Dame Irene Ward and Dame Joan Vickers). However, Michael Foot made up for the poor record of his party colleagues and ranks as an effective reformer of parliamentary law. As Employment Secretary, he oversaw the application of a body of industrial relations law to the staff of the House of Commons, and as Leader of the House he introduced a new legislative framework for it – the House of Commons (Administration) Act 1978 – and repealed the long outdated House of Commons Offices Act 1812. He even promised legislation to define the phrase 'proceedings in Parliament' in art 9 of the 1689 Bill of Rights,[5] but the government fell before this could be done. Moreover, he was the first Leader of the House to take seriously the need for proper medical facilities in the Palace of Westminster.

In opposition in 1975, Conservative spokesmen had approached reforms in a non-party spirit. For example, Mr Hayhoe said: 'I am sure that it is the intention of all hon. Members that labour legislation should be applied to those working within the House as we make sure that they [sic] are applied to those outside.'[6] And Mr (later Sir Leon) Brittan agreed:

> I think that all hon. Members would agree in the common aim, which is to ensure that those employed in this House enjoy the protection of legislation of the kind we have been discussing in the same way as do people employed elsewhere. I take this opportunity of welcoming the fact that a way has been found of ensuring that just that happens.'[7]

However, in 1980, after the Conservative Party's return to power, a further reform proposed by a Social Democrat (Mr John Grant) was voted down in a division on party lines. Speaking for the government, Mr (later Sir Patrick, then Lord) Mayhew resisted the move on the grounds that it would circumscribe the scope of the House authorities 'for applying employment legislation by analogy so far as was consistent with the requirements of the House of Commons'.[8] This harked back to the Hewart doctrine in the *Graham-Campbell* case that the 'internal affairs of the House' (staff matters, *inter alia*) were no concern of outsiders – judges included.

---

5   HC Deb, 6 February 1978, cols 1190-1192.
6   HC Deb, 30 July 1975, col 1919.
7   HC Deb, 29 October 1975, col 1698.
8   HC Deb, Standing Committee A, 1 April 1980, col 1738.

In the last two decades, the view has been taken that in general there is no realistic prospect of legislation about Parliament itself, to remove obscurities and to modernise the law. For example, when in 1984 it was agreed that the law on insane peers was in a mess,[9] Lord Whitelaw – then Leader of the House of Lords – deprecated the idea of legislation,[10] and his colleagues on the committee involved felt unable to press for it at an early date. The need for a definition of the Bill of Rights' phrase 'proceedings in Parliament' has been raised on various occasions – by four committees between 1967 and 1977[11] and by the then Clerk of the House of Commons in his memorandum on the 'Zircon' affair;[12] but nothing has been done. A definition of the phrase 'impeached or questioned' has now been imported into English law from an Australian statute.[13] As has been remarked, 'it is surely most unusual to find a judge in effect incorporating into English law the terms of a statute from another jurisdiction',[14] but, where imprecision has prevailed for over three centuries, clarification from whatever source is to be welcomed. When, very recently, a provision supplemental to the Bill of Rights was enacted,[15] its purpose was not to clear up obscurities, but rather to facilitate defamation actions by MPs and peers which had hitherto been barred.

It seems at present to be considered axiomatic that the two Houses must accept without complaint that the law applicable to them should be antiquated. As Patricia Leopold has written: 'Parliament does not have a good track record of reforming its own law'.[16] When a select committee produces a comprehensive report on a subject, as the 1967 Committee on Parliamentary Privilege did,[17] the chances are that most of its recommendations will be ignored. Perhaps the time has come to try a new approach, with an invitation to the Law Commissions to review and codify parliamentary law, weeding out obsolete statutes and outworn precedents. An efficient Parliament is surely entitled to a set of modern, relevant laws rather than a miscellany of ancient lumber.

---

9   See p 50, n 12 above and associated text.
10   Evidence taken by Lords' Committee (HL 254 of 1983-84) question 18.
11   See G F Lock [1985] PL 73; G F Lock (1983) ILJ 28 at 36.
12   First Report from the Committee of Privileges, (HC 365 of 1986-87) p 5.
13   *Prebble v Television New Zealand Ltd* [1995] 1 AC 321 at 333. Sir Clarrie Harders considers that s 16 of the Australian Parliamentary Privileges Act 1987 (adopted for wider application by the Judicial Committee) did not only codify existing law, but created new law; and so was contrary to s 49 of the Australian Constitution: see Sir C Harders (p 54, n 15 above) pp 37-39.
14   P M Leopold (1995) 14 LS 204 at 210.
15   In the Defamation Act 1996, s 13.
16   Leopold (p 51, n 16 above) at 218.
17   HC 34, 1967-68.

Chapter V

The application of the civil and criminal law to members of Parliament and parliamentary proceedings

Patricia M Leopold

Introduction

On the face of it, art 9 of the Bill of Rights 1689, which states that 'Freedom of speech and debates or proceedings in Parliament ought not to be impeached or questioned in any Court or place out of Parliament', would seem to provide members, officers of both Houses and strangers[1] with wide immunity from the civil and criminal law. If a civil or criminal action is commenced, then, provided the court is satisfied that the action, or evidence to be used in the action, is concerned with impeaching or questioning what was said or done in the course of a debate or proceeding in Parliament, it will (as appropriate) refuse to admit the evidence,[2] stay proceedings or decline jurisdiction. It is rare for civil or criminal cases to get to this stage,[3] since the knowledge that jurisdiction would be declined, or proceedings stayed is a disincentive to the commencement of an action. However, the position is more complicated, more controversial and more uncertain than might be supposed. The reasons for this are mainly difficulties and differences in the interpretation of art 9: what is covered by the phrase 'proceedings in Parliament'; and whether evidence of parliamentary proceedings can be used in a legal action, if such proceedings are not 'impeached or questioned' (whatever that may mean)? Even if a matter is a proceeding in Parliament, art 9 only provides that proceedings in Parliament *ought not* to be questioned in any 'court or place out of Parliament'. What is a 'place out of Parliament', does it include the media or the type of inquiry recently conducted by Sir Richard Scott?[4] Why is there a problem with prosecuting members for bribery? Since the prohibition in art 9 is in respect of places 'out of Parliament' it does not prevent

1 Strangers may, for example, give evidence to a committee or present petitions. However, strangers who provide information to members in their personal capacity by letter, personal interview or by film, are not protected by parliamentary privilege. See the Memorandum by the Clerk of the House in the First Report of the Committee of Privileges *Speaker's Order of 22 January 1987 on a Matter of National Security* (the Zircon affair) (HC 365, 1986-87) p 6.
2 Subject to Defamation Act 1996, s 13 (see p 80 below).
3 The decision in *Dillon v Balfour* (1887) 20 LR Ir 600 is one such case. Here, once the court was satisfied that the matter complained of was a proceeding in Parliament, it declined jurisdiction.
4 *Report on the Inquiry into the Export of Defence Equipment and Dual Use Goods to Iraq and Related Prosecutions*, 5 vols (HC 115, 1995-96).

Parliament, in the exercise of its penal jurisdiction, taking action against members or strangers, a procedure that is not without controversy. These are the issues to be examined in this chapter.

What are 'proceedings in Parliament'?

There are two aspects to the meaning of 'proceedings in Parliament'. First, with respect to the formal actions of the House and its members: one of the issues is whether the more extensive activities of members today, compared to 1689, are proceedings in Parliament. In 1967 the Select Committee on Parliamentary Privilege commented that:

> it cannot . . . be doubted that the modern limits of and application of (proceedings in Parliament), which may have been clear enough to the legislature in the 17th century, are no longer free from uncertainty.[5]

Today, this will include speaking in a debate, voting, giving notice of a motion, presenting petitions or committee reports and asking parliamentary questions.[6] The second aspect to this phrase is with respect to place. Erskine May states that 'not everything said or done within the precincts forms part of proceedings in Parliament'.[7] On the other hand, some parliamentary business conducted outside the precincts could amount to a proceeding in Parliament. In addition, as Erskine May notes 'Particular words or acts may be entirely unrelated to any business being transacted or ordered to come before the House in due course'.[8]

The meaning of 'proceedings in Parliament' has been considered from time to time both by Parliament and the courts, with both institutions claiming the last word.[9] It is possible by reference to parliamentary reports and decided cases to have a reasonable idea of what is a proceeding in Parliament. However, it is always possible for Parliament to change its mind or for a higher court to cast doubt on a previous court decision; it is also possible for a court to come to a conclusion that is not in accordance with Parliament's view of the matter. For example, in *Rost v Edwards*[10] Popplewell J decided, contrary to the opinion of the Solicitor-General, that the Register of Members' Interests and the practice and procedure relating to it was not a proceeding in Parliament, and that evidence could be led and challenged in connection with the Register.[11]

---

5 HC 34, 1967-68, para 74.
6 See Erskine May *Parliamentary Practice* (22nd edn, 1997) pp 95-97 for a further discussion.
7 *Erskine May* p 98.
8 *Erskine May* p 98. This was also the opinion of the Select Committee on the Official Secrets Act (HC 101, 1938-39) p ix.
9 The House of Lords in *Pepper v Hart* [1993] AC 593 made it clear that it is for the courts to determine the legal meaning of art 9. However, where Parliament's 'internal affairs' are concerned, the courts are normally willing to allow Parliament to interpret the phrase. In *R v The Speaker, ex p McGuinness* in the Northern Ireland High Court (3 October 1997, unreported), Kerr J suggested that a court: 'should be slow to reject a claim by the Speaker that an action taken by her to regulate the availability of facilities and services for MPs is a proceeding in Parliament' (transcript pp 7-8).
10 [1990] 2 QB 460.
11 The Attorney General lodged an appeal against this part of the decision, which had to be abandoned when the case was settled. For another privilege aspect of this case, which the Privy Council has since suggested was wrongly decided, see p 79 n 5 below. See also n 14 below.

Confusion and uncertainty can also be shown by reference to some of Parliament's own reports and decisions. In 1939 a select committee[12] had been confident that the dictum of O'Connor J in the Canadian case of *R v Bunting* that a member of Parliament was not amenable to the ordinary courts for 'anything he might say or do within the scope of his duties in the course of parliamentary business, for in such matters he is privileged and protected by *lex et consuetudo parliamenti*',[13] would command general assent. However, in 1958 the House of Commons refused to accept the recommendation of the Committee of Privileges that a letter written by a member to a minister on a matter within the scope of the duty of both the member and the minister, was a proceeding in Parliament.[14] Several parliamentary reports since then have recommended that the phrase should be defined by statute in order 'both to provide a more secure framework for decisions in individual cases and to help in judgments about how close to an undoubted proceeding an act done outside Parliament needs to be before it can properly benefit from the immunity conferred by privilege and declared by the Bill of Rights'.[15] One example was in 1987, when the Committee of Privileges was satisfied that private arrangements by a MP to show a film about Project Zircon[16] in a room within the precincts of the House did not fall within the concept of proceedings in Parliament. In response to a request from this committee, the Clerk of the House reviewed and commented on the variety of definitions proposed, and the committee commended the subsequent memorandum to the attention of the House as a helpful guide to any future consideration of the meaning of proceedings in Parliament. What appears to be clear is that any proposed statutory definition has to apply in respect of criminal as well as the civil liability of members, and that the definition should be concerned with determining whether or not proceedings were concerned with the transaction of parliamentary business and not the physical location of the proceedings.[17]

---

12   Select Committee on Official Secrets Acts (HC 101, 1938-39) para 7.
13   (1885) 7 OR 524.
14   HC Deb, vol 591, 8 July 1958, cols 208-346 (HC 34, 1957-58). An aspect of this matter was referred by the House to the Judicial Committee of the Privy Council for an opinion: *Re Parliamentary Privilege Act 1770* [1958] AC 331. At the time this was reported, such opinions could not contain any dissents, and it was not until 1985 that Lord Denning's dissent was published at [1985] PL 80. In this he suggested that the letter was a proceeding in Parliament and that it was for the courts in any case to decide whether or not a matter was a proceeding in Parliament; it was not for Parliament to use privilege to stop a legal action on the basis that it thought that the action was in respect of a proceeding in Parliament: 'Freedom of speech demands that the *courts of law* should protect the Member of Parliament, but not that Parliament itself should do so' (at 90). Interestingly, in an obiter dictum in *Rost v Edwards*, Popplewell J suggested that letters written by a MP to the Speaker and to another MP were governed by parliamentary privilege ([1990] 2 WLR 1280 at 1291).
15   *Erskine May* p 92.
16   See n 1 above. The government regarded the Zircon defence project to be a matter of national security, and it had successfully obtained an injunction preventing the disclosure of any information in connection with this project.
17   The word 'proceedings' is also found in the Parliamentary Papers Act 1840 in a context which suggests that it is used in the same sense as in art 9. Section 13 of the Defamation Act 1996, which was passed in an attempt to allow MPs, who so wish, to use parliamentary proceedings as evidence in libel actions, includes in sub-ss (4) and (5) what amounts to a partial definition of proceedings in Parliament. It remains to be seen if this definition, which is probably intended to be restricted to the application of s 13, is applied more widely. Another statutory reference to proceedings in Parliament can be found in s 6(3) of the Human Rights Act 1998. This clause specifically excludes a person exercising functions in connection with 'proceedings in Parliament' from the definition of a 'public authority'.

A further matter that has not been finally determined is in respect of criminal *acts* which could be regarded as having been committed in the course of proceedings in Parliament. Clearly, the fact that a criminal act is within the Palace of Westminster is not in itself enough to provide the protection of art 9. In *Bradlaugh v Gossett*[18] Stephen J said that he 'knew of no authority for the proposition that an ordinary crime committed in the House of Commons would be withdrawn from the ordinary course of criminal justice'. *Erskine May* says of this case that, since Stephen J immediately went on to refer to *Eliot's case*[19] where, although the court had left open the question whether an assault on the Speaker could have been decided by the King's Bench, it had accepted that nothing said by a member could be treated by the ordinary courts, 'it must be supposed that what the learned judge had in mind was a criminal act as distinguished from criminal speech'.[20]

There have been examples of criminal acts within the precincts of Westminster, which Parliament has considered but has made no suggestion of involving the police or the courts. In 1947 the Committee of Privileges Report in connection with an affray between a member and a lobby correspondent[1] was accepted by the House. A resolution was passed in which the House stated its 'determination to proceed with the utmost severity against such offenders in like cases'.[2] In 1988, when Ron Brown MP damaged the mace in the course of a heated debate, and failed to apologise in the way expected, the House exercised its penal powers not just in respect of the criminal damage, but in respect of the authority of the Chair.[3] An attempt to bring a private prosecution for criminal damage was halted by the DPP.[4]

Finally, even the proposition that no civil action may be taken against a member specifically in respect of something said in the course of a parliamentary debate, is not incontrovertible. Sir John Laws has commented that:

> I am not myself convinced that if a Member of Parliament were motivated by reasons of actual personal malice to use his position to defame, in the course of a debate, an individual outside Parliament, he should not as a result be subject to the ordinary law of defamation, and Article 9 could readily be construed comfortably with such a state of affairs.[5]

The particular problem of bribery of members of Parliament

The discussion so far has been concerned with the problems surrounding the meaning of the words in art 9 of the Bill of Rights. There are additional and rather different

---

18   (1884) 12 QBD at 284.
19   (1666) 3 State Tr 331-3.
20   *Erskine May* p 99.
 1   HC 36, 1946-47.
 2   HC Deb vol 433, 10 February 1947, col 41.
 3   See HC Deb vol 131, 19 April 1988, cols 929-953 for the debate on the motion to suspend Brown and to hold him responsible for the damage to the mace.
 4   *The Times*, 23 April 1988, 9 June 1988.
 5   Sir John Laws 'Law and Democracy' [1995] PL 72 at 76 n 14. See A Sharland and I Loveland 'The Defamation Act 1996 and Political Libels' [1997] PL 113 at 121 and n 24, where they state that: 'There is even some (US) authority for the proposition that a legislator's speech in the House or Senate may be the *subject* of a defamation action if the speaker has knowingly or recklessly disseminated lies.'

problems in respect to the application of both the parliamentary law and the substantive law of bribery to MPs whose corrupt activities are in connection with their parliamentary duties. It is a contempt of Parliament punishable by the House for someone to offer, or for a member to accept, a fee or reward for promoting, or opposing, any matter submitted to or transacted in Parliament.[6] However, in 1995 the Nolan Committee noted that 'the rules are much less explicit as regards restricting the freedom of Members to place themselves in situations where they are liable to be improperly influenced'.[7]

So far as the substantive criminal law is concerned, it was the opinion of the 1976 Royal Commission on Standards of Conduct in Public Life[8] that the offences created by the Public Bodies Corrupt Practices Act 1889 did not apply to MPs receiving rewards for doing or not doing something in respect of matters concerned with the House of Commons, since the House was not a 'public body' for the purpose of the Act. The 1976 Royal Commission also concluded that MPs were not 'public officers' for the purpose of the common law offence of bribery and breach of trust by public officers.[9] If these interpretations are correct,[10] then it must be noted that the failure of the substantive criminal law to apply to MPs is not as a consequence of art 9 of the Bill of Rights, but as a consequence of the defects in the existing law.[11] The Royal Commission suggested the law should be changed to ensure that bribery and attempted bribery of MPs was covered by the criminal law, but no action was taken. However, in 1992 charges were brought against several people including Harry Greenway MP for common law bribery. Buckley J rejected a defence application that it was not an offence to bribe a MP; the case collapsed because of evidential problems and the issue of the application of the common law of bribery offence to MPs has yet to be decided by an appellate court.[11a] The importance of art 9 was not overlooked by Buckley J, but he said that it was significant with respect to evidence and not as to the substantive law of bribery. The 1995 Nolan Report recognised the disparity between the decision of Buckley J and the conclusion of the Royal Commission and suggested that:

> it is quite likely the Members of Parliament who accepted bribes in connection with their parliamentary duties would be committing Common Law offences which could be tried by the courts. Doubt exists as to whether the courts or Parliament have jurisdiction in such cases.[12]

---

6 See the resolution of the Commons passed in 1695, CJ (1693-97) 331 (2 May 1695). There is no similar resolution in respect of the Lords, but Erskine May, by implication, accepts that bribery of a peer is likely to be regarded as a contempt: *Erskine May* p 112.

7 *Standards in Public Life: First Report of the Committee, Chairman Lord Nolan* 1995 (Cm 2850-I) para 35. In response to this report see now the Commons Code of Conduct (HC 688, 1995-96) pp 3-5.

8 The Salmon Commission, 1977 (Cmnd 6524).

9 This also meant that those offering bribes to MPs could not be prosecuted. The position with respect to the House of Lords may be different since Lords sit by virtue of their peerage and of their writ of summons: see *Erskine May* p 114.

10 For a criticism of the conclusions of the Royal Commission and a general discussion of the position of MPs see G Zellick 'Bribery of Members of Parliament and the Criminal Law' [1979] PL 31.

11 However, the then Prime Minister, Mr James Callaghan (as he then was), in the course of a debate on the Poulson affair in 1976, suggested that 'A Member who accepts a bribe in return for some action which is a proceeding in Parliament cannot be the subject of criminal proceedings' (HC Deb vol 917, col 1446).

11a The judgment is published at [1998] PL forthcoming.

12 Nolan Report, ch 1, para 104.

In consequence, Nolan recommended that the government should take steps to clarify the law relating to the bribery of, or receipt of a bribe by, an MP. In particular, Nolan suggested that there was a need to 'clarify or perhaps alter the boundary between the courts and Parliament' in respect of bribery of members. The previous Conservative government agreed the need for a clarification of the law, but felt that it was a matter of policy for the government and Parliament, rather than a matter of law for the Law Commission.[13] The Home Office has produced a discussion paper[14] in which it suggests that there are four options for the Select Committee on Standards and Privileges to consider: (i) to rely solely on parliamentary privilege to deal with accusations of bribery by members of Parliament; (ii) to subject members of Parliament to the present corruption statutes in full; (iii) to distinguish between conduct which should be dealt with by the criminal law and that which should be left to Parliament itself; (iv) to make criminal proceedings subject to the approval of the relevant House of Parliament.

There are potential problems with all these options. The first option would leave the investigation of allegations of bribery in relation to parliamentary duties to the Committee of Privileges and Standards, which, in the interests of fairness to anyone concerned, is not equipped to carry out such an investigation. In addition, the subsequent punishments available to Parliament are out of line with those available to the courts. It would also leave the conduct of a person bribing or being bribed by a member outside the normal law of the land. The second alternative, which would require a general review of the law on corruption, would be most in keeping with the notion of the Rule of Law. However, in order to implement such a change properly, Parliament will have to address the problem that, in some circumstances, it would be necessary to use parliamentary proceedings as evidence in the subsequent court proceedings. The third option would leave Parliament still in control over the application of at least part of the law of bribery, but it could be difficult to decide where the line between the courts and Parliament was to be drawn. The final option could be difficult to apply fairly. There have been several occasions where Parliament has had to decide matters connected with privilege and voting has taken place on plainly party political lines.[15] It would not improve public confidence in Parliament if matters such as when to require members to face criminal proceedings were seen

---

13   The Law Commission has produced a Consultation Paper (No 145) on corruption. In this it suggests a reconstruction of corruption into four offences. The Law Commission made no recommendations as to the application of the proposed law to members of Parliament, but assumed that: 'the position of members of either House, and of Ministers will be clarified by the Home Office review, and appropriate steps take, before we make our final recommendations' (at para 7.49).

14   *Clarification of the Law relating to the Bribery of Members of Parliament: a Discussion Paper,* (December 1996). The Joint Committee on Parliamentary Privilege considered the implications of the proposals for members: see HL 50, HC 401, 1997-98. The views of the Home Secretary are at HL 50-iii, HC 401-iii, 1997-98.

15   See eg the decision of the House in 1958 to ignore the recommendation of the Committee of Privileges in the Strauss case, and more recently the decision by the House that the (old) Committee of Privileges should be entitled to decide for itself how to conduct its investigation into the 'Cash for Questions' matter. A Labour motion calling for public hearings was defeated by 301 to 264 votes. HC Deb vol 248, 31 October 1994, cols 1217-1273. However, in the Garry Allinghan case in 1947, although there was a substantial Labour majority in the House of Commons, the House agreed to expel Allinghan, a Labour MP.

as a lottery. It would also be difficult for Parliament to make such a decision without first investigating the allegation.

Two recent government initiatives suggest that these matters will be taken further. These are commitment to reform the law on corruption in all areas of public life including the bribery of members,[16] and the establishment of a joint committee to undertake a general review of parliamentary privilege.[17] In deciding how to apply the law on corruption to members, it is to be hoped that Parliament will bear in mind the purpose of parliamentary privilege. In 1976, in the course of the House of Lords debate on the Salmon Report, Lord Salmon reminded members that art 9 of the Bill of Rights was 'a charter for freedom of speech in the House . . . not a charter for corruption'.[18]

The above discussion highlighted two problems with the application of the law of bribery to MPs, both of which have a more general application. The first is to what extent can evidence of something that is a proceeding in Parliament be used in a civil or criminal action? The second is how Parliament investigates and punishes breaches of privilege and contempt of Parliament, in particular where those breaches could also amount to civil or criminal wrongs.

The first of these problems involves a consideration of another area of confusion and uncertainty with respect to art 9. What does it mean to impeach or question proceedings in Parliament, and what is a place out of Parliament?

'Questioning' parliamentary proceedings in 'a court or place out of Parliament'

Evidence of what has been said or done in the course of debate or parliamentary proceedings can be referred to 'out of Parliament', provided that no attempt is made to 'question' or 'impeach' those proceedings. The prohibition on impeaching proceedings is straightforward, since it prevents actions directly against any member, officer or stranger for things said or done in the course of proceedings in Parliament.[19] However the interpretation of 'questioned' and 'place out of Parliament' are more controversial, and raise wider issues.

What does 'questioned' mean?

It was suggested above that, if the law on bribery is reformed so that MPs are fully subject to the criminal law, an associated 'privilege' problem will also have to be considered. As the law stands, if a member of either House is being prosecuted and either the prosecution or the defence seek to rely, as part of their evidence, on the speech or conduct of the member in the course of parliamentary proceedings, this could amount to 'questioning' proceedings in Parliament. This same problem, until

---

16 HC Deb vol 295, 9 June 1997, written answers, col 346.
17 HC Deb vol 295, 9 June 1997, written answers, col 320.
18 HL Deb vol 378, 8 December 1976, cols 611-671 at col 631. Lord Windlesham, in concluding the debate, optimistically suggested that the debate was: 'part of the process by which public policy is made or changed. It is hard to tell at what point public policy begins to shift, I do not think that I am alone in believing that changes are needed in the law and practice relating to corruption, and I hope that this debate will help towards that end' (at col 671).
19 But see the comment at p 74, n 5 and associated text.

recently, faced a MP who brought or sought to defend an action for libel in respect of something said not in the course of proceedings in Parliament, but where part of the evidence in the legal action was connected with parliamentary conduct.

The problem with the meaning of 'questioned' is that the:

> relatively clear protective principle [of art 9] has, over the years, become conflated with various wider claims, made by the Commons and conceded by the courts, as to the admissibility of evidence about proceedings in the House in actions of other kinds in which members or non-members may be involved.[20]

The courts are clearly wary about the need to refrain from 'questioning' proceedings in Parliament in the sense of questioning the motives or intentions of those who take part in parliamentary proceedings.[1] However, in *Pepper v Hart*[2] the House of Lords held that for a court to use ministerial statements as a guide to the construction of ambiguous legislation would not be to question proceedings in Parliament. Lord Browne-Wilkinson commented that he had no doubt that judges would be astute to ensure that counsel did not impugn or criticise a minister's statements or reasoning. It was not long before in *Prebble v Television New Zealand*,[3] Lord Browne-Wilkinson had another opportunity to consider the meaning of 'questioned'. The substance of the case was an action by the Hon Richard Prebble, a New Zealand MP and former government minister, for libel in respect of things said in the course of a television programme. The issue for the Judicial Committee of the Privy Council was whether art 9 prevented the defendant referring to statements made by Prebble in the House of Representatives in order to justify the allegations made by the defendant in the broadcast. The Judicial Committee agreed with the New Zealand Court of Appeal that to allow the defendant to use such evidence would be contrary to art 9. In coming to this conclusion, Lord Browne-Wilkinson referred with approval to s 16(3) of the Australian Parliamentary Privileges Act 1987, which provides that in court proceedings evidence in respect of parliamentary proceedings can not be used for the purpose of:

> (a) questioning or relying on the truth, motive, intention or good faith of anything forming part of those proceedings in Parliament; (b) otherwise questioning or establishing the credibility, motive, intention or good faith of any person; or (c) drawing, or inviting the drawing of, inferences or conclusions wholly or partly from anything forming part of those proceedings in Parliament.

Later, Lord Browne-Wilkinson summarised the position by stating that parties to litigation could not bring into question anything said or done in the House by suggesting that: 'the actions or words were inspired by improper motives or were untrue or misleading.'[4] The Judicial Committee acknowledged that there could be cases where the exclusion of material on the grounds of parliamentary privilege would make it impossible for the case to be decided and a stay would be required, but

---

20   G Marshall 'Impugning Parliamentary Impunity' [1994] PL 509 at 509.
1   *Church of Scientology of California v Johnson-Smith* [1972] 1 QB 522.
2   [1993] AC 593. See ch IX below.
3   [1995] 1 AC 321. See P M Leopold 'Free Speech in Parliament and the Courts' (1995) 15 LS 204.
4   *Prebble v Television New Zealand Ltd* [1995] 1 AC 321.

did not think that *Prebble* was such a case. Lord Browne-Wilkinson suggested that there was confusion in some of the cases between the right to prove the occurrence of parliamentary events and the embargo on questioning their propriety.[5] In consequence, there would be no objection to the defendants in *Prebble* referring to Hansard to prove what the plaintiff or other MPs had said in the House of Representatives, provided they did not allege impropriety. It would be for the trial judge: 'to ensure that the proof of these historical facts is not used to suggest that the words were improperly spoken or the statute passed to achieve an improper purpose'.[6]

A consequence of this decision was that not only could no direct action be taken against a member in respect of something said or done by him in the course of proceedings in Parliament, since that would be to 'impeach' free speech, but neither could there be any criticism or examination of something said in parliamentary proceedings as part of the evidence in an action which was not directly concerned with a parliamentary proceeding. Earlier in his opinion Lord Browne-Wilkinson had stated that art 9 was merely one manifestation of a wider principle, the respective constitutional roles of the courts and Parliament, from which it followed that the courts would not allow: 'any challenge to be made to what is said or done within the walls of Parliament in performance of its legislative functions and protection of its established privileges'.[7]

On the face of it, the decision in *Prebble* should have been welcomed by Parliament, since its wide interpretation of 'questioned' protected members, and indeed anyone, from any suggestion of misbehaviour in the course of parliamentary proceedings being raised in court. The public interest in the legislature exercising its powers freely on behalf of its electors was said to prevail over both the general need to protect free speech and the interests of justice in ensuring that all relevant evidence was before a court. Lord Browne-Wilkinson recognised that there was a risk that this approach could, depending on the situation, either prevent a MP from establishing his good name in the courts or prevent the media from making truthful disclosures about a member's misbehaviour in Parliament, since justification would be impossible. It was envisaged that it would only be in the most extreme circumstances that a case would have to be stayed.

It was not long before the application of the decision in *Prebble* came before an English court, in two cases involving MPs seeking to sue newspapers for defamation. In both cases the actions were stayed. In the first case, *Allason v Haines*[8] Owen J held that the defendant's pleadings indicated that they would seek to show that early day motions signed by Rupert Allason MP were inspired by improper motives or were activated upon improper behaviour, and that to do this would be contrary to *Prebble*. In the second case, Neil Hamilton MP sought to sue the *Guardian* for defamation in respect of articles alleging that he was paid money, which he did not declare in the

---

5   Ibid at 337. He in particular doubted if *Rost v Edwards* was rightly decided. This is clearly a reference to that part of *Rost v Edwards* where Popplewell J had held that the plaintiff MP could not, without leave of the House of Commons, call evidence as to his appointment or de-selection as a member of a House of Commons Standing Committee, since to do so would be to 'question' proceedings in Parliament.

6   *Prebble* [1995] 1 AC 321.

7   Ibid at 332.

8   [1995] NLJR 1576.

Register of Members' Interests, in return for, inter alia, asking parliamentary questions on behalf of Mohamed Al-Fayed. The defendant argued that it was not possible to inquire into the issues raised by the action without infringing parliamentary privilege. May J held that the case was so like *Prebble* that he had no option but to stay the proceedings. It is clear that May J had misgivings about the effect of this decision, and clearly doubted whether the use of the relevant parliamentary procedures would be an adequate substitute for a trial by judge and jury. He concluded by commenting that:

> Every judge is acutely aware that the ability of all persons to come to the courts to have their disputes tried and determined fairly, openly and according to law is a cardinal right upon which freedom under the constitution depends. The courts exist to try cases, not to decline to do so. In this instance statute and authority require the court to do just that.[9]

Section 13 of the Defamation Act 1996

Prebble left members in an awkward position. The Commons, by one of its own resolutions, in effect encourages members to bring civil actions in respect of alleged defamation rather than rely on the House's penal jurisdiction.[10] However, as a consequence of *Prebble*, as accepted in *Hamilton*, where either the plaintiff MP or the defendant to the libel action could not conduct the case without reference to parliamentary proceedings, the case would have to be stayed, and members would have to rely on Parliament's own procedures to investigate alleged contempts by the media. The injustice of this was raised in the House of Lords in the course of debate on the Defamation Bill 1996, and an amendment to the Bill was put forward by Lord Hoffmann in the course of the Lords' committee stage. The issues were not discussed fully until the third reading, when the pros and cons of allowing members in the position of Messrs Allason or Hamilton to decide to waive privilege and allow parliamentary proceedings to be 'questioned' as part of the evidence in a court were considered, as were several perceived defects in the content of the amendment.[11] One of the most persuasive voices in opposition to the amendment was Lord Lester, who doubted whether May J was right in his decision in the *Hamilton* case since, unlike *Prebble*, the issue was not Hamilton's behaviour in Parliament, but his behaviour outside Parliament. The amendment was passed by the Lords,[12] and despite some last-minute committee stage and third reading opposition, it was also agreed to by the Commons.

In consequence, it is now possible in a defamation action where 'the conduct of a person in or in relation to proceedings in Parliament is in issue' for that person[13] to decide to waive the protection whereby proceedings in Parliament could not be questioned. Section 13(2) provides that when the protection has been waived then:

---

9   (1995, unreported) transcript p 35.
10 HC Deb vol 943, 6 February 1978, col 1198.
11 HL Deb vol 572, 7 May 1996, cols 22-51. For a discussion of the views expressed in both Houses, and an evaluation of s 13, see Sharland and Loveland [1997] PL 113.
12 Lord Hoffmann abstained.
13 Which, in addition to members of either House, could also include others, such as witnesses before a House committee.

any such enactment or rule of law shall not apply to prevent evidence being given, questions being asked or suggestions, comments or findings being made about his conduct.

Section 13(4) makes it clear that this section does not –

affect any enactment or rule of law so far as it protects a person ... from legal liability for words spoken or things done in the course of, or for the purpose of or incidental to, any proceedings in Parliament.[14]

The immunity from civil or criminal actions for things said or done in the course of debates or proceedings in Parliament is unaltered.

There are potential problems and serious objections to s 13. What if two members are involved in a defamation action, but only one of them wishes to waive privilege? What if it is the defendant journalist who wishes to refer to parliamentary proceedings as justification, and the member refuses to waive privilege? Why should a privilege which belongs to the whole House be able to be waived by one member for his personal benefit? Since freedom of speech is a privilege of the House with an existence independent of art 9, should a member decide to use s 13 of the Defamation Act and waive the protection of art 9, the House could still consider the conduct or words in question and decide whether the member or the other party had committed contempt of Parliament. In this way there could be two inquiries, one in Parliament and one in the courts.

To return to bribery. Section 13 will make no difference to the position with respect to the use of parliamentary proceedings as evidence in respect of the prosecution of members for receiving bribes or strangers for offering such bribes. If Parliament decides to apply the statute law on corruption to members and to allow investigation and prosecution to be determined in the normal way, it will have also to decide what to do about the use of parliamentary proceedings as evidence in such a case. In many cases, no evidence of parliamentary proceedings will be required, the offer of a bribe will be the actus reus of the offence. If evidence of proceedings in Parliament is required, then the alternatives appear to be to accept that if a prosecution cannot succeed without 'questioning' proceedings in Parliament, then it will have to fail, and Parliament will have to rely on its own jurisdiction to deal with such cases. Alternatively, it will have to allow for the waiving of the protection in respect of 'questioning' proceedings in Parliament, as in s 13 of the Defamation Act. Whether the right to waive should be left to the defendant member, or be decided on by the House as a whole would have to be considered. It would be most strange to leave it to a member to decide, in circumstances where he is being prosecuted, whether or not to waive the protection of art 9. If Parliament decides that it should be for it to waive the protection, then there will be yet another anomaly between the application of the civil and criminal law to parliamentary proceedings, and an opportunity for partisan behaviour by Parliament.

An alternative approach to the problems and controversy illustrated above would have been for the courts to take account of the discretion art 9 gives to them. Article 9

---

14 A partial definition of what, in the context of this section, is included by proceedings in Parliament, is found in s 13(5). The Hamilton defamation action recommenced after the enactment of s 13, but was abandoned by Mr Hamilton on the eve of the trial.

provides that proceedings *ought* not to be questioned. This suggests that it would have been possible for the courts to distinguish between the different circumstances in which 'questioning' of proceedings arose. This could be the explanation for the decision in *Pepper v Hart*.[15] It could also be the explanation for the 'blind eye' turned by Parliament to media criticism.

Before turning to how Parliament itself can deal with breaches of privilege or contempt, this further incongruity in the interpretation and application of art 9 needs to be considered. Where, apart from the courts, is a 'place out of Parliament', and do the same restrictions on 'questioning' apply to such 'places'?

What is a 'place out of Parliament'?

One might have thought that the phrase 'place out of Parliament' in art 9 was as general as it is possible to be, but its interpretation in present-day conditions is not easy. There may be general agreement that 'place' excludes the media,[16] on the free speech argument presented by Lord Browne-Wilkinson who, in *Pepper v Hart*, noted that:

> . . . Members of Parliament must speak and act taking into account what political commentators and others will say. Plainly art 9 cannot have the effect so to stifle the freedom of all to comment on what is said in Parliament, even though such comments may influence Members in what they say.[17]

However, it may be recalled that it is only about 40 years since the rule was abolished prohibiting discussions on television on topics due to be debated in Parliament during a 14-day period prior to the debate. During the Australian case *R v Murphy*,[18] counsel for the President of the Senate first suggested that 'place' included the media, but that Parliament would take no action on media comments, even though they were prima facie a breach of art 9. He then changed tack and suggested that 'place' did *not* cover the media, but referred to 'a tribunal or other organ of State'. On this interpretation, 'place out of Parliament' would have included Sir Richard Scott's inquiry.[19] It was not conducted by a court, but the tribunal had some of the attributes of a court; it was a non-statutory, ad hoc, inquisitorial inquiry, and Sir Richard acted as 'detective, inquisitor, advocate and judge'.[20] In his report, Sir Richard severely criticised various aspects of parliamentary proceedings – the veracity of answers to parliamentary questions; a statement in the House of Commons by a minister; evidence to a select committee by a minister and a civil servant; and the choice of departmental witnesses for a select committee inquiry. But if Sir Richard had been debarred from making these criticisms, he would have been unable to do his job. However, the contrast is marked between the freedom he possessed as a one-man tribunal and the restrictions he would have had to observe as a judge in a court hearing. A Nelsonian blind eye

---

15 [1993] AC 593.
16 See eg the extensive criticism in the press of William Waldegrave in respect of the 'arms to Iraq' affair: *Independent,* 16 February 1995.
17 [1993] AC 593 at 638.
18 (1986) 5 NSWLR 18.
19 HC 115, 1995-96.
20 Lord Denning on his role in the inquiry into the Profumo Affair, 1963 (Cmnd 2152).

has been turned to the problem, which illustrates the point that art 9 'was passed to meet the needs of a very different age'[1] and that 'there can be a difficulty in the application to modern conditions of provisions enacted in very brief terms three centuries ago'.[2]

The 'questioning' of proceedings by Parliament and its penal jurisdiction

Speech and other proceedings in Parliament may be questioned by Parliament itself. Parliament has its own rules on behaviour and conduct, some of which are found in resolutions of the House, and with respect to these rules Parliament is said to be self-regulating. This is the penal jurisdiction of Parliament.[3] In certain circumstances, for a member to commit a civil or criminal wrong or to breach privilege or commit contempt of Parliament in the course of a proceeding in Parliament could give rise to an investigation by the House. It is not just members who may be subject to the penal jurisdiction of Parliament. Witnesses before parliamentary committees, journalists,[4] even lawyers acting for aggrieved clients, could commit contempt of Parliament and find themselves subject to Parliament's penal jurisdiction. Investigations into alleged breaches of privilege or contempt of Parliament are usually delegated to a Commons select committee – the Committee of Privileges[5] until 1995, when it became the Committee on Standards and Privileges. The final decision on the matter, including punishment, is for the House. Some of the problems with this arrangement, were summed up in 1992 as follows:

> There are no procedural safeguards. Accused persons may be condemned unheard, or summoned for cross-examination without legal representation or being given notice of the charges, and without any right to challenge the evidence given against them or to call witnesses in rebuttal. The Committee sits in secret, and reports in due course to the Commons. The House decides whether and what punishment to inflict, after a further debate in which biased MP's vote entirely as judges in their own cause. (These procedures) are in blatant breach of at least three articles of the European Convention on Human Rights.[6]

1   G Lock 'Parliamentary Privilege and the Courts: The Avoidance of Conflict' [1985] PL 73.
2   G Lock 'The 1689 Bill of Rights' (1989) XXXVII Pol S 542.
3   See *Erskine May* ch 9.
4   *R v Richards, ex p Fitzpatrick and Browne* (1955) 92 CLR 157. On the basis of old precedents, it would have been possible for Parliament to have acted against journalists for contempt of Parliament in respect of recent examples of aggressive reporting and comment on proceedings in Parliament.
5   Matters connected with members' interests were investigated by the Select Committee on Members' Interests, but there were anomalies and overlaps between this committee and the Committee of Privileges.
6   G Robertson and A Nicol *Media Law* (3rd edn, 1992) p 399. The European Court of Human Rights in *Demicoli v Malta* (1991) 14 EHRR 47 decided that the procedure in the House of Representatives for determining a question of privilege was in breach of the European Convention on Human Rights. The Human Rights Act 1998 makes it unlawful for a public authority to act in a way which is incompatible with the convention rights. However s 6(3) excludes Parliament and 'a person exercising functions in connection with proceedings in Parliament' from the definition of a 'public authority'. This will not prevent the European Court of Human Rights determining the compatibility of parliamentary proceedings with the convention.

The inquiries conducted by the Committee of Privileges were mainly concerned with issues of breach of privilege or contempt of Parliament where the 'defendant' was not a MP. The Committee of Privileges did not usually consider matters concerned with the conduct of members. Where such matters have arisen, the House has normally appointed a specific committee.[7] Whether such committees have been any better equipped to deal with the issues, is a moot point. There has been judicial concern as to whether parliamentary committees are the appropriate body to investigate members' conduct. In 1992, in the course of giving his decision in the *Greenway* case, Buckley J suggested that the Committee of Privileges was not well equipped to conduct an inquiry into a case of alleged corruption; that it was not an appropriate body to pass sentence and that he could not see that it would be in the interests of members for such allegations to be dealt with by such a committee. He went on to comment:

> The courts and legislature have over the years built up a formidable body of law and codes of practice to achieve fair treatment of suspects and persons ultimately charged and brought to trial. Again, unless it is to be assumed that his peers would lean in his favour why should a Member be deprived of a jury and an experienced judge to consider his guilt or innocence and, if appropriate, sentence? Why should the public be similarly deprived?[8]

The reference to the Committee of Privileges in 1994 of the allegations of members having been paid to ask parliamentary questions[9] was the first example since 1947[10] of the committee being asked to deal with a member's conduct. The alternative to this investigation would have been to report the members to the police for an investigation into what amounted to an allegation of bribery. The continued perceived uncertainty as to the application of bribery to members seems to have prevented this action.[11] The suitability of the Committee of Privileges for carrying out such an investigation was clearly even more suspect than its suitability to investigate 'ordinary' breaches of privilege and contempt. The committee concluded that the conduct of two of the members concerned had fallen below that which the House was entitled to expect from its members. It recommended, and the House agreed, that the members should be formally reprimanded and be suspended from the House with suspension of salary.

Until November 1995, a separate committee structure existed to consider complaints that a member was in breach of the House's own rules on the Register of Members' Interests. One of the last inquiries by this committee was in respect of allegations that Neil Hamilton MP had failed to register a 1987 complimentary stay at the Ritz Hotel in Paris. These and other allegations were also reported in the *Guardian* newspaper. The committee concluded that Hamilton had been 'imprudent' not to consult the Registrar as to the need to declare this hospitality. However, since a consequence of the allegations was Hamilton's resignation as a minister, no further action was

---

7   See eg Select Committee on the Conduct of a Member (HC 5, 1940-41); Select Committee on the Conduct of Members (HC 490, 1976-77).
8   See p 75, n 11a above.
9   HC 351, 1994-95.
10   HC 138, 142, 1946-47.
11   The Committee of Privileges doubted whether the offer of money to a MP to ask a parliamentary question or provide information was within the definition of bribery either at common law or in parliamentary law (HC 351-I, 1994-95) para 8.

required by the House. The committee decided, on a division, not to investigate an additional complaint that Hamilton had accepted cash and other payments from Mr Al-Fayed for carrying out parliamentary duties, on the basis that this could prejudice the libel action already started by Hamilton against the *Guardian*.[12] The possibility of reporting Hamilton to the police for a bribery investigation was not discussed. The general dissatisfaction with the procedural aspects of this affair was noted by the Nolan Committee. It also commented on the ad hoc basis upon which proceedings relating to the conduct of members were carried out, and suggested that there was a need for the public to be able: 'to see that breaches of the rules by its elected legislators are investigated as fairly, and dealt with as firmly, by Parliament as would be the case with others through the legal process.'[13]

The above summary suggests two separate but overlapping problems with the penal jurisdiction of Parliament. First, the procedure used and punishments available in respect of breaches of privilege and contempt have been unfair and unsatisfactory. Secondly, Parliament has lacked adequate procedures to investigate allegations of improper conduct by members.[14] The attempts to solve the first of these problems will now be considered.[15]

The procedure for investigation into breaches of privilege and contempt

The Nolan Report suggested that there should be new procedural arrangements for dealing with the conduct of members. An aspect of this was the creation of a new Select Committee on Standards and Privileges to take over the functions of the Committee of Privileges and the Select Committee on Members' Interests. The House accepted these proposals,[16] and in consequence there is now a different procedure for the investigation of the conduct of members and for matters relating to the privileges of the House.

The task of investigating 'traditional' matters of privilege remains little changed. It is still for the House to refer specific matters to the slimmed down[17] Committee on Standards and Privileges. Only one of the procedural changes[18] made to this

---

12 This was the action stayed by application of *Prebble*. It commenced again after the enactment of s 13 of the Defamation Act 1996, but collapsed.
13 Nolan Report para 92. See eg the Select Committee on the Marconi scandal in 1913, where the Liberal majority on the committee was able to secure a whitewash on Marconi share dealings by Lloyd George and Rufus Issacs (HC 152, 1913).
14 A third problem, the application of the law of bribery to members, has already been considered.
15 This chapter does not look at the special procedure for the investigation of conduct, except so far as there is an overlap between this and the procedure for the investigation of 'normal' privilege matters. One of the most controversial of the cases to be investigated by the newly created Parliamentary Commissioner on Standards was an expanded version of the complaint against Neil Hamilton which had not been investigated by the Select Committee on Members' Interests in 1995. This report and the subsequent reports from the Committee of Privileges and Standards suggest that there are still weaknesses and defects in the procedure (HC 30, 261, 1997-98).
16 After a report from the specially created Select Committee on Standards in Public Life (HC 637, 1994-95).
17 It now has 11 members.
18 The others include the power to *order* the attendance of members and to *require* members to provide specified documents to the committee (SO 149). This is the only select committee with such powers.

committee goes any way towards meeting the criticisms cited above. This is the decision that those who appear before the committee should be allowed to be accompanied by an adviser, although this adviser is not allowed to answer questions on behalf of a witness or to examine other witnesses.[19] One of the first investigations by the committee was in connection with allegations that David Willetts MP had brought improper pressure on the (old) Select Committee on Members' Interests.[20] In its conclusion, the committee indicated that it was concerned that much of the evidence, both oral and written submitted by Willetts was inaccurate. However, it did not take the next step of suggesting that this amounted to contempt of Parliament. Instead, it suggested that, in future, witnesses before the committee should be required to give evidence on oath. The effect of this was said to enable those who committed perjury to be prosecuted.[1]

A further weakness of Parliament's penal jurisdiction is the punishments available. Both Houses have power to imprison: the Lords for a specified term which may go beyond the duration of the session, the Commons only to the end of the session. This power has not been used since 1880, but it is theoretically still available, although it is in reality too extreme a punishment to be used. Even if it were considered appropriate, for example, for those found to have committed bribery, the term of imprisonment compares unfavourably with that available to those tried and convicted in court.

Other punishments available are reprimand and admonition. Only the House of Lords has a power to fine; neither House has a power to order the payment of damages. In recent years strangers have also been punished by the removal of lobby passes. Two additional punishments are available against members: suspension from the service of the House (with the possibility of loss of salary) and expulsion. The latter punishment in effect deprives the member of his livelihood.[2]

The whole procedure whereby Parliament investigates, judges and decides whether to punish those who offend against its rules looks inappropriate in respect of the more serious allegations of contempt or breach of privilege. There is a forceful argument to suggest that the Committee on Standards and Privileges is not a suitable place to investigate such allegations. There is clearly a need for Parliament to have jurisdiction to deal with the discipline of its members and strangers. Parliament has made a distinction between discipline and conduct in respect of its members. It probably ought to do the same with respect to strangers. The issue is: how could this be done? The attempt by Parliament to encourage members to seek redress in the courts for defamation proved problematical, and resulted in the ad hoc solution of s 13 of the Defamation Act. The alternative of allowing the Committee on Standards and Privileges to investigate such allegations, or allegations of criminal offences, is clearly not acceptable. A procedure whereby such allegations could be referred by Parliament to the High Court would be one solution. However, this would require a

---

19 This reform was introduced, in the interests of natural justice, primarily for the benefit of members whose 'conduct' was being investigated by the committee, and it was felt that it would be unfair that the 'accused' in traditional privileges cases, should be treated any less fairly.

20 This was in connection with the committee's investigation into the complaints against Hamilton and the Ritz Hotel etc.

1 Presumably, such a prosecution could require the questioning of proceedings in Parliament.

2 However, in respect of former MPs, the punishments available are limited to those available in respect of strangers.

clear statutory authority as to the use that could be made of parliamentary proceedings in such an action. To transfer the more serious matters to the courts would enable the imposition of appropriate penalties, after a fair hearing. Parliament would be able, where appropriate, to exercise its penal jurisdiction to respond to a court decision.[3] However, here and where Parliament is dealing with discipline, a more suitable range of punishments is required. To make this distinction in respect of disciplining members and strangers for minor contempts and breaches of Parliament's rules of behaviour would require a definitive list of contempts and rules of behaviour.

Conclusion

The present state of affairs with respect to the application of the civil and criminal law to members and proceedings in Parliament is a morass. It reflects in part the changing relationship between the courts and Parliament, with each institution both respecting the jurisdiction of the other and being watchful of encroachments. In this area, as in so many others, there have been ad hoc reforms without any attempt to look at the wider implications of the problem identified. Section 13 of the Defamation Act and the changes to the way Parliament investigates members' conduct are two examples. There are others. For example in 1967 the House clearly had in mind its 1958 decision that letters between members and ministers were not 'proceedings in Parliament' and therefore not covered by absolute parliamentary privilege when it enacted s 10(5) of the Parliamentary Commissioner Act 1967. This provides that for the purpose of the law of defamation, communications between the Parliamentary Commissioner and members are absolutely privileged, provided they are for the purposes set out in the Act. In 1976, when the Race Relations Act 1965 was being reformed, a provision was included to exclude from the criminal law 'fair and accurate reports of proceedings in Parliament' where those proceedings included words that, if said elsewhere, could have resulted in a prosecution for the offence of incitement to racial hatred.[4] However, there is no similar statutory protection for the reporting of fair and accurate accounts of parliamentary proceeding that could amount to criminal contempt of court, blasphemy or an obscene publication. If such reports are privileged, then it will have to be on the basis of an, as yet unrecognised, common law defence.[5]

The establishment of the Joint Committee on Parliamentary Privilege has given Parliament an opportunity to look at what its needs are today. Members, and those who assist Parliament, need to be able to speak and act freely without risk of legal action. By the same token, members and strangers should not abuse that privilege. Parliament must devise procedures to ensure that the uncertain limits of this privilege are clarified and, where this is not possible, that fair unbiased procedures exist to determine disputes.

3   Eg to expel or suspend a member.
4   There was no such provision in the 1965 Race Relations Act; see now s 26 of the Public Order Act 1986.
5   Section 15 of the 1996 Defamation Act provides a further example. It in part remedies the uncertain position of the broadcaster of parliamentary proceedings by providing a defence of qualified privilege for fair and accurate reports of proceedings in public of a legislature anywhere in the world. This still leaves the live broadcasting of criminal words said in the course of parliamentary proceedings unprotected.

Chapter VI

Legal advice and representation for Parliament

Barry K Winetrobe

Introduction

The idea of the autonomy of Parliament[1] should mean that, if Parliament is to be substantially independent of the Executive and the courts, it should have the benefit of legal advice and representation, from advisers who are independent of other branches of government. Should the fact that Parliament is not, in reality, independent of the Executive mean that it has less or no need for truly independent legal advice and representation? Is the role of the Attorney General, in particular, simply an extension of the role of the Executive generally in the activities of the legislature? If one approved, in theory, of independent legal advice for Parliament, would there really be sufficient work of a distinctive nature to make this a sensible, practical proposition?

When one takes account of the different personae of what we call Parliament, including its subordinate structures, as well as of the different categories of people and bodies which operate within it, one can see that it contains a complex web of legal advisers and 'clients', giving rise to all sorts of legal issues and problems, within the parliamentary system. Much of the complexity arises from Parliament's unique place in the constitutional and legal framework of the United Kingdom, developed piecemeal over centuries, as well as from its physical location – the Palace of Westminster being a royal palace, for example. The centrality of the notion of parliamentary self-regulation enforced through privilege means that Parliament's legal issues will cut across, as well as cover many of the ordinary matters of, civil or criminal law. The application of ordinary laws of the land to matters parliamentary is, in itself, a major and complex issue ranging from health and safety and employment law to perhaps more mundane matters such as the licensing laws.[2] Many of these issues have been clarified by statute, but doubtless there remain many grey areas, even in the context of 'proceedings in Parliament' (including the conduct of inquiries into breaches of privilege or rules on standards of conduct).[3]

---

1   On which, generally, see ch II above. While this chapter considers Parliament, attention is concentrated primarily on the House of Commons.
2   See *R v Graham-Campbell, ex p Herbert* [1935] 1 KB 594; G F Lock 'The application of the general law to Parliament' [1985] PL 376, and, generally, chs IV and V above.
3   The two Houses are, at time of writing, conducting a joint review of parliamentary privilege. For a discussion by the clerk of the House of Representatives of a recent New Zealand case, *Rata v A-G*, which found that even the caucus proceedings of parliamentary parties could be protected by parliamentary privilege as 'proceedings in Parliament', see D McGee 'Parliament and caucus' [1997] NZLJ 137; and ch V above.

As with any organisation, there will be legal questions relating to Parliament's own structure, operation and personnel. In addition, there will be similar legal relationships and problems between Parliament's 'micro-organisations'. These include:

- MPs and peers themselves in relation to their own staffs;
- the parliamentary parties and their staffs;
- other independent and semi-independent organisations – post office, travel office, police and security, media etc;
- other individuals – constituents, visitors, lawyers and others for House of Lords cases etc – who are on the premises from time to time.

As part of Parliament's operation at a 'micro' level, members of Parliament and peers, and their staffs on their behalf, will require all kinds of advice that could be classified as legal, especially in relation to their parliamentary duties. In practice, much of this will be dealt with by them in a routine way, often with the assistance of external bodies and persons such as pressure groups or party officers. Much of the rest will be treated as matters of parliamentary procedure, law and practice (including, for example, guidance on the boundaries of privilege), and will therefore be the province of the Clerks of both Houses, who are not, in general, legally qualified in the conventional sense. The research and information staff of both Houses, some of whom have legal backgrounds, will also provide assistance in the non-procedural aspects of parliamentary work, such as the interpretation of the content of legislation, policy briefings and advice on constituency problems and grievances.

Developments of the legislative process which aim to provide a greater input for 'outsiders' at the pre-parliamentary stage (such as the practice of departments' producing draft bills) and for parliamentarians at the pre-parliamentary and parliamentary stages (such as the involvement of departmental select committees in legislative initiatives and the use of mixed 'select/standing' committees in both Houses[4]) may lead to members of both Houses requiring access to independent sources of legal advice on the meaning and drafting of proposed legislation and amendments. This is often necessary to counterbalance the increasing volume of 'partial' advice and lobbying directed at parliamentary legislators from interested parties and pressure groups, and from ministers in charge of legislation, and their officials.[5] Recent, not altogether happy, experience of legislation in contentious areas such as the community charge/poll tax, dangerous dogs, child support, criminal justice and firearms, as well as the increasing complexity of legislation (primary and secondary) of a regulatory type,[6] demonstrates a need and a demand for more substantial and expert 'in-house' advice. The growing impact of *Pepper v Hart*,[7] with ministers regularly being asked to explain or interpret their legislation in ways which may ultimately be considered by the courts, also means that members of both Houses need to be clear as to the meaning and effect of all forms of ministerial utterances.

---

4   In particular, Commons Special Standing Committees and Lords Special Public Bill committees.
5   Recent improvements in the provision of explanatory material on Bills may actually enhance the need for such independent advice for parliamentarians.
6   Mirrored by the evolving scrutiny function over the agency-structured, contracted-out, managerialised public service.
7   [1993] AC 593: see ch IX below.

The involvement of Parliament, as an organisation in its own right, in what might be termed the 'real world' appears to be growing, especially in the extent to which it mirrors developments in the rest of the public service. Changes under the present government to the management of government departments and their officials have had their effect, albeit sometimes in a modified way, on Parliament and its staff and other personnel. This is most marked in attempts to introduce more effective and accountable management through, inter alia, defined financial systems, and revised pay and personnel policies. Although Parliament as an employer is obliged by statute to operate 'broadly in line'[8] with the civil service, the current policy of a shift away from a uniform service-wide approach to personnel requires Parliament as much as any other public sector employer to have access to appropriate advice on issues such as the negotiation of pay and reporting systems to the negotiation of contracts and disputes as they may arise *uniquely* within its precincts.

It may be suggested that those who work within Parliament may, to some extent, come to take Parliament's unique legal position somewhat for granted, not in the sense, of course, of feeling that they can flout the law, but that they sometimes do not have a sufficient appreciation of developments in the law which would, but for Parliament's special position, apply to them in their parliamentary work. This has been demonstrated in recent years where the combination of technological developments and the impact of governments' public sector policies has made it necessary for Parliament, like other parts of the public sector, to act, in many situations, more like an ordinary legal person transacting legal business and involving itself in legal relationships with various external bodies, than it has been used to doing hitherto. Traditionally, in many of these quasi-commercial areas Parliament has been used to having outside governmental agencies acting on its behalf. An example of this is the Central Computer and Telecommunications Agency (CCTA) in the information technology (IT) field, who, directly or through their contracted lawyers, and with the Treasury, will advise parliamentary officials on various matters such as the application of domestic and European public procurement regulations, and provide standard contracts or model clauses for various areas of parliamentary procurement and other commercial activities. On the very rare occasions when legal action is required involving, directly or otherwise, Parliament or one or other of its Houses or staff in the IT area, the CCTA may well be involved along with the Treasury Solicitor.

Examples of other novel areas include questions of copyright, especially since the initiation of the concept of 'parliamentary copyright' under the Copyright, Designs and Patents Act 1988, where Parliament has been seeking to deal with these complex legal issues through internal control mechanisms. It is unclear to what extent all potentially affected areas of the two Houses were fully involved in the 1988 legislation itself and regulations made thereunder. Another area is the Data Protection Act 1984, where it is understood that Speaker's Counsel (and his Lords equivalent) advised the Houses that it did not apply directly to Parliament. Ultimately, it was agreed, following parliamentary discussions with the Data Protection Registrar, that the two Houses would comply with the Act by analogy, with the Computer Officer acting as Parliament's data protection officer and 'registrar'.

---

8   House of Commons (Administration) Act 1978, s 2(2).

Finally, the growing scope and extent of European law must be considered. If European law is supreme throughout the Union, as applied by the European Court of Justice and accepted by the United Kingdom courts in the *Factortame* sense,[9] then, logically, it could override any domestic rule of law which provides immunity to certain unique constitutional institutions such as Parliaments. EU regulations and directives, especially in the health and safety and employment fields, are being applied within Parliament. Whether this is because Parliament is, or believes it is, bound by law from such sources, or simply because it chooses to apply them in the way that it chooses to apply some domestic laws, is not entirely clear.[10] There may not yet have been any litigation where a United Kingdom court has rejected any parliamentary privilege point on the grounds of European supremacy, but such a situation may not be far off. A position of Parliament being bound by European-inspired laws, but not by purely domestic laws, could not only inflame Euro-sceptics but could be as severe a blow to the constitutional 'separation of powers' relationships between Parliament and the other two organs of government, as it has been to the constitutional doctrine of the supremacy of Parliament itself.

A related point, in this respect, is the application of the European Convention on Human Rights to Parliament. The Human Rights Bill 1997-98 expressly excludes from the definition of a public authority subject to its provisions, 'either House of Parliament or a person exercising functions in connection with proceedings in Parliament'.[11] The apparently deliberate use of the 'proceedings in Parliament' test in the proposed statutory exclusion may well give rise to the sorts of legal difficulties as to the scope of the exclusion that arise in the field of parliamentary privilege. It appears that the provision is intended primarily to cover Parliament in its legislative and related functions, such as suspension by the House of Commons of its members, but not to more domestic matters where Parliament is acting, for example, as the employer of its staff, a contractor of services and supplies or a manager of property. In these domestic areas, the government apparently believes that the application of the convention would not impinge on the privileges or sovereignty of Parliament in its constitutional sense.

But for this provision, it may have been possible for domestic courts to feel that they could inquire into the conduct of Parliament's 'disciplinary' procedures,[12] as the European Court of Human Rights did in 1991 in relation to the Maltese House of Representatives.[13] Indeed, it may be that the domestic courts or the Strasbourg court may, at some future point, entertain a complaint against Parliament, perhaps on the

---

9   [1990] 2 AC 85 and [1991] 1 AC 603.

10 Giving evidence to the Joint Committee on Parliamentary Privilege on 16 December 1997, the then Clerk of the House of Commons, Sir Donald Limon, noted EC contracts and tendering laws 'which we have to take into account. I do not think there is any suggestion that Parliament is exempt from them, certainly. If it ever went to European Court, I do not see our case standing up well' (HC 401-ii, 1997-98) Q57.

11 Clause 6(3). 'Parliament' does not include the House of Lords in its judicial capacity: cl 6(4).

12 See the views of the Committee on Standards and Privileges and of the Parliamentary Commissioner for Standards on the special procedures adopted for the Hamilton/Al-Fayed case: 8th report of 1997-98 (HC 261, 1997-98).

13 *Demicoli v Malta* (1991) 14 EHRR 47, noted by the Clerk of the House of Commons and the Clerk Assistant in their evidence to the Joint Committee on Parliamentary Privilege (minutes of evidence, 2.12.97 (HC 401-i, 1997-98) p 9, para 28).

ground that the exemption for Parliament from the Bill's provisions is itself incompatible with the convention.

Separation of powers and legal advice for Parliament

It is a distinctive feature of the British system of government that many of its actors are able, often required, to wear more than one hat in their public, and sometimes private, personae. This exercise in political millinery need not necessarily cause any ethical or practical difficulties in cases where the practice is accepted by custom or convention or legitimised by law. However, it does rest on the belief that those performing such a potentially delicate balancing act manage to operate in their various guises as if there were 'Chinese walls' between them. Other than in obvious areas, such as the statutory rules on members' disqualification, the traditional 'gentlemanly' ethos of British public service has preserved, or appeared to preserve, the integrity of this arrangement. But we have seen in recent years that greater political polarisation in certain areas has led to the replacement of these unwritten understandings by formal statements of conduct, such as the statutory provisions on 'twin-tracking' in local government.

The provision of legal advice and assistance to Parliament is an area where these difficulties can be thrown into sharp relief, especially at the highest levels. It is, at the very least, curious that in a case as crucial to the relationship between Parliament and the courts as *Pepper v Hart* in the House of Lords, Parliament was represented by a senior member of the government, and the case was argued before a bench which included one of the most senior Cabinet members.[14] This is not to suggest, of course, that any of these, or other, legal actors who have to wear many hats have not performed all the various functions diligently and with the utmost integrity. All Law Officers will have given Parliament the full benefit of their legal expertise, as they would to any client, if not more so, and any judge, whether or not a current or former minister of the Crown, will try, with complete fairness, any case involving Parliament.[15] The real question is whether it is proper for these political/legal actors to be placed in such situations, both in terms of abstract constitutional propriety and practical utility to all concerned, and especially to Parliament itself.

Speaker's Counsel

In an article in 1982, Sir Robert Speed, a former Speaker's Counsel, described the role and function of this important office.[16] Having outlined its history and development

---

14   Even if the Lord Chancellor, Lord Mackay of Clashfern, did, as it were, 'take Parliament's side' in his dissenting opinion.

15   The role of the Law Officers is considered below. Where the Law Officer are also Members of Parliament, the constitutional position becomes even more complex, as they will have the usual duties to their constituents and to their parties (to be exercised as would ministers, subject to the provisions of the Ministerial Code, presumably). Similar party considerations apply to Law Officers (and the Lord Chancellor) in the House of Lords.

16   Sir R Speed 'Speaker's Counsel' (1982) LXIII Parliamentarian 15. See also the brief description of the history and role of the office in the report of the Select Committee on House of Commons (Accommodation), (HC 184, 1953-54) Appendix L, s 3B.

since 1838, including the recommendations of the 1851 Select Committee on Private Bills,[17] and the office's functions in relation to private bills, statutory instruments and European legislation, Speed noted that, in addition to these main functions, 'Speaker's Counsel is called on to advise on a great variety of legal problems raised by Members, select committees and departments of the House'. However, he pointed out that 'some legal problems do not arise because the courts do not interfere in the conduct by Parliament of its own internal proceedings (virtually anything done within the four walls of the precincts of the House)'.[18] He claimed that, apart from the statutory provisions directly applying to, or concerning the House, 'the Speaker himself seldom needs advice from Counsel. Every problem connected with the proceedings of the House is a matter of procedure which falls within the responsibility of the Clerk of the House'. In relation to other members, they seek advice, sometimes on the law of disqualification, or 'whether some problem in which they are interested requires legislation and, if so, what form the legislation should take'. Departmental select committees may appoint outside lawyers to advise them on detailed questions of law concerning the subject of their inquiries, 'but if this is not done, legal points may arise in the course of their inquiry and then the committee will come to Speaker's Counsel', as they 'cannot get advice from the Law Officers or departmental lawyers since they advise the Government and are not truly independent in a matter on which the committee are investigating the activities of a department'.[19]

Speed noted that House departments may all require advice 'on a wide variety of problems'. For example, the Fees Office may seek assistance on 'difficult problems of construction' of the various resolutions and statutory provisions concerning members' pay and pensions, such as 'whether an elected Member unable to take the oath or his seat was entitled to his salary'.[20] He also mentioned the definition of 'officer' for the purposes of the legislation providing excusal from jury service, and whether and how far it was wider than the internal term 'officer of the House', and issues of copyright for the House Library, as well as new problems relating to parliamentary broadcasting.

In so far as the main task of Speaker's Counsel has historically been in relation to private legislation, and therefore to the Chairman of Ways and Means rather than the Speaker, the title of the office was thought to have been somewhat misleading. By the middle of the nineteenth century, 'he had practically ceased to advise the Speaker on any matter at all'.[1] Mr J Booth, the first holder of the office, told the 1847-48 Select Committee on Private Bills that he acted as counsel to the Speaker 'to a small extent only; the Speaker sends for me occasionally to consult me; for instance, there have been questions lately on some of the Election Acts on which he has desired my

---

17 On the history, see O C Williams, *The Historical Development of Private Bill Procedure and Standing Orders in the House of Commons* (1948) vol 1, pp 95-103.
18 (1982) LXIII Parliamentarian 15 at 18, citing as an example the licensing laws and the *Herbert* case (see n 2 above).
19 Ibid.
20 Presumably referring to the Bobby Sands case in 1981. Similar issues have arisen with the election of two Sinn Fein members in the 1997 general election. See ch IV above.
1   *Williams* p 97. He describes the title as one which 'has remained an anomaly ever since' (p 98).

opinion',[2]   The Speaker himself told the 1851 Select Committee on Private Business that Speaker's Counsel was seldom required to give any legal advice to him.[3]

The advisory role of Speaker's Counsel was described in evidence to the 1954 Select Committee on House of Commons (Accommodation) as the

> general duty of advising the Speaker upon all legal points which do not fall within the sphere of procedure and thus within the responsibilities of the Clerk of the House. His advice is also constantly sought by Members of the House, especially upon statutory instruments, but also generally upon legal matters ranging over the whole field of modern government.[4]

In a modern context, the advisory work can be divided into a number of distinct roles:[5]

(i)   *Advice for the Speaker*: In practice this function rarely arises except in relation to the Speaker's statutory functions – eg Parliament Acts, Recess Elections Act 1975, House of Commons (Administration) Act 1978 – since procedural matters will be for the Clerk of the House. The Speaker has traditionally been the conduit between the House of Commons and the world outside, be it the other House, the Crown or other persons or bodies.

(ii)   *Advice for members*: In addition to legal advice on policy issues, constituents' grievances and the interpretation or application of existing or proposed legislation, members may seek guidance on a number of more 'domestic' matters, such as the potential application of the House of Commons Disqualification Act 1975; issues of parliamentary and legal privilege (especially in relation to their correspondence to and from constituents, ministers and others), and so on.

(iii)   *Advice for select committees*: Departmental select committees will generally appoint their own advisers, including legal specialists where their general remit or particular inquiry warrants it. Other committees of a more specialised or domestic nature may seek advice from Speaker's Counsel. Examples of the former include committees dealing with deregulation, delegated legislation or EU law, and of the latter include the Standards and Privileges Committee. In some cases, resort may be had to the Law Officers by such committees.

(iv)   *Advice for House departments and the House of Commons Commission*: While the Clerks will be expert in procedural matters, they may seek advice, sometimes on members' behalf, on issues such as disqualification or liability for jury service. The Serjeants may seek guidance on their security functions (eg powers of arrest, detention and exclusion). The Library and the Official Report may inquire about copyright. In addition, the application of internal rules, such as the use of the portcullis emblem, may give rise to approaches to Speaker's Counsel. Advice may also be given directly to the House of Commons Commission on its statutory powers, and on employment and health and safety legislation. Speaker's Counsel

---

2   First report (HC 32, 1847-48) Q267.
3   First report (HC 35, 1851) Q11. Booth, the Counsel to the Speaker, told that committee that he gave the Speaker assistance generally in any legal questions coming before him (Q36).
4   HC 184, 1953-54, p 147.
5   This list is based in part on a note kindly supplied by Speaker's Counsel.

may also advise on the potential effect on Parliament of relevant or important case law.[6]

(v) *Advice for officers*: The Parliamentary Commissioner for Administration, the Parliamentary Commissioner for Standards and the Comptroller and Auditor General may seek guidance on their powers and duties.

(vi) *Advice for the Parliamentary Pensions Trustees*: The complex parliamentary pensions legislation, in the 1972, 1976, 1978 and 1987 Acts, can give rise to legal problems upon which advice may be sought by the trustees from Speaker's Counsel.

The Treasury Solicitor

The Treasury Solicitor is Head of the Government Legal Service, and provides legal advice to government departments and other public bodies, especially those who do not have their own solicitors or legal advisers.[7] The office is an ancient one, currently established by the Treasury Solicitor Act 1876. Staff of this department will, from time to time, provide legal advice and assistance to Parliament and act as its legal representatives in appropriate cases.[8]

The Speaker may feel it expedient to place the defence of officers of the House subject to legal proceedings because of their conduct in obedience to the orders of the House 'in the hands of the Government', and the latest edition of *Erskine May* cites examples of Crown Counsel being briefed on behalf of the House: (a) by the Treasury Solicitor during the 1997 dissolution, and in the following session against an application for leave to apply to judicial review of certains actions of the Parliamentary Commissioner for Standards (the Hamilton case): and (b) also in 1997, by the Crown Solicitor of Northern Ireland in a similar application against certain actions of the Speaker (the Sinn Fein Members case).[9]

The Law Officers

The role of the Law Officers of the Crown, and, in particular, the Attorney General,[10] as legal advisers to Parliament is crucial not only for the substantive function, but for the constitutional questions it raises in the context of this subject.[11] The major study is that by Edwards,[12] who deals in detail with the parliamentary role of the Attorney

---

6 A recent example was the 'EU/Parliamentary sovereignty' part-time workers case, *R v Secretary of State for Employment, ex p Equal Opportunities Commission* [1995] 1 AC 1.

7 The Solicitor to the Secretary of State for Scotland is the Scottish equivalent.

8 A useful guide to the history and functions of the office is contained on the department's web-site: http:\\www.open.gov.uk/tsd.

9 (22nd edn, 1997) p 126 and n 4. See also ch IV above.

10 For an internal view see eg the press release issued from the Attorney General's Chambers to coincide with the Scott Report on 15 February 1996, *The role of the Attorney General*.

11 For an analysis of the Attorney General's various roles in the context of the 'arms for Iraq' affair, see D Woodhouse 'The Attorney General' (1997) 50 Parliamentary Affairs 97. She asserts that 'in constitutional terms the position of the Attorney General is at best awkward and at times barely sustainable' (at 97).

12 J Edwards *The Attorney General: Politics and the Public Interest* (1984) ch 8. See also his earlier *Law Officers of the Crown* (1964) chs 3 and 12.

General. He notes that, while the Law Officers' role in relation to the House of Lords has gone, the Lower House 'continues to exhibit its expectations that one or other of the Law Officers of the Crown should make himself available to guide the Commons on legal questions pertaining, for example, to the meaning and legal implications of proposed legislation, the privileges of the House or the conduct and discipline of Members of Parliament'.[13] For example, Harold Wilson, when Leader of the Opposition in 1963, claimed that:

> the Attorney-General, whoever he may be, is not only the legal adviser to the Crown and to the government. He is also a servant of this House. It is, from time to time, his duty to advise the House on legal matters – a duty going beyond his responsibility to the government and the Crown – and [he] like his predecessors, has frequently accepted this duty and has told us that it was his duty to advise this House in a particular legal sense.[14]

The parliamentary role of the Law Officers relates not only to legislation but to Parliament's direct and indirect scrutiny functions, including both internal matters, relating to privilege and conduct, and external matters concerning the public administration. They may, for example, act upon an order of the House or following a direction given by a minister, in defence of officers of the House who are the subject of legal proceedings in relation to their conduct in obedience to the orders of the House.[15] No Law Officer sits on the Committee on Standards and Privileges, the successor to the Committees on Privileges and on Members' Interests, though those who are members of the House attend, participate 'and may give such other assistance to the committee or sub-committee as may be appropriate', but cannot vote, make a motion, move an amendment or be counted in the quorum: SO No 149(9).[16] The Select Committee on Standards in Public Life, which examined how to take forward the Nolan Report[17] as it related to the conduct of members, considered the role of the Attorney General on its proposed new committee on standards and privileges:[18]

> The Committee, or any Sub-Committee, should be able to invite the Attorney General to assist them in their deliberations and evidence-taking (including cross-examination), but it would not be necessary for the Attorney to be formally appointed to the Committee for this purpose. (There is a precedent, in the form of the Select Committee on Conduct of Members in the mid 1970s, for the Attorney, although not appointed to the Committee, to be able to take part in proceedings, while not being able to vote). The Attorney's role in this respect would not, however, preclude the Committee from seeking other specialist

13   *The Attorney General* p 207.
14   HC Deb vol 678, 27 May 1963, col 993.
15   *Erskine May* p 126, which cites nineteenth century examples such as *Burdett v Abbot* (1811) 14 East 1 and in relation to Bradlaugh in the 1880s.
16   The Law Officers have a similar role in relation to Commons standing committees: SO No 87.
17   *First Report of the Committee on Standards in Public Life* May 1995 (Cm 2850).
18   *First Report of the Select Committee on Standards in Public Life* (HC 637, 1994-95) appendix 2, para 17. In his evidence to the Joint Committee on Parliamentary Privilege, the Attorney General, John Morris, said that, because of the demands imposed on its members by its wide remit, he had argued successfully for the Law Officers not to be members of the Standards and Privileges Committee but able 'to attend its meetings, take part in its deliberations, receive papers and give such assistance to the Committee as may be appropriate'. He described that as 'a satisfactory arrangement' (HC 405-v, 1997-98) Q231.

legal advice, if it wished, although such specialist advisers would not be able to take part in any public proceedings of the Committee.

In his evidence to the select committee, the Clerk of the House noted that the Attorney General had, for many years, been a member of the Committee of Privileges and had customarily led its questioning: 'His advice and the advice of his Office has been available to the Committee by virtue of his membership.' He cited the example of a different approach in the 1976-77 select committee on the conduct of members, and concluded that:

> the experience of Attorneys General and their broad knowledge of the law and parliamentary law, has been of great value to the Committee of Privileges. It is important that this assistance should be available to the Committee for Standards when needed and that the appropriate power be granted by the House.[19]

The present Attorney General, John Morris, described the parliamentary aspect of his role when giving evidence to the current Joint Committee on Parliamentary Privilege in February 1998:[20]

> ... I attach great importance to my role as an adviser to Parliament. I am always at the House's disposal if my advice is needed and it has been on a few occasions since I took office. I am glad to say that my office has good working relations with the House authorities so the system works well. As the Committee will be aware, the Attorney may intervene in court proceedings to assert the privileges of either House, either of his own motion or, more usually, at the request of the House authorities or indeed the trial judge. Such cases have usually arisen where parties seek to question proceedings in Parliament contrary to Article IX of the Bill of Rights. In that way, the Attorney performs the important function of representing the interests of Parliaments in the courts and I would expect that function to continue.

Responding to further questions, he said that the House authorities the Attorney General would deal with were the Speaker and the Clerk, the Leader of the House, and to the House of Commons and its committees and members. He thought that the Attorney General was available to be consulted by individual members on privilege matters: 'He is a Member of the House; I am an adviser to the House. It has not actually happened in my time . . . There is no reason in principle why not.' Lord Mayhew of Twysden, a former Law Officer, immediately concurred, and went further:

> Law officers have always regarded themselves as available to all members of the House of Commons. It has not arisen in the case of the House of Lords, to my knowledge, but all Members of the House of Commons, regardless of party, on any matter touching the law or conduct which they wish to consult them on. Obviously, it is treated wholly as a matter of confidence.[1]

---

19 HC 637, 1994-95, p 11, para 50.
20 HC 405-v, 1997-98, Q231.
 1 Ibid, Q255.

The Law Officers have traditionally often played an active legal role in tribunals of inquiry, set up by resolution of both Houses of Parliament under the Tribunals of Inquiry (Evidence) Act 1921. This has, from time to time caused controversy, as in the Aberfan case,[2] or if a tribunal be established or proposed to investigate a matter in which the Law Officers were apparently significantly involved (as in the 'arms to Iraq' affair, ultimately investigated by the non-statutory Scott Inquiry). The 1966 report of the Salmon Royal Commission on Tribunals of Inquiry recommended that the Attorney General's[3] role as counsel to such tribunals should be discontinued.[4]

One aspect of the duality of the Law Officers' role is the confidentiality of their opinions within government.[5] The fact that the Law Officers' opinions are almost invariably kept confidential from Parliament, even in situations where Parliament's need for them may be thought to be clear (in the legislative function, for example) perhaps suggests that the Law Officers' governmental role, at least in this respect, is superior to their parliamentary personae.

Yet, far from being concerned at the theoretical or practical implications of the constitutional duality of the Law Officers' parliamentary role, a survey of the historical development of the role would appear to suggest the contrary. Members of Parliament appear to have sought to ensure the continuing availability of the Law Officers as Parliament's legal advisers in the face of their other competing functions, whether professional or ministerial. It may well be, of course, that this desire is not totally unconnected with the practical realities of the party political atmosphere of Parliament, especially in the House of Commons. For example, recourse or attempted recourse to the Law Officers during the legislative process of a particularly controversial measure can drag out the process and raise the potential of differences of legal interpretation between legal and departmental ministers which can be exploited by the measure's opponents.

This has been seen in recent years, for example, over legislation affecting the United Kingdom's relationship with the European Community and Union. This can occur where the Law Officers' parliamentary and ministerial functions may not be in perfect harmony. Where, for example, the Law Officers have advised one course of action or one interpretation of a statutory provision or case law, but a minister has chosen to adopt a different course of action or interpretation for policy reasons, should the Law Officers be required to discharge their duty to Parliament by revealing, when asked, their own views, or support their ministerial colleagues by sticking to the policy line? As Law Officers are ministers of the Crown, they are bound by ministerial responsibility, both collective and individual. Because of their peculiar ministerial functions, they act both in their own right and in conjunction with their fellow ministers. This provides unique opportunities for their political opponents to seek to exploit any potential or actual differences between the Law Officers and their

---

2   See the adverse comments to the Attorney General's statements on the role of the press (HC Deb vol 734, 27 October 1966, cols 1315-1320) and the Prime Minister's statement (HC Deb vol 735, 1 November 1966, cols 254-264).

3   And the Scottish Law Officers, where appropriate.

4   1966 (Cmnd 3121).

5   See para 24 of the Ministerial Code (July 1997) (formerly *Questions of procedure for ministers*). Paragraph 22 states that written opinions of the Law Officers, unlike other ministerial papers, can be made available to succeeding administrations.

ministerial colleagues, as well as any perceived failings by the Law Officers in their own right. It is in this respect that the doctrine of the confidentiality of Law Officers' advice, enforced in various ways such as the Ministerial Code, is potentially of significance. A revelation that a minister has acted, or wished to act, contrary to the clear legal advice of a Law Officer can measure high in the political Richter scale.[6]

Why are parliamentarians apparently so unconcerned by the constitutional ambiguities inherent in the various roles of the Law Officers? Is it that they are unaware of any theoretical difficulties, or is it that they feel that the benefits both in terms of substantive legal assistance and in partisan terms, as noted above, outweigh any disadvantages? Are they dazzled by the thought that legal figures of such seniority and status as the Law Officers are willing, indeed required, to attend upon them when they wish? Perhaps few, if any, of them have even seriously considered the possibility that Parliament as a whole, or each House individually, could or should have senior legal advisers of their own whose sole function is to provide legal advice and assistance to Parliament in all its various guises. Perhaps they think that this function is already undertaken by officers such as Speaker's Counsel.

Advice from other House departments

In the sense that all the work of Parliament actually or potentially takes place within a context of 'parliamentary law', much of the advice and assistance which staff of the two Houses provide for their members can be said to be 'legal advice'. For example, the clerks of both Houses, whether providing procedural advice or administrative assistance to the operation of the Houses, operate within a framework of the 'law and custom of Parliament' (only a relatively small proportion of which is statutory or judge-made). Within this exclusive jurisdiction (its very exclusivity, and relative ease of alteration and amendment of the rules, impose responsibilities as well as rights), the clerks have a central role in parliamentary law, acting as its permanent custodians and providing authoritative interpretations, either directly or through the Houses, their chairs and committees. For example, in the Commons, rulings from the Chair have a particular status, which Erskine May describes as 'an obvious parallel to the decisions of judges in the courts. The House of Commons has its own body of case-law'.[7] Standing orders, sessional orders and resolutions (Parliament's internal 'legislation'), and, where appropriate, rulings from the Chair, will be drafted by, or with the assistance of the clerks, requiring drafting skills.[8] No formal legal training

---

6   The Westland episode in 1985-86 is an example of this.
7   *Erskine May* p 7. Redlich emphasised the 'predominantly judicial character of the office of Speaker': J Redlich *The procedure of the House of Commons* (1908) vol II, pp 148-150.
8   Such skills will also be deployed when assisting in the drafting of amendments to Bills before Parliament, as private members, other than those high in the sessional ballot or those whose legislative proposals have the support of the government, will not have formal access to specialist drafters. It was estimated, for example, that the Video Recordings Act 1984 would have cost £9,000-£10,000, had the text not been supplied by the Home Office (D Miers and A Page *Legislation* (2nd edn, 1990) p 102 n 15). Even select committees may suffer from the absence of drafting expertise, as when the 1954 House of Commons (Accommodation) Committee wished to append to its report a draft Bill on its proposed House of Commons Commission but 'they regret that the assistance of a Parliamentary Counsel was not made available to them for this purpose' (HC 184, 1953-54, para 52).

in the conventional sense is required, as the law of Parliament is almost entirely 'internal' and 'on-the-job' training is provided.[9]

Parliament's research and information staff provide advice and assistance to members in their various duties, whether in the course of parliamentary proceedings (in the Chambers, committees or all-party groups), policy-making, or constituency work. They can be said to be providing 'legal advice' in the sense of discovering, interpreting and explaining existing actual or potential law, as it is before Parliament or applied to constituents, for example. While there are no professional, practising lawyers as such on the staff, there are an increasing number, especially in the Commons staff, with a legal background in one of the United Kingdom jurisdictions, and a variety of specialisms in relevant fields. Some deal directly with obvious 'legal' areas – for example the operation of the legal system and profession, civil and criminal law, constitutional law – while others apply their skills to specific areas, such as housing or business law. In addition, they will provide colleagues (and, where consulted, staff in other departments) with guidance of a legal nature, in the same way as, for example, the statistical, economics and science specialists do.

Whether or not the 'constituency welfare' role of the modern MP is regarded as a proper or effective use of limited parliamentary resources, there is no doubt that this role is a substantial and increasing aspect of parliamentary life, and this is reflected in the work of those staff who provide research and information services. The provision of 'legal advice' in this sense is more akin to that in a citizen's advice bureau than in a professional firm, as staff cannot and would not seek to provide a full legal service for Commons members and, through them, for their constituents. In many cases, the advice and assistance may simply amount to a general explanation of the application of the relevant law to particular circumstances, and suggestions as to sources of more specialist advice or redress (professional lawyers, ombudsmen and other complaints procedures, regulatory and other public bodies and so on). Inevitably, given the traditional specialisms of professional practitioners, parliamentary staff may often provide more detailed assistance with, say, members' constituents' immigration, social security or housing problems than with their conveyancing or tax problems.

In the House of Lords, the 'equivalent' officers to Speaker's Counsel are the Counsel to Chairman of Committees. As with their Commons counterparts, much of their time is devoted to committee work, such as those on Scrutiny of Delegated Powers and on Statutory Instruments. In addition, they also provide general legal advice to the House, its members and staff as required, and may liaise as appropriate with Parliamentary Counsel, for example on the form and content of deregulation orders. The House of Lords is, of course, a repository of legal expertise, derived in part from its judicial role, and active and retired judges and other practitioners can and do play a full role in the legislative and scrutiny work of the House, not least when complex legal or constitutional matters are involved.[10]

---

9   In this sense, as well as in the methods of appointment, the clerks of both Houses resemble the senior levels of the civil service.

10   Eg such members were instrumental in the creation in recent years of enhanced scrutiny procedures for delegated legislation, especially of the increasingly common 'Henry VIII' form, such as deregulation orders under the Deregulation and Contracting Out Act 1994 and the proposed remedial orders under the current Human Rights Bill.

External legal assistance

From time to time, Parliament may employ specialist external legal advice. A recent example of this arose in relation to Parliament's response to the privatisation of HMSO, in particular the contractual agreement with the Stationery Office. This was based on the existing 'supply and service agreement' (SSA) with HMSO, which was not a formal legal document. The government offered to provide advice on the conversion of that agreement into an enforceable legally binding contract,[11] but in the event the House of Commons decided to commission its own, independent legal advice from the firm of Denton Hall.[12] The draft contract that was subsequently prepared took account, among other things, of a number of stipulated principles, laid down by the Speaker and the House of Commons Commission soon after the government's intention to privatise HMSO was announced, and intended to safeguard the House's interests.[13] This new draft formed the basis of the relevant contracts entered into by both Houses, or more precisely by their corporate officers, on their behalf, with the Stationery Office and for the separate contracts for the provision of electronic publishing services. Parliament's own lawyers were closely involved in this and related matters.

While staff brought in as specialist advisers by select committees may, in appropriate inquiries, have legal backgrounds or expertise, generally committees (other than those Speaker's Counsel assists) will not employ legal specialists as such. A recent exception which perhaps proves the rule was the appointment of external counsel to assist the Parliamentary Commissioner for Standards in the major and complex 'Hamilton/cash for questions' investigation. The Committee on Standards and Privileges agreed to the Parliamentary Commissioner's request for more overall resources for his office, which included the appointment of Nigel Pleming QC 'to provide legal assistance'.[14] This sort of appointment (the other two extra staff were Commons clerks) was understandable given the quasi-judicial nature of the Commissioner's (and the committee) function; the complexity of the particular case coming so early in the life of the new Nolan-inspired arrangements,[15] and the controversy surrounding the inquiry's inquisitorial procedures.[16] The committee is, at the time of writing, reviewing the relevant procedures in the light of the Hamilton case, and it may be that, notwithstanding the general desire which there seems to be

---

11 HC Deb vol 268, 19 December 1995, written answers, col 1092. For the Lords position see HL Deb vol 568, 18 January 1996, cols 705-706, and the report of the Committee on House of Lords Offices (HL 12, 1995-96).
12 See House of Commons Commission Annual Report 1995-96 (HC 612, 1995-96) paras 16-19, and more generally the exchange of letters between the Speaker and the government (HC Deb vol 268, 11 December 1995, written answers, cols 453-455; 19 December 1995, written answers, cols 1091-1093).
13 In the Speaker's letter of 28 November 1995 (see n 12 above).
14 First special report October 1996 (HC 34, 1996-97) para 3. According to Robert Sheldon, who chairs the committee, Mr Pleming 'acted as counsel to Sir Gordon's inquiry and as a specialist adviser to the Committee' (HC Deb vol 301, 17 November 1997, col 89).
15 See further ch II above.
16 See generally D Woodhouse 'The Parliamentary Commissioner for Standards: lessons from the "cash for questions" inquiry' (1998) 51 Parliamentary Affairs 51.

to regard that case as exceptional, internal and external[17] pressures may eventually lead to the appointment of a permanent or semi-permanent legal officer in Parliament to ensure that internal investigatory practices adhere, as far as possible, to generally accepted procedural norms.

Mention should also be made briefly of references to the Judicial Committee of the Privy Council. The Crown may refer any matter to it for an advisory opinion, including disqualification from membership of the House of Commons[18] and parliamentary privilege,[19] under s 4 of the Judicial Committee Act 1833.

The future

The forms of legal advice and assistance required at Westminster are varied and complex, reflecting the interrelationships existing in a legislature, especially one where the government is inextricably linked with the legislature. This means that the numerous interests, some of which have been outlined in this chapter, will not always be complementary to each other and may even be diametrically opposed.[20] The 'legal quality' of advice and assistance will also vary from basic information on 'the law', on the one hand, to advice to and representation on behalf of Parliament (or one of its constituent parts) in actual or potential litigation[1] on the other. By no means all the providers of 'legal' advice and assistance described in this chapter will be legally qualified in the conventional sense, still less will they be professional legal practitioners. Nor will all of them recognise that they are fulfilling such 'legal' functions.

This complex web makes any general conclusions difficult, if not impossible, especially if they are aimed at providing a neat, all-inclusive description and explanation of what happens in this field. In one sense, advice to the institution of, and actors in, Parliament is no more legal than similar administrative functions in any body, such as companies, local authorities or even families, which is to some degree regulated by law (even if it is not all law of its own making). What makes the parliamentary situation different is that Parliament is the state's supreme legislative body and paramount democratic forum, and legal advice (broadly defined) about the processes of law making itself attains a peculiar importance.

Constitutional and political developments may generate within Parliament new or greater demands for legal advice and assistance of the types described in this chapter. For example, the Human Rights Bill (going through Parliament at the time of writing[2]), if and when enacted, may well be a significant source of such demand in a number of ways. Ministers in charge of Bills will be required either to issue a

---

17 The possibility of judicial scrutiny of quasi-judicial parliamentary procedures and practices by domestic or European courts in such circumstances has already been noted.

18 *Re Macmanaway* [1951] AC 161.

19 *Re Parliamentary Privilege Act 1770* [1958] AC 331.

20 A simple example is advice and assistance on the form, content and effect of a proposed legislative amendment, and on its parliamentary procedure, given to both those supporting and those opposing it.

1 Inevitably, an institution such as Parliament will be at the receiving end of some unconventional or eccentric legal challenges, as when a writ was issued in Sheffield in 1988 against 'Parliament' by a person who described himself as 'The Christ', seeking recognition by the defendant of the plaintiff's 'rightful sovereignty' over, and 'rightful ownership' of, the United Kingdom and £100m damages.

2 References are to the original version of the Bill, as introduced in the Lords in October 1997 (HL Bill 38).

statement that a Bill is compatible with European Convention rights or that such a statement of compatibility cannot be provided for a Bill which should nevertheless be proceeded with.[3] The Houses may conceivably wish to have an independent opinion on compatibility, before or during such a Bill's passage, especially if the present government's proposed changes to the legislative process involve more extensive and formalised pre-legislative scrutiny of proposed legislation by Parliament. This may be through some form of committee-based arrangement, or perhaps by a parliamentary committee on human rights suggested by the government in its October 1997 White Paper.[4] Presumably, advice will also have to be provided to members other than ministers who either wish to move amendments to government Bills, or promote their own Bills, on the compatibility of their legislation in convention terms. This could be done by clerks as an aspect of parliamentary procedure, or there could be a role for professional legal advice, perhaps on a 'Speaker's Counsel' model.

Other constitutional developments which may have a legal impact on Parliament include the application of a Freedom of Information Act, and legislative jurisdictional questions between Westminster and devolved parliaments in the United Kingdom, especially the Scottish Parliament, as envisaged under the Scotland Bill. Again, these novel situations could generate demands which may be seen by members of both Houses of Parliament as more legal than strictly procedural. The opportunities provided by the creation of new devolved bodies within the United Kingdom may itself provide the opportunity for fresh and radical thinking as to the needs and requirements of a modern Parliament, including its need for independent legal support. The Scottish Parliament, in particular, especially its Presiding Officer, will require some form of advice on the vires of legislative proposals. This could be regarded as a 'parliamentary' matter, to be dealt with by clerks, but it is likely that there would be some role here for professional legal advice, perhaps from an Edinburgh equivalent of Speaker's Counsel.

The traditional scope of parliamentary privilege is something that may be under threat in the near future on a number of fronts. The outcome of the review currently being undertaken by the Joint Committee on Parliamentary Privilege may lead to a 'modernisation' of the content and ambit of privilege, and the abandonment of some aspects which may be regarded as either obsolete or inappropriate. The fact that Parliament was willing to legislate on core aspects of privilege in the Defamation Act 1996, not to mention the unusual way in which s 13 of that Act was introduced and approved, may reduce some of the inhibition which Parliament (and the courts) may have had in tackling such a sensitive constitutional issue. The courts, progressively more used to the widespread application of judicial review principles (especially fairness and natural justice), and mindful of the many challenges from Europe and elsewhere to the traditional, rigid view of parliamentary sovereignty, may be more willing to entertain action alleging unacceptable action by Parliament

---

3   Clause 19. The statement would be part of the explanatory material published with a Bill when first introduced in either House, alongside the existing Explanatory and Financial Memorandum (see the Home Office White Paper *Rights brought home: the Human Rights Bill*, 1997 (Cm 3782) paras 3.2-3.3).

4   Ibid, paras 3.6-3.7. There could be a joint committee of both Houses, or separate committees in each House.

or its officers.[5]   The Clerk of the House of Commons, in his evidence to the joint committee, has recognised that the growing involvement of Parliament in the 'real', commercial world puts old notions of privilege under strain:

> Another question which springs to mind is what adjustments are needed now that Parliament has given itself several – I was going to say quasi-executive functions – really executive functions in recent years. For example, by taking over the works and buildings and its own printing arrangements, we are in the commercial field; I am the Corporate Officer and people can sue me – and are doing so – and privilege . . . impinges on that. Is that any longer sustainable or sensible? That is a very important side-issue we are going to have to deal with.[6]

There may come a time when one or both Houses of Parliament may consider that they should have their own distinct legal office or offices, comprising staff who will have the resources and expertise to carry out (directly or otherwise) many of the functions described in this chapter, and other new legal functions that may emerge in the future. Such an innovation may solve any constitutional dilemma that may be felt by Parliament's traditional resort to the legal resources and officers of the Executive, such as the Law Officers and the Treasury Solicitor. Subject to suitable demarcation between a 'Parliamentary Legal Office' and the proper role and function of other departments (such as the procedural expertise of the clerks), and agreement by all concerned as to how it could serve all the various 'clients' within Parliament, such an innovation may enhance Parliament's 'legal' work, and thereby the prestige of Parliament itself.

5   Though see *R v The Speaker, ex p McGuinness* (3 October 1997, unreported), the case in Northern Ireland concerning the two Sinn Fein Members' challenge to the Speaker's decision that they were not entitled to any parliamentary facilities because they had not taken the oath, where Kerr J, at first instance, refused to review her action on grounds of 'exclusive cognisance': see ch IV above.

6   HC 401-i, 1997-98, Q35, and see his memorandum, para 13.

Chapter VII

The law relating to members' conduct[1]

Michael Rush

> We recommend that the House [of Commons] should draw up a Code of Conduct setting out the broad principles which should guide the conduct of Members, and that this should be restated in every new Parliament.
>
> The Nolan Committee, para 2.89[2]

Introduction

The House of Commons lays claim to a number of 'ancient and undoubted rights and privileges', the most important of which is freedom of speech. Parliamentary privilege is a complex matter, which lies beyond the scope of this chapter,[3] but the rights and privileges of Parliament are acknowledged by the courts. Among the other privileges claimed is the 'exclusive cognisance of proceedings', that is the right to regulate its own proceedings or operation. This means that the House of Commons has the right to regulate the conduct of its members, including the right to punish MPs who are found to have breached parliamentary privilege or have been found in contempt of the House. Such punishment may range from an admonition, through suspension from the service of the House (with or without pay), to expulsion in the most serious cases. Until 1868, when jurisdiction was transferred to the courts, the Commons decided the outcome of disputed elections, such as those involving allegations of the bribery or corruption of electors. But the House has always resisted suggestions that its right to regulate the conduct of members should pass to an extra-parliamentary body or authority.

---

1   This is a revised version of an article first published in (1997) 3 Journal of Legislative Studies. The author gratefully acknowledges the helpful comments from the readers to whom the original article was referred and to Oonagh Gay of the House of Commons Library, who provided much of the information on which the article and this chapter are based.
2   Committee on Standards in Public Life (the Nolan Committee), *First Report*, 1995 (Cm 2850-I) para 289.
3   For a detailed account of parliamentary privilege see Erskine May *Parliamentary Practice* (22nd edn, 1997) chs 5-11. See also chs IV and V above; G Marshall 'Parliamentary Privilege' in S A Walkland (ed) *The House of Commons in the Twentieth Century* (1979) pp 204-246; G Marshall 'Parliamentary Privilege' in M Ryle and P G Richards (eds) *The Commons Under Scrutiny* (1988) pp 212-228.

For much of its history, the Commons has exercised its jurisdiction over privilege largely through the Committee of Privileges, which dates from the seventeenth century, but in 1974 the House established a Select Committee on Members' Interests. Both committees were creatures of the House and, although they possessed the usual powers of select committees to send for papers, persons and records, like other select committees they could only make recommendations to the House.

The whole question of the conduct of members, how and by whom its should be regulated, became a contentious issue in the 1990s, culminating in the appointment in October 1994 of the Committee on Standards in Public Life (the Nolan Committee). This followed allegations of impropriety against two Conservative MPs (Neil Hamilton and Tim Smith) made by Mohamed Al-Fayed, the owner of Harrods department store. These were the latest in a series of allegations about the conduct of ministers and members of Parliament in Britain.[4] One of the most damaging was the 'cash for questions' affair, in which reporters from *The Sunday Times*, posing as businessmen, approached a number of MPs and asked them whether they would table Parliamentary Questions in return for payment. Two Conservatives (Graham Riddick and David Tredinnick) agreed and found themselves at the centre of suggestions that this was merely the tip of an iceberg of parliamentary corruption. This case was preceded and followed by other allegations of the acceptance of inappropriate gifts or favours from businessmen, while revelations about the sexual lives of a number of ministers had resulted in several resignations.[5]

Further disquiet was caused by ex-ministers acquiring lucrative jobs in the private sector soon after leaving office, in some cases involving businesses or industries which had had direct dealings with their former departments. Yet another area of concern was appointments to quangos (quasi-autonomous non-governmental organisations), particularly those with executive powers.[6] And last, but by no means least, the government had earlier referred allegations that ministers had broken their own policy guidelines and misled Parliament over the supply of arms to Iraq, to a judicial inquiry, headed by Sir Richard Scott.[7]

All this contributed to a general atmosphere of what became known as 'sleaze' – that corruption and questionable behaviour generally had become increasingly common in British political life. The 'cash for questions' cases were referred to the House of Commons' Privileges Committee, but it was almost inevitable that sooner or later the government would appoint an extra-parliamentary body to examine the wider implications of these matters, to bring forward proposals for restoring public confidence in politicians and political life, and thus seek to relieve pressure on the

---

4   See F F Ridley and A Doig (eds) 'Sleaze': Politics, Private Interests and Public Reaction' (1995) 48 Parliamentary Affairs (special edn) 551-749.

5   See D Woodhouse *Ministers and Parliament: Accountability in Theory and Practice* (1994) and R Brazier 'It *is* a constitutional issue: fitness for ministerial office' [1994] PL 431-451.

6   Although the *number* of non-departmental public bodies (NDPBs – the term used by the government for quangos) had declined from 2,167 in 1979 to 1,345 in 1994 (including a decline in executive bodies from 492 to 325, the public expenditure involved had risen from £8.51bn in 1979 to £15.08bn in 1994, and the number of posts in executive bodies was 3,850. In addition, there were a further 5,015 executive posts in NHS bodies (Nolan Report, paras 4.5-8).

7   *Inquiry into the Export of Defence Equipment and Dual-Use Goods to Iraq and Related Prosecutions* (HC 115, 1995-96) (the Scott Report).

government itself. Lord Nolan, a senior judge, was therefore asked to chair a committee to 'examine current concerns about standards of conduct of all holders of public office, including arrangements relating to financial and commercial activities . . .'[8] The committee decided 'to concentrate on three of the subjects which appeared to give rise to the greatest public concern, namely issues relating to Members of Parliament, Ministers and Civil Servants, and executive Quangos and NHS bodies'.[9] This chapter concentrates on the Nolan recommendations on the conduct of MPs, its proposal that there should be a code of conduct for members of Parliament, the introduction of a code in July 1996, and the implications these have for the outside interests of MPs. In announcing the appointment of Lord Nolan, the then Prime Minister said that the committee had been asked to produce a report on these matters within six months, but he made it clear that the government envisaged Nolan continuing to operate beyond that deadline to consider other areas and aspects of public life.[10]

The Nolan proposals

At the beginning of its first report, the Nolan Committee set out what it called 'The Seven Principles of Public Life'. These were 'Selflessness, Integrity, Objectivity, Accountability, Openness, Honesty, and Leadership' and should, in the committee's view, be observed by all those engaged in public life, no matter in what capacity. The report contained 55 recommendations, of which 11 concerned the conduct of Members of Parliament. These fell under six headings: paid outside employment; parliamentary consultancies; disclosure of interests; conflicts of interest; a code of conduct; and the enforcement of obligations. The only recommendation requiring legislation was that the law on the bribery of MPs should be clarified. All other recommendations concerned matters that required changes in the procedures or practice of the House of Commons.

One of the issues that had received a good deal of media attention and had become a cause for public concern was that of consultancy work done by MPs. In particular, some members had consultancy agreements with public relations or lobbying firms and Nolan noted that the 1995 Register of Members' Interests recorded 26 MPs with such agreements and a further 142 who had consultancies with other business associations, constituting 29.7% of members, excluding ministers and the Speaker.[11] This led Nolan to recommend that contracts on parliamentary consultancies or sponsorship should be deposited with the Registrar of Members' Interests and that the annual remuneration from such contracts should be declared.[12] The committee stopped short of recommending a ban on contracts with lobbying firms, but did recommend a ban on contracts with firms which provided 'paid parliamentary services to multiple clients'.[13] It also stopped short of recommending an immediate

---

8 Nolan Report, Terms of Reference.
9 Ibid, letter from Lord Nolan presenting the report to then Prime Minister, John Major.
10 In November 1997 Sir Patrick Neill (now Lord Neill) replaced Lord Nolan as chair of the Committee on Standards in Public Life. The committee has since been examining the financing of political parties.
11 The Nolan Report, para 2.13.
12 Ibid, para 2.70.
13 Ibid, para 2.59.

ban on paid advocacy. It did so partly on the grounds that such 'arrangements . . . have been made perfectly lawfully and are often of very long standing', but mainly because 'so many Members . . . would be excluded from particular pieces of business, there would be a short term disruption of the business of the House', the 'impact on the income of many Members', and the effect on the sponsorship of Labour candidates by trade unions and the Co-operative Party which would disturb 'the equilibrium of party political funding'. The question of a total ban should be left for further consideration.[14]

In proposing a code of conduct for MPs, Nolan included a draft code in its report. Although the draft code included rules relating to financial interests in particular, Nolan argued 'against unduly prescriptive rules'[15] and recommended that the code –

> should avoid the type of detailed code which can give rise to anomalies, but should set out principles clear enough to enable appropriate decisions to be made. It ought to be supplemented by detailed guidelines from time to time.[16]

In short, Nolan proposed a code which accords with the English common law tradition of leaving much detail to emerge through case law, in this instance the case law of parliamentary reports and resolutions.

To enforce the obligations that its recommendations and a code would place upon MPs, Nolan recommended the appointment of a Parliamentary Commissioner for Standards (PCS), whose status would be essentially similar to that of the Comptroller and Auditor-General and the Parliamentary Commissioner for Administration (PCA) in that the holder would be an Officer of the House of Commons. The PCS would have the authority to send for persons, papers and records and would report to a sub-committee of the Privileges Committee, which would break with its traditions and in the future normally meet in public.

The parliamentary response

The government's formal response to Nolan was in the form of a White Paper, in which it said that the recommendations relating to MPs were essentially a matter for the House of Commons, although it reaffirmed an earlier commitment to consolidate the law on corruption.[17] Following all-party discussions, a Select Committee on Standards in Public Life was set up in June 1995 to consider the Nolan recommendations on the conduct of MPs. In its first report, the committee recommended a draft resolution:

> That the House endorses the principles of a Code of Conduct, and instructs the appropriate Select Committee to prepare such a draft Code for approval as soon as possible,

---

14 Ibid, paras 2.52-2.53.
15 Ibid, para 2.87.
16 Ibid, para 2.89.
17 *The Government's Response to the First Report from the Committee on Standards in Public Life* 1995 (Cm 2931) p 2. In December 1996 the Home Office issued a discussion paper, 'Clarification of the law relating to the Bribery of Members of Parliament'. See also *Legislating the Criminal Law: Corruption* Law Com No 248 (HC 524, 1997-98).

taking into account the suggestions of the Nolan Committee and any relevant overseas analogues . . .[18]

This was one of five resolutions passed by the Commons on 19 July 1995. The other four related to the establishment of a new Select Committee on Standards and Privileges, which was to take over the functions and responsibilities of the existing Privileges Committee and the Select Committee on Members' Interests (thus rejecting Nolan's recommendation that a sub-committee of the Privileges Committee deal with complaints), the extension of the requirement to declare an interest in all procedures requiring written notice, and the arrangements for the appointment of a Parliamentary Commissioner for Standards and other matters on the declaration of interests, and the need for further consideration of the Nolan recommendations on consultancies.[19]

In its second report, the Select Committee on Public Standards took up another of the Nolan recommendations – that the resolution passed by the House of Commons on 15 July 1947, which prohibited members from making any agreement restricting his or her freedom of speech and action in Parliament, be restated, since it regarded some of the activities of MPs brought to its attention as in breach of the spirit, if not the letter of the resolution.[20] The 1947 resolution followed a report by the Privileges Committee dealing with a complaint by W J Brown MP that the trade union to which he belonged and by whom he was sponsored, being dissatisfied with his performance, had sought to punish him by ending the sponsorship.[1] The select committee linked this with Nolan's proposed ban on contracts with firms with multiple clients and its rejection of a total ban on paid advocacy, which it regarded as impractical. The select committee therefore recommended an amendment of the 1947 resolution which would ban *all* forms of paid advocacy.[2] (It should be noted, however, that Nolan's proposed code of conduct stipulated: 'A Member must not promote any matter in Parliament in return for payment.') The committee also recommended that MPs who were members of delegations to ministers or civil servants should record relevant interests in the Register of Members' Interests,[3] endorsed Nolan's recommendation that appropriate employment contracts should be deposited with the Registrar, but recommended against the disclosure of the remuneration received under such contracts.[4]

On 6 November 1995 the House of Commons passed a further series of resolutions arising out of these two reports. Standing orders were amended to establish a new Committee on Standards and Privileges and the office of Parliamentary Commissioner for Standards. The 1947 resolution was amended, clearly banning paid advocacy. Members were prohibited from initiating or participating in delegations to ministers or civil servants on matters affecting '*only the body*' (author's italics) from which they have paid interests (a narrowing of the committee's recommendation). All existing

18 Select Committee on Standards in Public Life, *First Report* (HC 637,1994-95) para 48.
19 See HC Deb vol 263, 19 July 1995, cols 1674-1739. Unlike the office of Parliamentary Commissioner for Administration (the ombudsman), the office of PCS is not established by statute.
20 Nolan Report, para 2.45
1 See Committee of Privileges, *First Report* (HC 118, 1946-47).
2 Select Committee on Standards in Public Life, *Second Report* (HC 637,1994-95), para 18.
3 Ibid, para 31.
4 Ibid, paras 38-49.

and future agreements involving the provision of parliamentary services by members must conform to the amended 1947 resolution and copies deposited with the PCS. Finally, rejecting the committee's recommendation against the disclosure of payments under such agreements, the House voted in favour of disclosure. The latter were to be reported in bands of up to £1,000, between £1,000 and £5,000, and bands of £5,000 thereafter.[5]

Devising a code of conduct

One of Nolan's reasons for recommending a code of conduct was that, although it regarded *Erskine May* as 'a thorough guide to the procedures and rules of Parliament, it is a very weighty document, and we doubt that it is closely read by all Members'.[6] There is a further problem in relying on *Erskine May* for guidance: new and updated editions are published at relatively lengthy and not entirely regular intervals. The current edition was published in 1997; the two previous editions were published in 1983 and 1989 respectively. Thus, while the changes arising from the Nolan Report and the two reports of the Select Committee on Standards in Public Life are, of course, reflected in the current edition, no periodic amendments or addenda to *Erskine May* are issued, so that any further changes would not be found in *Erskine May* until the next edition is published. By contrast, a new edition of the standing orders of the House of Commons is published whenever necessary and, in the meantime, any amendments are published separately as addenda. The annual publication of *Erskine May* is not a practical proposition and, even if it were, would only ameliorate but not solve the problem. It is surely time that *Erskine May* were published in looseleaf form (and on the internet) in similar fashion to *Halsbury's Statutes*.

There is a specific section headed 'Misconduct of Members or Officers' and, following Nolan, a chapter entitled 'Rules governing the conduct of Members and the disclosure of financial interests in the House of Commons',[7] but there are other references scattered through *Erskine May*. The section of *Erskine May* entitled 'Misconduct of Members or Officers' in fact is limited in its scope, covering bribery and corruption, the provision of professional services connected with parliamentary proceedings, and the advocacy of matters in which a member has been concerned professionally, although there is a textual reference to the later section on the declaration of interests.

Bribery is defined in *Erskine May* as:

> The acceptance by a Member of either House of a bribe to influence him in his conduct as a Member or of any fee, compensation or reward in connection with the promotion of, or opposition to any bill, resolution, matter or thing submitted or intended to be submitted to either House or to a committee is a contempt.[8]

---

5   See HC Deb vol 265, 6 November 1995, cols 604-699.
6   Nolan Report, para 2.88.
7   *Erskine May* pp 111-119 and 420-428.
8   Ibid, p 112.

The entry continues by pointing out that MPs found guilty of acce[...] been expelled from the House, leaving it unclear whether the crimina[...] extends to MPs – hence Nolan's recommendation that the law shoul[...] This provision has always been interpreted narrowly, covering cases on[...] [...]e intention is to bribe and acceptance indicates a willingness to act corruptly, [...]er than broadly, covering the provision of services – such as 'cash for questions' – otherwise regarded as legitimately provided. The prohibition on professional services is certainly a narrow one, aimed essentially at lawyer-MPs, who may not act as counsel in any proceedings, nor advocate or promote matters with which they have been professionally concerned.[9]

Elsewhere in *Erskine May* there is a reference to a clear prohibition on voting on matters in which the member has a personal pecuniary interest, but this is drawn very narrowly:

> No Member who has a direct pecuniary interest in a question is allowed to vote upon it; but, in order to operate as a disqualification, this interest must be immediate and personal, and not merely of a general or remote character.[10]

Thus, it is entirely in order for MPs to vote on tax proposals, for example, since these have general application, even though some members might be directly affected and others not. In fact, the disallowance of votes on questions of public policy is rare and the most recent case cited in *Erskine May* occurred in 1892.[11] More common is the disallowance of votes on private bills, which have limited applicability to named localities or persons. A member nominated to serve on a committee on an opposed private Bill must sign a declaration that his or her constituents have no local interest and that the member him/herself has no personal interest in the Bill concerned.[12]

The Register of Interests

Apart from the specific matter of votes, it has long been the practice that MPs are expected to declare a pecuniary interest relevant to the proceedings when making a speech in the House or in a standing committee or examining a witness in a select committee. This was formalised in a resolution passed by the House of Commons in 1974, following a select committee report which led to the setting up of the Register of Members' Interests. The 1974 resolution states:

> That, in any debate or proceeding of the House or its committees or transactions or communications which a Member may have with other Members or with Ministers or servants of the Crown, he shall disclose any relevant pecuniary interest or benefit of whatever nature, whether direct or indirect, that he may have had, may have or may be expecting to have.[13]

---

9   Ibid, pp 115-116.
10   Ibid, p 361. In the case of standing (or legislative) committees on public bills, the committee itself determines whether a member has a personal pecuniary interest in a vote (*Erskine May* p 706).
11   Ibid, p 362. In 1986 the Speaker ruled that members of Lloyd's could vote on an amendment to the Financial Services Bill relating to Lloyd's.
12   Ibid, pp 363 and 903.
13   HC Deb vol 874, 22 May 1974, cols 537-538.

At the time, this requirement did *not* apply to the asking of questions for oral or written answer, nor to the tabling of Early Day Motions (EDMs) (essentially expressions of backbench opinion) or amendments to bills. However, from the 1993-94 session onwards, the initial sponsors of EDMs were required to declare any relevant interests,[14] and this was extended to all those who added their names or tabled an amendment to an EDM, to the tabling of questions and amendments to bills in 1995, following the first report of the Select Committee on Standards in Public Life, as noted above. This leaves only supplementary questions not requiring a declaration of interest, on the grounds that it would be an unnecessarily cumbersome procedure and further truncate Question Time.

A second resolution passed in 1974 authorised the establishment of a Register of Members' Interests, the first edition of which was published in 1975. It has been published annually since, except for a four-year gap when the Select Committee on Members' Interests declined to publish the register in protest against the refusal of the House to take action against a small number of MPs who refused to register their interests, the most notable of whom was Enoch Powell.[15] *Erskine May* details the registration requirements, whose operation was the responsibility of a senior member of the Clerk's Department and was overseen by the Select Committee on Members' Interests. Since its inception, the rules of registration have been modified and refined, but the Nolan Committee recommended a number of changes to clarify the requirements, two of which have already been noted – the depositing of contracts involving the provision of parliamentary services by MPs and the declaration of the amounts received under such contracts. Nolan also recommended that entries in the register should be made more informative, that the register should be updated by electronic means, and that members should be given better and more frequent guidance on registration. The responsibility for compiling and maintaining the register has now been passed to the newly-appointed PCS, who has taken steps to clarify the entries in the 1996 and later registers. The electronic updating of the register, possibly through the Parliamentary Data and Video Network, is being explored. In October 1993 the Registrar of Interests issued guidance on registration in the form of *Rules on the Registration and Declaration of Financial Interests* and one of the resolutions passed by the House on 19 July 1995 supported the recommendation of the Select Committee on Standards in Public Life that the Clerk of the House should prepare new written guidance to be given to all MPs. It was envisaged that this would include explanations of the proposed code of conduct.

The various rules governing the compilation of the register require members to register interests under nine heads, with a discretionary tenth head 'for use by Members wishing to register interests, including unremunerated interests, which do not fall within any of the specific categories but which they consider to be relevant to the definition of the Register's purpose'.[16] The nine specific categories are listed in Appendix 1.

---

14 See Select Committee on Members' Interests, *First Report* (HC 326,1991-92) para 84.

15 For an account of the events leading to the establishment of the register and subsequent developments, see M Shaw 'Members of Parliament' in M Rush (ed) *Parliament and Pressure Politics* (1990) pp 92-107.

16 Introduction *Register of Members' Interests*, October 1997 edn [New Parliament] (HC 291, 1997-98) pp iv-v.

Only 20.0% of MPs returned nil entries in the October 1997 register (the first of the new Parliament) and nearly a quarter of these (4.9%) were ministers, which in part reflects the requirement that ministers dispose of shareholdings or place them in blind trusts.[17] What these figures suggest is extensive outside interests in general, and significant extra-parliamentary income in particular, among MPs. But behind such basic figures lie considerable variations in the number and types of interests held and the levels of extra-parliamentary income, both within and between parties. For example, in October 1997, 12.6% of Labour back-benchers recorded nil entries, compared with 1.8% of the Conservatives. Further analysis is beyond the scope of this chapter, but these variations need to be borne in mind, as does the fact that only remuneration for the provision of parliamentary services needs to be declared; amounts of other extra-parliamentary income do not have to be declared, making a detailed analysis of all extra-parliamentary income impossible.[18] However, under the new rules, the 1997 register does focus attention on the provision of parliamentary services by MPs, which was one of the major concerns of Nolan and remains highly pertinent to a code of conduct.

The 1947 resolution

The 1947 resolution, referred to above, declares:

> . . . that is it inconsistent with the dignity of the House, with the duty of a Member to his constituents, and with the maintenance of the privilege of freedom of speech, for any Member of this House to enter into any contractual agreement with an outside body, controlling or limiting the Member's complete independence and freedom of action in Parliament or stipulating that he shall act in any way as the representative of such outside body in regard to any matters to be transacted in Parliament; the duty of a Member being to his constituents and to the country as a whole, rather than to any particular section thereof.[19]

Nolan pointed out that the 1947 resolution appears at odds with the requirement to register –

> any pecuniary or other material benefits which a Member receives which might reasonably be thought by others to influence his or her actions, speeches or votes in Parliament, or actions taken in his or her capacity as a Member of Parliament . . .[20]

As Nolan acknowledges, however, the 1947 resolution was passed following the complaint by a W J Brown that his trade union was seeking to punish him for his

---

17 See Cabinet Office *Ministerial Code* (July 1997) paras 117-119.
18 The largest extra-parliamentary income in 1996 – between £100,000 and £110,000 – was declared by Roy Hattersley, Labour MP for Birmingham (Sparkbrook), and the smallest – up to £1,000 by a number of members.
19 See Committee of Privileges, *First Report* (HC 118, 1946-47) and HC Deb vol 440, 15 July 1947, col 365.
20 Select Committee on Members' Interests, *First Report* (HC 326, 1991-92) para 27, cited in the Introduction to the October 1997 edition of the *Register of Members' Interests* (HC 291, 1997-98) p iii.

actions as member of Parliament, not a complaint that the member was engaged in what is now called paid advocacy. It was concerns about the latter that led Nolan to recommend a ban on multi-client consultancies and the Select Committee on Standards in Public Life and the House to go much further, and ban paid advocacy altogether. Thus it was that the 1947 resolution was amended by adding the following:

> and that in particular no Member of the House shall, in consideration of any remuneration, fee, payment, reward or benefit in kind, direct or indirect, which the member or any member of his or her family has received, is receiving or expects to receive
> (i)   advocate or initiate any cause or matter on behalf of any outside body or individual or
> (ii)   urge any other member of either House of Parliament, including Ministers, to do so by means of any speech, Question, Motion, introduction of a Bill or amendment to a Motion or Bill.[1]

The code of conduct

The task of drafting a code of conduct was passed to the new Committee on Standards and Privileges, which reported in July 1996.[2] The committee in fact produced a short code of conduct – a little over two pages – and a much more extensive 21-page *Guide to the Rules relating to the Conduct of Members*. The code and guidelines were the subject of a short debate the day before the summer recess and were approved without a division.[3]

In producing a short code and extensive guidelines, the committee was following the Nolan recommendation that the code should set out broad principles accompanied by detailed guidance. Essentially, what the committee has done is to put into a systematic and succinct form the resolutions relating to the conduct of members passed by the House, the rules concerning the register of interests, and the guidance found in *Erskine May*, and added, for greater clarification, explanatory guidelines where appropriate. If the committee, as its terms of reference required it to do, examined 'any relevant overseas analogues', it is silent on the matter.[4]

---

1   HC Deb vol 265, 6 November 1995, col 661.
2   Committee on Standards and Privileges, *Third Report: The Code of Conduct and the Guide to the Rules relating to the Conduct of MPs* (HC 604, 1995-96).
3   HC Deb vol 282, 24 July 1996, cols 392-407.
4   In 1992 the Commonwealth Parliamentary Association published a report on conflict of interest. Not surprisingly, they found that codes of conduct were more commonly applied to ministers than legislators and only four countries had codes for MPs. These were Belize, Papua-New Guinea, the Solomons, and Tanzania. Seven out of ten Canadian Provinces had codes, some of limited scope. Registers of interests were more common, with 20 Commonwealth members having registers. A more recent study by the Directorate-General for Committees and Delegations of the European Parliament showed that registers exist in ten out of the 15 member countries (DOC EN\CM\268\268837, 24 March 1995). However, as far as can be ascertained, only the German Bundestag has a code of conduct for members. See Gerard Carney *Conflict of Interest: A Commonwealth Study of Members of Parliament* Legal Division, Commonwealth Secretariat, London (December 1992) pp 83-109 and Appendices A and G. A joint committee of the Canadian Senate and House of Commons has produced a draft code of conduct, but it has not yet been published.

The code proclaims its purpose as being 'to assist Members in the discharge of their obligations to the House, their constituents and the public at large.'[5] It then states that MPs have obligations to the monarch, the law, to Parliament and then, in Burkean mode, 'a general duty to act in the interests of the nation as a whole; and a special duty to their constituents'.[6] This is followed by Nolan's seven principles of public life and by the setting out of more specific obligations: to avoid conflicts of interest; to maintain the integrity of Parliament; not to accept bribes; to register their interests, to act openly with ministers, other members and public officials; not to act as paid advocates; not to make improper use of parliamentary allowances; and not to misuse confidential information. The detailed guidelines are divided into three sections – on the registration of interests, the declaration of interests, and paid advocacy. A further section deals with the procedure for complaints.

Nolan's argument for a code of broad principles with detailed guidelines is sensible enough, as is its desire to avoid 'unduly prescriptive rules', but the guidelines produced by the committee and adopted by the House go into considerable detail. Whether they prove 'unduly prescriptive' remains to be seen, although some misgivings were expressed during the debate.[7] Having been adopted by resolution of the House, the guidelines will acquire a status which is less than that of standing orders but considerably greater than mere advice. In particular, they will inform the work of the PCS and the deliberations of the Committee on Standards and Privileges. It is clear from the treatment in *Erskine May* of the conduct of members, the operation of the register of interests since 1975, and the recent developments pre- and post-Nolan, that MPs need detailed advice. If some of the guidelines prove to be 'unduly prescriptive', let them be modified; less detail is likely to give rise to more accusations of failing to meet appropriate standards of conduct, not fewer.

The new rules in practice

Between November 1995, when the Commons strengthened the rules governing the conduct of members, and February 1998, the Committee on Standards and Privileges published 25 reports, of which 21 concerned complaints against 41 members. In 14 cases the committee upheld the complaints, recommending in one case that the member concerned should be suspended from the service of the House for a week. This recommendation was accepted by the House of Commons.[8] In five others of the 14 cases where the complaint was upheld, the committee reported that it would have recommended periods of suspension, but was unable to do so because the individuals were longer members of Parliament, a matter which is discussed below. In addition, the committee agreed with the PCS that another case would have involved a breach of the rules, had the November 1995 resolutions been in force at the time of the alleged

---

5   House of Commons *The Code of Conduct together with The Guide to the Rules Relating to the Conduct of Members* (HC 688, 1995-96), para I.
6   Ibid, para II.
7   See speeches by Gary Waller (Cons) and Sir David Mitchell (Cons) (HC Deb vol 282, 24 July 1996, cols 399-401 and 401-402.
8   See Committee of Standards and Privileges, *Fifth and Sixth Reports: Complaint Against Mr Robert Wareing* (HC 182, 1997-98 and HC Deb vol 299, 30 October 1997, cols 1051-1052.

misconduct,[9] and, in another, that the rules had been breached in the spirit but not the letter.[10]

In the three sessions preceding the introduction of the new rules, only five cases in all were referred to the former Committee of Privileges and the former Select Committee on Members' Interests. That there has been a flurry of cases since the new rules is not surprising: there is inevitably uncertainty over interpretation, especially concerning the definition of paid advocacy, and allegations of breaches of privilege and failure to declare interests have long been a part of the party battle in the House of Commons.

Twenty-five of the 41 complaints against members related to allegations concerning relations with Mohamed Al-Fayed and Ian Greer, the former public relations consultant. Two others involved complaints from members of the public. The remaining 14 complaints were made by MPs of parties other than that of the member against whom the complaint was made, which is the past has largely been the norm.

Breaches of privilege

In dealing with all these cases, the Committee on Standards and Privileges decided to draw a distinction between those alleging a breach of privilege and those alleging misconduct.[11] The cases involving alleged breaches of privilege continue to be dealt with in the traditional way, in that the committee takes oral and written evidence from those involved and the PCS is not therefore involved in such cases. This practice was followed in the two cases concerning allegations of improper pressure being brought to bear on the Select Committee on Members' Interests. Both cases arose out of a complaint that Neil Hamilton (then MP for Tatton and a former Minister of State at the Department of Trade and Industry) had failed to declare interests in the Members' Register. The first involved an allegation that, in 1994, David Willetts, then a government whip but subsequently Paymaster-General, had sought to influence the committee's handling of the Hamilton case through its chair, Sir Geoffrey Johnson-Smith. The committee concluded that a conversation between Sir Geoffrey and Mr Willetts about the Hamilton case should not have taken place and expressed concern that Mr Willetts 'should dissemble in his account to the committee', an action which the committee believed 'substantially aggravated the original offence'.[12] Mr Willets subsequently resigned his ministerial post. The second case related to an allegation that Andrew Mitchell, a government whip who was also a member of the Select Committee on Members' Interests, had sought to use his position as a whip to influence Conservative members of the committee. The Standards and Privileges Committee accepted Mr Mitchell's assurance that he had not done so, but recommended

9 See Committee on Standards and Privileges, *First Report: Complaint against Mr Patrick Nicholls* (HC 148, 1995-96).
10 See Committee on Standards and Privileges, *Fifth Report: Complaint against Marjorie Mowlam* (HC 636, 1995-96).
11 See Committee on Standards and Privileges, *First Special Report* (HC 34, 1996-97) para 6.
12 Committee on Standards and Privileges, *First Report: Complaint of Alleged Improper Pressure Brought to Bear on the Select Committee on Members' Interests in 1994* (HC 88, 1996-97) para 38.

that, in future, the main parties in the House should not appoint whips to any quasi-judicial select committee.[13]

Misconduct cases – procedural issues

Cases concerning the alleged misconduct of members, mainly matters that would previously have been dealt with by the Select Committee on Members' Interests, and now, of course, alleged breaches of the code of conduct, initially entail an investigation by the PCS, and it is his report that forms the basis for the committee's subsequent inquiry. In most cases, the committee does not take oral evidence and bases its report to the House on the PCS's report to the committee. However, where the member complained against wishes to challenge the PCS's findings by giving oral evidence, then the committee normally holds one or more sittings for that purpose.[14] This occurred in the case of Neil Hamilton, but it raised important questions about the procedures adopted by the committee, particularly the absence of a clearly-defined appeal procedure. The committee found that Mr Hamilton's conduct 'fell seriously and persistently below the standard which the House is entitled to expect of its members',[15] but did not take evidence from anyone other than Mr Hamilton. It thus based its report on the oral evidence from Mr Hamilton and the oral and written evidence contained in the PCS's report, thereby denying him the opportunity to challenge his accusers' evidence directly. Furthermore, there was no opportunity for him to appeal against the committee's findings. The committee acknowledged that the role of the PCS and the committee was more like that of an investigatory or prosecuting counsel and a tribunal and that no satisfactory appeal mechanism exists. It therefore decided to examine this matter further and invited interested parties to submit evidence to it.

Clearly, there are serious problems with the existing arrangements, especially the absence of an appeal procedure. This has been publicly recognised by Martin Bell, the Independent MP who defeated Hamilton in 1997, running on an 'anti-sleaze' ticket. In written evidence to the Committee on Standards and Privileges, academic members of the Study of Parliament Group (SPG) argued that a clearly-defined disciplinary process is needed for the effective enforcement of the Code of Conduct.[16] This should involve five stages:

13 See Committee on Standards and Privileges, *Third Report: Complaint of Alleged Pressure Brought to Bear on the Select Committee on Members' Interests in 1994 [Further Report]* (HC 226, 1996-97).
14 The PCS normally relies on written evidence from complainants, the members against whom allegations have been made, and any other material witnesses, but he may conduct oral hearings if he deems it appropriate. This occurred, for example, in the case of allegations made by Mohamed Al-Fayed against Michael Howard, the former Home Secretary, and in the cases of the 25 members subject to other allegations involving Mr Al-Fayed.
15 Committee on Standards and Privileges, *Eighth Report: Complaints from Mr Mohamed Al-Fayed and Others against 25 Members and Former Members: Second further report: Mr Neil Hamilton* (HC 261, 1997-98) para 7.
16 Academic members of the Study of Parliament Group *Minutes of Evidence Presented to the Committee on Standards and Privileges* (January 1998).

1. An initial investigation to determine whether a prime facie breach of the code has occurred.
2. A further or full investigation once a prime facie case has been established.
3. A hearing before an appropriate body to determine whether a breach has occurred by testing the evidence assembled.
4. The determination of an appropriate penalty where it is found that a breach has occurred.
5. Provision for an appeal against the finding and/or penalty.

The SPG proposed four grounds for appeal: 'procedural irregularity; the manifest unreasonableness of the findings; significant new evidence; and the disproportionality of the penalty.' The SPG envisaged that stages 1 and 2 of the disciplinary process – the investigatory stages – would be the responsibility of the PCS; that stages 3 and 4 – hearing and determination of a penalty – would be the responsibility of a penal drawn from the Standards and Privileges Committee; and that stage 5 – the appeal – would be the responsibility of either a separate appeal panel drawn from the committee or all the members of the committee other than those involved in stages 3 and 4. Crucially, however, it argued that stages 3, 4 and 5 must operate judicially and that this would include the calling of witnesses by the member accused of misconduct and the right of that member to cross-examine any other witnesses. As at present, of course, it would be open to any member accused of misconduct to accept the findings of the PCS and allow the committee or panel to proceed directly to stage 4. The findings and recommendations of the committee and of any appeal would remain subject to the approval of the House, particularly where they involved the suspension or expulsion of a member, but it was suggested that findings would be 'deemed to have been approved by the House, unless negatived by a vote within a specified period (say ten sitting days)'. In order to avoid the disciplinary procedure having to cope with complex cases alleging corruption, the SPG favoured their transfer to the criminal courts, although this would require the clarification of the law on bribery recommended by Nolan.

Sanctions and sponsorship issues

The Standards and Privileges Committee's experience since 1995 also highlights two other problems, one relating to Parliament's ability to impose penalties on former members and the other to the question of financial sponsorship. The complex investigation concerning allegations against 25 members involving Mohamed Al-Fayed began in 1996, but the committee did not report until after the general election of 1997.[17] Of the 25 members being investigated, no fewer than 22 either retired or were defeated in the election and, more importantly, none of the five against whom complaints were upheld was a member of the new Parliament. In each case, the committee reported that, had they still been members, it would have recommended a period of suspension, in three cases a *substantial* period of suspension. But since the subjects of these findings were no longer MPs, no penalties could be imposed.

---

17 See Committee on Standards and Privileges, *First Special Report* (HC 34,1996-97), in which the committee reported that it had approved the appointment of a QC and another senior clerk to assist the PCS in his investigation.

The issue of sponsorship relates to what is meant by 'paid advocacy'. Throughout its history, the Labour Party has operated a system of financial assistance to, or sponsorship of, parliamentary candidates, mostly involving individual trade unions, but also a smaller number supported by the Co-operative Party.[18] Since 1933, sponsorship has been governed by the Hastings Agreement between the party, the unions and the Co-operative Union. In most cases, it has entailed the payment of a proportion of the candidate's election expenses, up to a maximum of 80% of the legal maximum, but often less in practice. Sponsorship has also usually involved an annual donation to the member's local party and, in some cases, financial or other assistance to the member. For most of the period since 1945, about 25% of Labour candidates and between 40% and 50% of Labour MPs have been sponsored by trade unions, but in recent elections the proportion of union-sponsored MPs has increased, and in 1992 it was 64.6% (175). No limit was ever imposed by the party on the number of candidates and MPs the unions could sponsor, nor on whether particular constituency parties could select a union-sponsored candidate. Understandably, the unions mostly preferred to sponsor candidates in Labour-held seats or marginal constituencies which the party could reasonably hope to win at the next election. The number of candidates sponsored by the Co-operative Party, however, has always been much smaller and, since the imposition of an agreement by the Labour Party in 1959, sponsorship by the Co-operative Party has been subject to restrictions in both the number and electoral status of seats. This forced the Co-operative Party to sponsor a number of seats which Labour neither held nor expected to win. In 1992 5.2% (14) of Labour MPs were elected as Labour-Co-operative candidates.

However, sponsorship has presented the Labour Party with a problem, related partly to its desire to distance itself from the unions and partly by the rule changes of 1995, particularly over paid advocacy. Consequently, at the 1997 general election only 8.4% (35) of Labour MPs declared union sponsorship in the Register of Members' Interests and only 0.2% (1) Co-operative Party sponsorship.[19] In most cases, sponsorship was transferred from individual candidates to the local party organisation, although it could be argued that this follows the letter more than the spirit of the code of conduct. Some Labour members also adopted the practice of soliciting donations towards their election expenses from unions, but ensured that no single donation exceeded 25% of their total election expenses, which meets the existing rules on the declaration of interests; this too might be seen as following the letter rather than the spirit of the rules.

Blind trusts

A related matter was the establishment of blind trusts by a small number of front-bench Labour MPs when in opposition to pay for research assistance and other costs of their front-bench responsibilities. It was argued that, since the beneficiaries of such trusts did not know who had contributed to them, they could not be influenced and

18 See M Harrison *Trade Unions and the Labour Party since 1945* (1960) pp 80-88, 92-94 and 262-303; M Rush *The Selection of Parliamentary Candidates* (1969) pp 165-204 and 228-242; W D Muller *The Kept Men? The First Century of Trade Union Representation in the British House of Commons, 1874-1975* (1977).
19 Register of Members' Interests, October 1997 edn (HC 291, 1997-98).

therefore did not need to be declared. Initially, this argument was accepted by the PCS, but he later changed his view and ruled that blind trusts should be declared.

The Standards and Privileges Committee has recognised that, inevitably, the new rules would produce uncertainties, some of which can and have been resolved by rulings by the PCS, but others, such as sponsorship, leave questions unanswered, and it was for this reason that the committee published a consultative paper on sponsorship in July 1997.[20] Such uncertainties, however, raise the wider question of what are acceptable and what are unacceptable outside interests for members of Parliament.

The code of conduct and outside interests

Codes of conduct are recommended, proposed or put in place precisely because legislators have outside interests, especially those of a pecuniary nature or some other personal benefit. The nature and extent of the interests inevitably has implications for the role or roles of legislators. Leaving aside the executive recruitment role typical of parliamentary systems, where ministers are drawn entirely or substantially from the legislature, legislators may be said to perform at least four major roles – those of law-makers, executive scrutineers or watchdogs, supporters of a political party, and, of course, representatives. The mix of roles varies from individual to individual, system to system, and over time, but in each role the question of outside interests remains important.

Outside interests are inevitable, but are paid interests legitimate? Various grounds can be put forward to justify outside paid interests:

1. An association with an organisation which predated the member's election: eg director of a business; maintaining professional links; and, in the British case, trade union or Co-operative Party sponsorship.
2. Maintaining or developing interests which may be of benefit to the member as an elected representative: eg association with economic activities important to the legislator's constituency; maintaining or developing specialised knowledge in areas of local, regional, national or international importance; generally keeping in touch with the 'real world'.
3. It is beneficial to advance or defend outside interests in particular policy areas in which the member holds or develops strongly-held personal views.
4. It will increase the effectiveness of the member if he or she acquires the services of a research assistant or other staff partly or wholly funded by an outside organisation or receive other logistic support.
5. A member needs to supplement the legislative salary by outside earnings to fulfil parliamentary duties more effectively and/or to maintain the standard of living enjoyed before election.
6. A member may be wish to exploit his or her position as a legislator for personal gain.[1]

---

20 Committee on Standards and Privileges, *Fourth Report: The Register of Members' Interests, Category 4, Sponsorship* (HC 181, 1997-98).
 1 Minutes of Evidence, Select Committee on Members' Interests, *First Report* (HC 326, 1991-92) p 75, written evidence presented by the author.

These are not mutually exclusive categories – and the last is to be deplored – but others may be deprecated to varying degrees by legislators themselves and by members of the public. The Nolan Committee recommended that 'Members of Parliament should remain free to have paid outside interests unrelated to the work of Parliament'.[2] However, Nolan acknowledged that there was a widespread view that MPs 'should have no outside paid interests, and that their only earned income should be their parliamentary salaries'.[3] Indeed, this was the view of the majority of people who wrote to Nolan on the matter. Such a view would not, of course, preclude unearned income from, for instance, investments, but it would preclude income from, among other activities, company directorships, professional practice (such as the law or accountancy), and journalism. However, Nolan argued:

> we . . . consider it desirable for the House of Commons to contain Members with a wide variety of continuing outside interests. If that were not so, Parliament would be less well-informed and effective than it is now, and might well be more dependent on lobbyists. A Parliament composed entirely of full-time professional politicians would not serve the best interests of democracy. The House needs if possible to contain people with a wide range of current experience which can contribute to its expertise.[4]

and reinforced this view by adding:

> . . . the House of Commons should contain Members from a wide variety of backgrounds. We should be worried about the possibility of a narrowing in the range of able men and women who would be attracted to stand for Parliament if members were banned from having any outside paid interests. We believe that many able people would not wish to enter Parliament if they not only had to take a substantial drop in income to do so but also ran the risk of seeing their source of income disappear altogether if they were to lose their seats. Some of our witnesses regretted the tendency for Members of Parliament to be drawn increasingly from those who had no employment experience outside the political field.[5]

The Nolan recommendations on paid outside interests and the arguments raised in their favour raise important questions: First, should legislators be full-time or part-time? This produces a supplementary, but at least as crucial, question: to what extent are members of any given legislature full-time in practice? Second, to what extent is extra-legislative income, whether related or not to legislative services, regarded as a necessary supplement to their legislative income? And third, to what extent can paid outside interests be justified as a means of keeping in touch with the 'real world'?

It would be sensible to take the supplementary question first. Clearly, the answer will differ from legislature to legislature, but in the British case, historically membership of the House of Commons was part-time for all but a handful of 'professional' politicians: the House met for a limited period of the year, the volume of business was much smaller than today, committee activity was much lower, and

2   Nolan Report, para 2.21.
3   Ibid, para 2.17.
4   Ibid, para 2.19.
5   Ibid, para 2.20. Though such a tendency exists, its extent is exaggerated.

the demands of constituents were limited in scope and number. Not only did most members have no difficulty in combining their parliamentary duties with various extra-parliamentary activities, but for many it was a necessity, since MPs were not paid until 1911. However, there has been a massive expansion in parliamentary activity since the last century and the demands upon MPs and their time have grown enormously. A survey conducted on behalf of the Top (now Senior) Salaries Review Body in 1971 led the Review Body to conclude that 'by any reasonable standard . . . most Members must be considered as working on a full-time basis'.[6] Similar surveys carried out in 1975, 1978, 1982 and 1996 confirm this judgement.[7] In short, whatever outside interests MPs may have, being a member of Parliament is now their principal activity, taking up most of their 'normal' working hours, and anything else is additional.

Should legislators be full-time or part-time? Some light on this is thrown by a survey conducted by members of the SPG on the socialisation of MPs.[8] Two questionnaires were sent to MPs first elected at the 1992 general election and one to a control group of longer-serving MPs. The first questionnaire to new members was sent immediately after the election but before the meeting of Parliament. It was therefore largely concerned with measuring the expectations of newly-elected MPs. The second, sent 18 months after the election, was concerned with how far their expectations had been borne out by experience. Simultaneously, a questionnaire asking essentially the same questions was sent to a sample of longer-serving members. New MPs were overwhelmingly of the view that the job of the member of Parliament should be full-time: this was the view of no fewer than 94.7% in the first survey and 93.7% in the second. Indeed, in the two major parties it was only new Conservatives – 10.7% in the first survey and 16.7% in the second – who thought it should be part-time. Longer-serving Labour members were also overwhelmingly in favour of a full-time role, although one did think it should be a mixture of full-time and part-time. In contrast, only 57.1% of longer-serving Conservatives thought it should be full-time and 35.7% part-time, leaving 7.1% who thought it should be a mixture. Where the 1992 intake differed was that Conservatives frequently qualified their support for the full-time role by saying that it should not preclude the pursuit of outside interests, principally on the grounds that it kept MPs in touch with the 'real world'. As might be expected, this view was echoed among longer-serving Conservatives.

The SPG research can also throw some light on the second question – is extra-parliamentary income a necessary supplement to the parliamentary salary? On a scale of 1 (highest) to 5 (lowest) both new and longer-serving members were asked whether

---

6   Top Salaries Review Body (TSRB) *Ministers of the Crown and Members of Parliament* December 1971 (Cmnd 4836) para 25. See also M Rush 'The Professionalisation of the British Member of Parliament' in *Papers in Political Science: 1*, Department of Politics, University of Exeter (1989).

7   See TSRB *Report No 8*, 1976 (Cmnd 6574) Appendix A; TSRB *Report No 12*, 1979 (Cmnd 7598), Appendix C; TSRB, *Report No 20*, 1983 (Cmnd 8881-II) s 1; and Review Body on Senior Salaries, *Report No 38* (Cm 3330-II) s 2.

8   Unpublished research by the Study Group on New Members, Study of Parliament Group. The response rates to the three questionnaires were 61.4%, 49.6% and 31.2% respectively. The research was supported by a grant from the Nuffield Foundation. Evidence based on this research has been presented to the Nolan Committee and the Senior Salaries Review Body.

they thought the parliamentary salary was too high, about right, or too low. There was a marked contrast between Conservative and Labour respondents. Before arriving at Westminster no new Conservative MP thought the salary too high, only 25% thought it about right and the remaining 75% thought it too low. After 18 months' experience, these views had hardened: only 16.7% thought the salary about right and 83.3% too low. This was broadly in line with longer-serving Conservatives, although they felt somewhat less strongly – one actually thought the salary too high, 20% about right and 75% too low. On the other hand, 55.5% of the new Labour members initially regarded the salary as about right, compared with 13.4% who thought it too high and 28.8% too low. Eighteen months later, these views had shifted to 59.0% (about right), 5.1% (too high) and 35.9% (too low) and, unlike the Conservatives, contrasting with longer-serving Labour MPs, none of whom thought the salary too high, 38.7% about right and no less than 61.3% too low. The substantial increase in salary from £35,085 to £43,000 in 1996 has modified these views, but it has not fundamentally altered the party divide: a third questionnaire to the 1992 intake (administered in November 1996) found that 50% of the Conservatives now thought the salary about right and 42.8% still thought it too low. In contrast, 63.6% of the 1992 Labour MPs now regarded the salary as about right and as many as 31.8% thought it too high. The 1992 intake were also asked whether their pre-election income had been higher, about the same or lower than the parliamentary salary. Of Conservatives, 75% had previously earned higher incomes, 14.8% about the same and only 11.1% less than the parliamentary salary. Conversely, 63.6% of new Labour members had earned less, 29.5% about the same, and only 6.8% more.

The third question – to what extent do paid outside interests help legislators keep in touch with the 'real world'? – is the most subjective. A cynical, but not necessarily facetious, response is: who does live in the 'real world'? We all live in our own worlds. Moreover, a distinction needs to be drawn between recruiting a wide range of men and women (and, indeed, many more women) in socio-economic terms and experience and keeping in touch with the 'real world' after election.[9] The level of legislative salaries and the provision of services and faculties are likely to be major factors influencing the supply side of legislative recruitment: poor salaries, actually or relatively, and inadequate backup will have a deterrent effect. There are, of course, other deterrent factors, such as unsocial hours and disruption of family life. On the other hand, the ability to supplement the legislative salary through paid outside interests almost certainly offsets some of the financial deterrents for would-be legislators.

Keeping in touch with the 'real world' needs to be argued in its own right and not in financial terms. Membership of various organisations, contacts with other organisations and individuals, formal and informal networks, and the like can all help legislators keep in touch. None of these need necessarily involve financial relationships. Other people in other occupations have to maintain contact with the 'real world' by such means. However, legislators can and do argue that continuing to practise as a lawyer or accountant, or being a company director, or pursuing some other occupation,

---

9   In the 1992-97 Parliament there was the unusual case of Sir Paul Beresford, Conservative MP for Croydon Central, who was appointed Parliamentary Under-Secretary in the Department of the Environment, but was given permission to continue to practise as a dentist one day a week while holding ministerial office.

does allow them to keep in touch with reality in a more effective way than various forms of networking; they are better-informed, they argue, because they are *active* in the real world. However, as the SPG survey data show, this is much more commonly a Conservative than a Labour argument. The significance of this is that, although Parliament largely affects not to recognise parties, parties are the engines of legislatures: it is one thing not to recognise them, it is quite another to ignore the differences between them when considering rules and regulations.

At this point a further distinction needs to be made and that is between paid outside interests which are not directly related to the provision of legislative services and those which are – parliamentary consultancies. The House of Commons has banned paid advocacy, but MPs may continue to act as paid advisers to companies, trade associations, trade unions, pressure groups, and other organisations. Yet advice can be just as valuable, sometimes more valuable than advocacy. Whether such organisations should be able to purchase advice from legislators is a moot point: the right of outside interests to make representations to legislators is not in dispute; the right buy their advice is.

From the member's point of view, the 'actively involved' argument can be used to support the case for legislative consultancies and some would argue that they would not advise those with whom they lack sympathy or for whose interests they lack concern. From the outside interests' point of view, it can be argued that it is better that they get good advice from 'insiders' than less good advice from elsewhere. However, all these views rest on considerable assumptions, beg many questions, and provide less than categorical answers.

Conclusion

What are the implications of the adoption of a code of conduct for British MPs? The House of Commons is not the first the field, but such legislatures remain a distinct minority in the world. None the less, codes of conduct for legislators are likely to become more common, partly as a response to particular incidents, but mainly because they are part of a wider demand for greater accountability in liberal-democratic political systems. The existence and development of codes is likely to increase the pressure on legislators to reveal more information about their financial affairs, including details of earned and unearned income, either publicly or to a named official. This raises questions about the roles of legislators, particularly about the acceptability or not of paid outside interests. A major factor here is whether the legislators and those they represent take the view that membership of a legislature should be a full-time occupation: an affirmative answer means that pay, services and facilities must be adequate to recruit and retain high calibre legislators. Developments in these areas, however, may have a general impact on legislative recruitment and a differential impact on the ability of parties to attract able would-be parliamentarians.

Arguably, the British House of Commons is undergoing a significant change of culture, as the pressure to be a full-time MP grows and hardens and the parameters of acceptable outside interests narrow. In such circumstances, a clear code of conduct and sufficiently detailed guidelines will facilitate and smooth that change. But what remains crystal clear is that there will be no going back: codes of conduct are here to stay and legislators will have to bite the bullet on the question of outside interests.

Chapter VIII

The Parliamentary Ombudsman: a successful alternative?

Philip Giddings

A successful transplant

It is 30 years since the legislation setting up the United Kingdom Parliamentary Commissioner for Administration (PCA) came into effect. Over that period, the traditional preference in British political culture for political, as opposed to legal or judicial, methods of dealing with complaints about the action or inaction of public authorities has begun to wane. A decline in confidence in the efficacy of Parliament has been accompanied by increasing resort to the courts of law to challenge public authorities. Thus, the introduction of revised procedures for judicial review has significantly extended the scope for challenging the decisions of public authorities in the courts.

At the same time, the procedures of the courts themselves have come under criticism for their complexity, length and expense. Restrictions on legal aid, arising largely because of the need to limit public expenditure, have meant that access to the courts has increasingly been confined either to the very rich – who can afford to pay for themselves – or the very poor, who still qualify for legal aid. Anxieties about the implications of these constraints upon the general public's access to justice were evident in the 1995 report on the civil justice system, in which Lord Woolf gave powerful endorsement to alternative forms of dispute resolution, including ombudsman schemes.[1]

Thus, the PCA scheme has evolved in a period in which criticism of the two main traditional mechanisms for dealing with complaints against public authorities – Parliament and the courts – has led to increasing interest in alternatives. An ombudsman scheme is clearly an alternative to the judicial process for resolving complaints – and in the form of the PCA it can also be seen as an alternative to the *political* process in that it provides an alternative, that is to say an *additional*, route for a member of Parliament dealing with a constituent's complaint against a public authority. In this chapter we shall review the way the PCA scheme has developed from this 'alternative' perspective.

---

1 Lord Chancellor's Department *Access to Justice: Interim Report of the Lord Chancellor on the Civil Justice System in England and Wales* (June 1995) p 139.

This 'alternative' feature of an ombudsman scheme was, in fact, one of the main reasons for resistance to setting up such a scheme in the first place. The British preference for political, as opposed to legal or judicial, methods of dealing with complaints against public decision-makers manifested itself particularly in the role of the constituency member of Parliament as grievance chaser. For some, this preference was a reason for rejecting any idea of an ombudsman-type institution, as was evident in the Macmillan government's rejection of the JUSTICE recommendations in November 1962.[2] But the determined opposition of Whitehall and other constitutional conservatives at this time was overcome when Harold Wilson's government was elected in 1964.[3]

The British variant of the Scandinavian ombudsman institution has, in the ensuing 30 years, become a universally accepted and well-established part of our parliamentary arrangements. Initial opposition to the PCA concept on the grounds that it would undermine parliamentary sovereignty and ministerial responsibility has been shown to be not well-founded. Indeed, its very success, together with other developments like the Citizen's Charter and the acceptance of growing judicial activism in the field of administrative law, might suggest that the British cultural preference for the political method of complaint-redress has now changed, reflecting a decline in confidence in our political system and, perhaps especially, our politicians.

The attractiveness of an ombudsman scheme as an alternative to the courts of law and tribunals is that it not only provides objectivity and impartiality but is also informal, quick and cheap (actually free to the complainant). In recent years there has been a marked growth in use of the Parliamentary Commissioner's Office, judged by the recent rapid expansion in his case-load since 1991 (see Table VIII.1).

Table VIII.1: The PCA's growing case-load

Year	New cases	Cases brought Forward	Total cases
1989	677	260	937
1990	704	298	1002
1991	801	278	1079
1992	945	310	1255
1993	986	398	1384
1994	1332	458	1790
1995	1706	651	2357
1996	1933	883	2816

Source: PCA *Annual Report 1996* (HC 386,1996-97) March 1997, p 37.

There has also been a growth in the number of ombudsman-type institutions in both public and private sectors: the British and Irish Ombudsman Association currently

2   Whyatt Committee *The Citizen and the Administration* a report by JUSTICE (1971).
3   For an account of the origins of the PCA, see F Stacey *The British Ombudsman* (1971).

lists some 19 United Kingdom members, eight in the public and 11 in the private sector – five of which are nevertheless statutory. The latter include ombudsman schemes for: the insurance industry (1981); the banks (1986); building societies (1987 – statutory); personal investments (1989); legal services (1990 – statutory); corporate estate agents (1990); pensions (1991 – statutory); funeral services industry (1994); and social housing (1997 – statutory). In addition to these ombudsman schemes, the government has established a number of internal complaints adjudicators in areas such as: prisons (1993); the inland revenue (1993); customs and excise (1995); and national insurance contributions (1995) – the latter three now being combined in one Adjudicator's Office (May 1993).

The Parliamentary Commissioner Act 1967 was a cautious reform. Initially, it was heavily criticised for its timidity: 'Ombudsman or Ombudsmouse?' was the subtitle of an early article on the scheme.[4] This was not a promising beginning for an institution the effectiveness of which would depend upon the co-operation of ministers, MPs and senior civil servants. But the early caution seems to have been well justified in terms of the subsequent expansion and cloning of the institution so that most of the public service is now covered by one ombudsman or another. The British PCA is clearly an example of a successful institutional transplant and its success became evident within a few years of its establishment, well before the era of the Citizen's Charter.[5] There are clear lessons here about how resistance to constitutional and administrative reform within government can be overcome: an evolutionary approach is more likely to be successful in British administrative culture, if success is judged by the long-term acceptability of the reform.[6]

Not only has the PCA survived its unpromising beginnings and the ombudsman concept expanded to become an accepted part of British administrative arrangements, but it has proved a successful adaptation of the Scandinavian original, providing an alternative to both political and judicial modes of complaint-handling. It has been particularly successful in achieving compliance from governmental authorities with PCA recommendations, notwithstanding initial reservations from sceptics of the limitations of the original statutory framework. One feature of that framework which is not often remarked on is that correspondence between MPs and the ombudsman enjoys absolute privilege in the law of defamation – in contrast to the lack of protection of correspondence between MPs and ministers.[7]

In line with the classical concept of a governmental ombudsman, the PCA is empowered only to make recommendations. He has no authority to impose his findings, or to make binding orders or awards. If his recommendations are to be implemented, they, and the findings on which they are based, must first be accepted

4   W B Gwyn 'The British PCA: Ombudsman or Ombudsmouse?' (1973) 35 Journal of Politics 45-69; compare the same author's 'The Ombudsman in Britain: a qualified success in government reform' (1982) 60 Public Administration 177-195.

5   W K Reid, Evidence to the PCA Select Committee, First Report, *The Powers, Work and Jurisdiction of the Ombudsman* (HC 33-II, 1993-94) Q22, November 1993.

6   See P Giddings and R Gregory 'Transplanting an Institution: the Evolution of the British Parliamentary Ombudsman', paper presented to a Workshop of Parliamentary Scholars and Parliamentarians, Berlin, August 1994.

7   Decision of the House of Commons in the *Strauss* case: HC Deb 591, 8 July 1958, cols 208-347. Erskine May (22nd edn, 1997) p 96.

by the administrative authority against whom the complaint was originally made. The basis upon which an administrative authority – in practice, usually a government department – accepts the PCA's recommendations is two-fold: acknowledgment of the calibre of the investigative research and persuasive argumentation in the report; and what has come to be called respect for the (moral) authority of the PCA as an impartial investigator.

On this basis, almost all of the PCA's recommendations have been accepted by government, even in those cases where ministers/permanent secretaries have not been persuaded that they are themselves guilty of maladministration or that an injustice had been inflicted. The roll-call here over the years is impressive: Sachsenhausen;[8] Barlow Clowes;[9] compensation for chicken farmers;[10] Disability Living Allowance;[11] Child Support Agency;[12] and, most recently, if still a little speculatively, Channel Tunnel Rail Link blight.[13]

In some instances, no doubt, 'respect for the PCA's Office'[14] may have been a convenient cover for appeasement of a political interest.[15] But the fact remains that government itself has recognised, particularly in the slaughtered chickens and Channel Tunnel Rail Link cases, that it is highly exceptional for a department even to contemplate declining to accept and implement the PCA's findings. And that exceptionality has in turn reinforced the moral authority of the office. So the PCA achieves near to 100% compliance without having any formal powers of enforcement. Some mouse!

Those substantial successes need to be kept in mind when looking at the criticisms of the effectiveness of the PCA scheme as a form of dispute resolution. Some of these criticisms date back to the deliberately cautious way in which the scheme was set up in the 1960s. Others have emerged more recently, either in the context of the development of other government policies in relation to the public service (eg the Citizen's Charter), or as a result of growing pressure for wider administrative or constitutional reform – such as open government, a written constitution, patriation of the Human Rights Convention – reflecting the decline in confidence in traditional mechanisms.

---

8 See R Gregory and P Hutchesson *The Parliamentary Ombudsman: A Study in the Control of Administrative Action* (1975) chs 11 and 12.

9 See R Gregory and G Drewry 'Barlow Clowes and the Ombudsman' [1991] PL 192, 408.

10 Third Report of the PCA Select Committee, *Compensation to Farmers for Slaughtered Poultry* (HC 593, 1992-93), and the government's Reply (HC 947, 1992-93).

11 PCA Sixth Report of 1992-93, *Delays in Handling Disability Living Allowance Claims* (HC 652).

12 Third Report of the PCA Select Committee, *The Child Support Agency* (HC 199, 1994-95) and the government's Reply, 1995 (Cm 2865). But see also PCA Third Report *Investigation of complaints against the Child Support Agency* (HC 20, 1995-96).

13 Sixth Report of the PCA Select Committee, *The Channel Tunnel Rail Link and Exceptional Hardship* (HC 270, 1994-95) and the government's Reply (HC 819).

14 The expression used by the government in the Barlow Clowes case (see HC Deb 1989-90, vol 164, cols 201-212) and also in the Channel Tunnel Rail Link case (see PCA Select Committee Fifth Special Report, *The Channel Tunnel Rail Link and Exceptional Hardship – the Government Response* (HC 819, 1994-95).

15 *Independent*, 20 December 1989, commenting on the Barlow Clowes case. See R Gregory and G Drewry 'Barlow Clowes and the Ombudsman – Part II' [1991] PL 441.

Criticisms and challenges

Maladministration

To begin with, we consider a feature of the PCA scheme which occasioned much criticism in the early years of the scheme although that criticism seems to have largely disappeared as a consequence of its pragmatic development: the limitation of the PCA's competence (the grounds on which he is empowered to make criticisms and therefore recommend redress) to maladministration. Together with an explicit debarring of the PCA from investigating the merits of decisions, the confining of his investigations to alleged maladministration was part of the adaptation of the ombudsman concept to fit the British doctrine of ministerial responsibility. Ministers could be expected, it was argued, to account to Parliament for the merits of decisions taken by them or on their behalf, no doubt because 'merits' are inherently 'discretionary' and therefore to be accounted for to the House as a whole. As for matters administrative, officials could answer to committees on behalf of ministers without imperilling the doctrine of ministerial responsibility. So, it was reasoned, an Officer of Parliament modelled on the Comptroller and Auditor General could safely report to MPs on administrative defects.

Maladministration was deliberately left undefined in the 1967 Act, with guidance as to its intended meaning being provided only in the celebrated Crossman catalogue of examples, the most significant words of which are the last three: 'and so on'.[16] Unlike New Zealand – another Westminster-type system, but one which preceded the United Kingdom in making provision for an ombudsman – neither the statute nor the unofficial catalogue included decisions which were simply 'wrong'. But the doctrines of 'constructive maladministration' and 'the wrong decision', endorsed by select committee[17] reports in 1968 and 1971 and in debate in the House,[18] and the ingenuity of successive Commissioners have produced a situation in which neither the PCA nor the select committee – nor, one suspects, government – consider 'maladministration' to be a significant limitation upon the PCA's activity. Where avoidable injustice to individual citizens results from a decision, that in itself is now taken as prima facie evidence of maladministration – since it is an obligation of good administration to avoid such consequences if possible.

Sir William Reid, who retired as PCA in January 1997, has pointed out that 'to define maladministration is to limit it. Such a limitation could work to the disadvantage of individual complainants with justified grievances which did not fit within a given definition'. He went on to supplement the Crossman catalogue with one of his own.[19] The two together (reproduced in Appendix 2) now constitute a wide category of administrative fault – a quarry for the Commissioner's investigations which is both broad and deep.

---

16 The full 'Crossman Catalogue' is reproduced in Appendix 2.
17 The Select Committee on the Parliamentary Commissioner for Administration, which became the Select Committee on Public Administration in 1997.
18 Second Report from the Select Committee (HC 350, 1967-68) pp vi-viii; Second Report from the Select Committee (HC 513, 1970-71) HC Deb 1978-79, vol 959, col 922.
19 PCA Annual Report 1993 (HC 112, 1993-94) para 7.

Use of the term 'maladministration' does, however, still have one significant disadvantage: its potential deterrent effect on complainants considering whether their complaint is likely to fall within the PCA's jurisdiction. Whilst there is an MP filter, it is reasonable to assume – presumably – that MPs can overcome this deterrent effect. But the term is likely to be perceived as inherently obscure to the average citizen, not to mention the socially or educationally disadvantaged.

The MP filter

In recent years, the MP filter – the requirement that cases should be referred to the PCA through members of Parliament rather than by citizens directly – has displaced maladministration as the most criticised feature of the PCA scheme. Again, it was a feature which was deliberately included to adapt the ombudsman concept to the United Kingdom's parliamentary context and to circumvent anticipated opposition from MPs keen to defend their constituency post-bags. It has been defended pragmatically as a way of reducing the PCA's case-load to a manageable size, building on the point that, when the PCA scheme was introduced, the United Kingdom was by far the largest state to contemplate an ombudsman scheme. It remains true that the PCA's case-load is low in comparison with international counterparts (only the French médiateur and Sri Lanka have similar filter mechanisms) but, as Table VIII.1 clearly shows, during Sir William Reid's tenure of the office (1990-96) there was a very substantial increase in cases: new cases increased nearly three-fold and the number of investigations completed more than doubled.

The qualitative effectiveness of the MP filter is more problematic. Every year something like 70% of the cases referred by MPs to the PCA are not admitted for investigation. Because of the complexities surrounding the PCA's jurisdiction, MPs were in fact encouraged by the PCA in 1993 to refer cases if they were in any doubt.[20] So the evidence suggests that relatively few MPs consciously operate the filter as a form of quality control – though it is likely that some cases that might have become PCA cases are instead successfully resolved by MPs.

However, the evidence also suggests another kind of selectivity: a proportion of MPs who never use the PCA at all. In the early years of the scheme, the proportion of non-referring MPs was substantial – in some years, more than half and at best a third, as Table VIII.2 indicates. Determined efforts by the select committee and the PCA to make the office known and some significant successes by the PCA in high profile cases like Barlow Clowes have led to a significant increase in the number of MPs referring cases in the last three years, but even 1994, with 501 MPs referring cases (then an all-time high), saw around a quarter of Members referring not even one.

20 PCA, *Fifth Report* (HC 569, 1992-93) para 18.

Table VIII.2

Year	No of MPs referring cases
1967	428
1972	306
1977	401
1982	389
1987	379
1990	361
1991	432
1992	460
1993	429
1994	501
1995	546
1996	566

Source: PCA *Annual Reports.*

Why have so many MPs not referred cases to the PCA?[1] Is it that they always succeed in resolving their constituents' complaints satisfactorily? Or is governmental maladministration selectively distributed so that some parliamentary constituencies are immune to it? Some MPs who comment on this suggest that the reluctance to use the PCA is explained by the length of time the PCA process takes: MPs want to reply to their constituents within a few weeks, not wait many months. The average time taken by the PCA to complete an investigation and report to the referring MP in 1996 was 88 weeks – see Table VIII.3 below. What such comments do not reveal is what MPs do with cases which they are unable to resolve by their own efforts and which could be referred to the PCA if they were willing so to do.

A survey of MPs conducted for the select committee in 1993[2] found that the majority of MPs were then opposed to removing the MP filter. However, the breakdown of responses – 69% of Conservative respondents were against, whereas 53% of Labour MPs responding were in favour – suggests that the change in the majority party in Parliament after the 1997 general election may lead to a change in parliamentarians' collective view on this issue. Indeed, in the 1993 survey the highest level of support for removing the filter was found amongst the more recently-elected Labour MPs – ie those elected in 1983 or since (58%). Moreover, in evidence to the select committee in 1992, the PCA stated that it had seemed to him for some time that it was 'potentially disadvantageous' that complainants had to approach him through an MP[3] – and putting the onus on the MP to refuse to allow an investigation for a constituent who has requested it directly has gone some way to remove its worst effects.

---

1   Note that ministers can, and do, refer cases to the PCA like any other MP.
2   First Report of the PCA Select Committee of 1993-94 *The Powers, Work and Jurisdiction of the Ombudsman* (HC 33).
3   Ibid, Evidence, 5 May 1993, Q1.

Removal of the filter could be expected to lead to a substantial increase in the number of cases reaching the PCA (as happened with the local government ombudsmen when direct access was permitted) which would require a significant injection of resources and perhaps regional ombudsmen to cope. It is also argued that the filter ensures that MPs, through their constituency case-work, are kept in touch with the way in which governmental administration actually affects ordinary citizens. As that argument assumes that direct access to the ombudsman would lead to a significant reduction in MPs' constituency correspondence, it could actually increase support amongst MPs for direct access.

A related issue, and a critical one should the MPs' filter be removed, is public awareness of the PCA. A survey carried out in March 1995 found that less than half (46%) of respondents had 'heard of' the Parliamentary Ombudsman.[4] However effective a complaint-handling mechanism may be when in operation, potential complainants with justified grievances need first to know that it exists, and then how to bring it into play, if it is to be of any help to them. Publicity campaigns and outreach programmes are a common feature of other ombudsman jurisdictions, often with an emphasis on reaching disadvantaged citizens. This issue of visibility closely connects with accessibility – whether the procedures adopted by an ombudsman (eg requiring forms to be filled in or letters to be written) deter the less literate or less determined complainants.

Limited jurisdiction

The third issue raised about the PCA scheme concerned the limitations upon jurisdiction which are, in effect, limitations upon access to justice if the PCA is perceived as a form of alternative dispute resolution. As time has gone on, a number of these have been removed or covered by the creation of other ombudsman schemes, such as those for local government and the national health service. The general approach adopted by successive PCAs has been to press the boundaries of jurisdiction to their furthest limit in favour of the citizen.[5] It is also worth noting that the PCA's jurisdiction has not been curtailed by developments such as the setting up of 'Next Steps' executive agencies and that 'privatised' and 'contracted-out' activities[6] conducted 'on behalf of' government departments and public-sector bodies are still within his remit.[7] In this respect, the apparatus of public accountability has remained intact.

Nevertheless, two significant jurisdictional anomalies do remain, upon which the select committee has repeatedly pressed government, to no effect – personnel matters and contracts. Here the official apologia for the PCA's remit comes back to haunt its progenitors. For if ministerial responsibility is the guide to the PCA's remit, as was

---

4   MORI *Local Government Ombudsman. Omnibus Report. Research Study Conducted for the Commission for Local Administration in England* 10-13 March 1995, p 2. Interestingly, the figure for the Local Government Ombudsman was 47% and for the Banking Ombudsman 46%.

5   See eg PCA: *Annual Report 1979* (HC 402) para 6.

6   See *Second Report of the PCA of 1990-91* (HC 299, 1990-91) para 5 and *Fourth Report from the PCA Select Committee, 1990-91* (HC 368, 1990-91) pp x-xi.

7   *Fifth Report of the PCA, 1993*, HC 569, para 5. See also, P Giddings (ed) *Parliamentary Accountability: A Study of Parliament and Executive Agencies* (1995) pp 139-152.

argued when the original legislation was being considered in the 1960s, then these matters very definitely fall within the ambit of administrative decisions which one would expect to be subject to PCA investigation. Nor does the availability of other forms of redress save the argument, since there is precedent within the legislation for allowing the PCA discretion to take on cases where, in his view, it would be unreasonable to expect the complainant to pursue other available remedies.

Some recent cases have shown how far the PCA has been able to push the limits of his jurisdiction. In the slaughtered chickens case he was able not only to overturn a ministerial decision on the method of calculating compensation, but also successfully to press the case for requiring the ministry to apply the revised method of calculation to all poultry farmers who had been incorrectly compensated. In the Channel Tunnel Rail Link case he has overturned what the Transport Department had seen as a ministerial policy decision about the limits of compensation for planning blight – a victory achieved with the aid of the select committee, who took evidence from the Transport Secretary himself as well as the Permanent Secretary of the Department. In the Barlow Clowes case, the government's eventual decision to accept his recommendations even though they did not agree with them led to payments of 'compensation' totalling £150m.[8]

The accountability of the PCA

Such cases illustrate the significance of some of the PCA's decisions. Significant sums of public money may be involved. And as the PCA's case-load has grown, so have people's expectations about the effectiveness of public sector complaint-handling mechanisms, no doubt encouraged by the importance given to such mechanisms in the Citizen's Charter programme. As, inevitably, these expectations are not fulfilled in every case, they lead to questions about the accountability of the PCA. Again, such questions are particularly important when the PCA scheme, as a form of alternative dispute resolution, is viewed as an alternative to political or judicial methods. To whom is the Commissioner accountable? To whom can the citizen go if he is dissatisfied with the way the PCA has dealt with his case?

One indicator of complainants' higher expectations may be the increase in the amounts of correspondence coming back to his office after a decision has been given with which the writer disagrees: in 1996 the PCA reported that such 'come-back' correspondence increased by 45% the number of analyses required by his screening directorate alone.[9] All of which underlines the issue of the PCA's accountability: to whom is this independent complaint-investigator accountable? *Quis custodiet custodem ipsum*?

Before responding directly to that question, we need to register two important preliminary points. First, we need to keep in mind that impartiality is fundamental to the ombudsman concept. It is not the ombudsman's role to take the citizen's side against the administration or vice versa. He makes an impartial and disinterested assessment of the complaint – which is complied with precisely because it is impartial and disinterested, thorough and well-argued. Independence is crucial to that impartiality –

8   See R Gregory and G Drewry 'Barlow Clowes and the Ombudsman Part II' [1991] PL 408.
9   PCA *Annual Report for 1996* (HC 386, 1996-97) p 4.

independence of the government, in both its bureaucratic and ministerial forms, and of Parliament in its political form. Accountability and oversight must, therefore, be held in tension with independence.

Secondly, we need to remember the basic case for setting up an ombudsman-type institution. This was not only that traditional political/parliamentary modes of redressing citizens' grievances were perceived to be inadequate, but also that courts, and to a lesser extent tribunals, were not seen as likely to provide a satisfactory *alternative*. What was needed was a remedy which was informal, cheap and quick – the precise opposite of judicial means of redress. This was the line of reasoning which received powerful endorsement in Lord Justice Woolf's 1995 Report on Access to Justice: 'Ombudsman schemes provide many advantages to the complainant. They are free, and complainants do not need the assistance of lawyers'.[10] The latter point is important, as with lawyers there so often comes a change to a more rule-based culture – a feature which some have detected in some private-sector ombudsman schemes in which the ombudsman is empowered to make binding awards and thereby acts as de facto arbitrator.

It may be as well that Lord Woolf did not include 'speed' in his list of the potential advantages of ombudsman schemes since that is one aspect in which the PCA scheme is clearly vulnerable to criticism, as Table VIII.2 shows. But, particularly in the era of the Citizen's Charter, there is little doubt that an ombudsman scheme provides an important supplement – along with other forms of alternative dispute resolution (ADR) – to the parliamentary and judicial mechanisms for dealing with citizens' grievances against public authorities.

Table VIII.3 throughput times

Year	Average time in weeks and days*	Number of cases taking More than twelve months
1989	65.4	n/a
1990	64.4	41
1991	58.3	23 (12%)
1992	53.6	42 (16%)
1993	58.5	101 (30%)
1994	70.4	151 (36%)
1995	74	n/a
1996	88	n/a

* Average time taken to complete a full investigation and report on it to the MP who referred the complaint.

Source: PCA *Annual Reports*.

Those two points having been made, the British PCA scheme does nevertheless provide for a form of public accountability of the Parliamentary Ombudsman. Its primary mode is the PCA Select Committee. Although the committee's performance

10 Lord Chancellor's Department *Access to Justice: Interim Report to the Lord Chancellor on the Civil Justice System in England and Wales* (June 1995) p 139.

has sometimes been lack-lustre, there is no doubt that its existence was a significant factor in establishing the PCA scheme as an accepted and respected part of the Whitehall-Westminster nexus. It may not have the same clout as the Public Accounts Committee, but there is little doubt that neither permanent secretaries nor ministers relish having to appear before such a select committee to explain their departments' misdemeanours or, worse, their unwillingness to accede to the PCA's recommendations. Certainly, the Commissioners themselves have greatly valued the select committee connection and ombudsmen in other jurisdictions look upon it with envy. The absence of the equivalent of select committee follow-up has been offered as a reason for the fact that the local government ombudsmen have been less successful than the PCA in achieving compliance with their recommendations from public authorities of which they have been critical. Recently, the Australian Commonwealth Ombudsman has remarked upon the advantage which the select committee form of linkage with the legislature can provide.[11]

To be appreciated is not, however, the same as to be effective: indeed, it can suggest a cosiness which would make the external critic suspicious. But there does seem to be sufficient evidence of the select committee reinforcing the PCA's gradualism in establishing and expanding the office's remit and subsequently its 'administrative audit' activity to justify concluding that this part of the machinery set up by Harold Wilson's government has indeed worked successfully as a support mechanism. Can the same be said of the select committee's effectiveness as a mode of accountability? The PCA reports to Parliament annually, quarterly and on what he judges to be special occasions. The committee considers his reports and questions him about them – but the committee has taken very great care not to allow itself to become a form of appeal against the PCA's findings or recommendations. Is this classical form of accountability adequate? Those complainants who do not consider that the PCA has dealt adequately with their case may not think so.

Although there is no provision for appeal against the PCA, it should be noted that the PCA, like the Local Government Ombudsman, is not immune from judicial review. Although the courts have recognised that the PCA Act provides the Commissioner with a very wide discretion, the courts have explicitly held that there was nothing about the role of the PCA, or the statutory framework within which he operated, 'so singular as to take him wholly outside the purview of judicial review'. However, 'it did not follow that the court would readily be persuaded to interfere with exercise of the commissioner's wide discretion'[12] and it did not do so when a complainant, Miss Dyer, sought review of the PCA's decision not to re-open an investigation into her complaint.[13]

Although the courts have thus held that the PCA's discretion is so widely drawn that it is unlikely to provide fertile ground for pursuing challenges to his findings, such a challenge is possible and was successfully made in the *Balchin* case in 1996.[14] In this case the PCA had found that the Secretary of State for Transport had not acted maladministratively when confirming road orders relating to a by-pass scheme

---

11 D Pearce 'The Commonwealth Ombudsman: the Right Office in the Wrong Place' (1997, unpublished).
12 *R v Parliamentary Comr for Administration, ex p Dyer* [1994] 1 All ER 375.
13 PCA *Annual Report for 1993* (HC 290, 1993-94).
14 *R v Parliamentary Comr for Administration, ex p Balchin* [1996] NPC 147.

sponsored by Norfolk County Council.[15] That PCA report was the subject of judicial review proceedings as a result of which the PCA was required by the court to determine the complaint afresh on the grounds that he had omitted to consider a particular issue. Although that reconsideration has yet to be completed, it is a clear demonstration of the power of the court to direct the PCA to consider a case again.

Thus, although the PCA is an independent and impartial officer of Parliament with a very wide discretion to investigate cases where maladministration by a governmental authority has been alleged, he is accountable to Parliament through the select committee and, like any other public official created by statute, subject to the rule of the law. Within that framework, he provides an effective alternative to the courts or parliamentary politics as a means of resolving citizens' complaints against the administrative actions of public authorities within his jurisdiction.

The future

There are three possible developments which may significantly affect the future development of the PCA scheme: proposed legislation to provide 'Open Government'; a change in the PCA's relationship with the Health Service Commissioner arising from the reform of NHS procedures; and the possible removal of the 'MP filter'.

Pressure for greater openness in British public administration has already had an impact on the PCA scheme. In its initiative on access to official information in 1993[16] the Conservative government effectively extended the PCA's remit by providing that complaints about breaches of the non-statutory Code of Practice on Access to Government Information could be referred to the PCA. This was based on the proposition that failure to adhere to the official codes constituted evidence of maladministration. This extension of jurisdiction did not prove as productive as was anticipated,[17] though the Commissioner was very robust in the few cases he had to deal with.[18]

The PCA Select Committee conducted an extensive inquiry into the workings of the Access to Government Information Code in the 1995-96 Session, and reported in March 1996. The committee endorsed the ombudsman/information commissioner model for external review of Freedom of Information complaints, but went on to recommend a Freedom of Information Act.[19] The Labour Party's general election manifesto contained a commitment to a Freedom of Information Act[20] and the new government published its proposals in a White Paper at the end of 1997.[1] Although these proposals envisage that an Information Commissioner will be set up separately from the PCA's office, there is no doubt that the introduction of statutory rights to

15 PCA *Sixth Report* (HC 307, 1994-95) p 37.
16 *Open Government*, 1993 (Cm 2290).
17 See PCA Second Report, 1994-95 *Access to Official Information: the First Eight Months* (HC 91, 1994-95); also PCA *Annual Report for 1995* (HC 296, 1995-96) p 5 and *Annual Report for 1996* (HC 386, 1996-97) p 32.
18 PCA *Annual Report for 1995* (HC 296, 1995-96) pp 47-52 and *Annual Report for 1996* (HC 386, 1996-97) pp 28-33.
19 Second Report from the PCA Select Committee *Open Government* (HC 84, 1995-96) paras 109 and 126.
20 The Labour Party *Because Britain Deserves Better* (1997) p 33.
1   1997 (Cm 3818) *Your Right to Know: the Government's Proposals for a Freedom of Information Act*.

official information will have a significant effect upon British administrative culture. How this will affect the type and number of cases coming to the PCA remains to be seen.

As well as the official information role given to him by government in 1993, the PCA has since 1974 also had a special role in relation to the National Health Service. In that year, with the establishment of the health service ombudsman schemes, the three Health Service Commission (HSC) offices[2] and that of the PCA have been held by the same person in plurality. This arrangement has continued with the most recent appointment of Mr Michael Buckley, who succeeded Sir William Reid in January 1997. Following the report of the Wilson Committee in May 1994,[3] the NHS complaints system has undergone a major restructuring, which included significant extensions to the HSC's jurisdiction so as to remove the exclusion of complaints involving matters of clinical judgement and complaints about family practitioner services and the creation of an integrated NHS complaints system. The necessary legislation was passed in 1996 and the new arrangements came into effect on 1 April of that year.[4]

It is not yet clear what the effect of the new NHS complaints system will be on the volume of complaints reaching the HSC. The extension of jurisdiction could lead to a significant increase; the introduction of the two-stage procedure and the requirement that the HSC must be satisfied that these complaints procedures have been invoked and exhausted before accepting a complaint may lead to a reduction.

So the PCA is entering into a period of uncertainty in terms of these linkages with health service and open government cases. Changes here could bring to an end the arrangement by which the same individual has been able to hold these offices in plurality. And that, in turn, could lead to quite significant changes in the PCA's way of working. Even more significant changes might follow if the Labour government's modernisation programme includes the abolition of the MP filter, thus allowing citizens direct access to the Parliamentary Ombudsman.

Conclusion

In this chapter we have reviewed the evolution of the United Kingdom Parliamentary Ombudsman scheme in the light of growing interest in different forms of alternative dispute resolution. We have seen that, in spite of initial opposition to the very idea of an ombudsman in Britain, the 1976 Act did enable the Ombudsman institution to take root and develop and that the PCA has demonstrated an impressive ability to achieve governmental compliance with his recommendations. Anxieties about the doctrine of ministerial responsibility, the concept of maladministration and limited jurisdiction have been largely overcome. Concerns about accountability have been met with the development of the select committee and limited judicial review but doubts about access, and particularly the MP filter, remain.

---

2   The legislation established separate offices for England, Wales and Scotland: National Health Service (Scotland) Act 1972 and National Health Service Reorganisation Act 1973, subsequently consolidated as the Health Service Commissioners Act 1993.
3   Department of Health *Being Heard* (May 1994).
4   Health Service Commissioners (Amendment) Act 1996.

Developments in regard to open government, NHS reforms and the possible removal of the MP filter could bring significant changes, but the British PCA scheme has already proved its worth as an adaptation of the ombudsman concept to a political culture which preferred political to legal/judicial methods of resolving individual citizen's grievances and complaints about administrative action. The initial caution of the 1967 Act has been justified by the way in which the scheme has not only become established but has been used as a pattern for other public- and private-sector schemes. Thirty years on, we may be moving into a period in which legal/judicial methods are perceived by some to be more attractive. Others are attracted by alternative forms of dispute resolution. In such a climate, the Parliamentary Ombudsman scheme may be viewed as a valuable bridge between the unpredictability of the political process and the more rule-based culture of the independent arbitrator.

Chapter IX

Hansard and the interpretation of statutes

Geoffrey Marshall

The common law rule

Until 1992 the English common law system rejected the explicit recourse to legislative materials as evidence of legislative intention for the purpose of interpreting statutes. Since the common law rule excluding such materials has been changed by the House of Lords and in part abandoned, it is worth reflecting a little on the historical and constitutional bases of the principle that it embodied. From the thirteenth to the sixteenth century in England, statutory interpretation passed through several stages. At first, the idea that the law-maker was the best interpreter was encouraged by the fact that legislation was the work of the King and a small group of councillors and judges. Hengham CJ needed no gloss on the statute because he had played his part in its making. If judges did not know what the law-makers intended, they could consult their colleagues. In 1366 Thorpe CJ and a fellow judge 'went together to the council where there were a good dozen bishops and earls and asked those who made the statute what it meant. The archbishop told them what the statute meant'.[1]

The development of parliamentary legislation changed this intimate relationship of legislator and adjudicator. Statutes became more detailed legislative texts. The judges came to see themselves, not as councillors, but as a body independent of both the legislature and executive. They began to develop a body of rules for the exposition and interpretation of the statute law.[2]

They could not find guidance in reported proceedings, since there were no official reports of debates. Indeed, it was an unlawful breach of privilege to make such reports. The journals of the two Houses contained a history of the formal stages of Bills and the amendments made in the course of their passage. But these records were held inadmissible for purposes of interpretation. 'The sense and meaning of an Act of Parliament', it was supposed, 'must be collected from what it says . . . not from the history of changes it underwent in the House where it took its rise. That history is not known to the other House or to the Sovereign'.[3] So the exclusion of the courts from

---

1 T F T Plucknett *A Concise History of the Common Law* (2nd edn, 1936) p 293. See also W Holdsworth *A History of English Law* (1924) vol 2, p 308.

2 See S E Thorne's Introduction to *A Discourse on the Exposition and Understanding of Statutes* (1942) p 8, and T F T Plucknett *Statutes and their Interpretation in the First Half of the Fourteenth Century* (1922).

3 *Millar v Taylor* (1769) 4 Burr 2303 at 2332.

parliamentary inquiry owes something to the conscious growth of a separation of powers. It takes something also from parliamentary privilege and perhaps something from the doctrine of the sovereignty of the Queen-in-Parliament. In expounding that doctrine in the nineteenth century, it was held that when an Act had received the royal assent, 'no court of justice can inquire into the manner in which it was introduced into Parliament, what was done previously to its being introduced, or what passed in Parliament during the various stages of its progress through both Houses'.[4]

Though the rules of interpretation as they developed in the nineteenth century alluded frequently to the principle that a statute was to be expounded 'according to the intent of them that made it', it was equally asserted that the legislature must be presumed to have intended what they have actually expressed and that 'the object of all interpretation of statutes is to determine what intention is conveyed, either expressly or implicitly, by the language used'.[5] The conclusion gets some reinforcement from the idea of Parliament as a formal aggregate of the three estates of the realm, each estate independent of the other. There is thus no common intention. The meaning attached to statutory words by individual members of the three estates cannot control or be authoritative as to the construction of them.[6] That view was sometimes expressed in the Privy Council, particularly by Lord Haldane, and may have influenced some Commonwealth judges. So, in South Africa in 1951, it was said that:

> Evidence that every member who voted for a measure put a certain construction upon it cannot affect the meaning which the courts must place upon the statute.

The sovereign will, it is added, is the product not of a number of individuals but of an impersonal Parliament. Parliament –

> is an abstract concept. Its sovereign powers are exercised by human beings, but that does not make them individually or jointly sovereign. Legislative powers were conferred on Parliament, not on them.[7]

Perhaps the idea owes something also to Professor A V Dicey's exposition of the rule of law.[8] The authority of the courts, he thought, was emphasised by the fact that Parliament, though sovereign, could speak only through the joint action of its constituent parts and in no other way. The coexistence of two legislative chambers with the Crown prevents the confusion of resolutions of either House with laws.[9] Dicey rightly thought this to be an important principle, where one chamber dominated the other and that chamber had come to be dominated and controlled by the executive government. It remains in the United Kingdom essential to remind the members of the majority in the House of Commons that they are not Parliament. The views of

---

4   *Edinburgh and Dalkeith Rly Co v Wauchope* (1842) 8 Cl & F in 710 at 724-725.
5   *Re Mew and Thorne* (1862) 31 LJBcy 87.
6   *Dean of York's case* (1841) 2 QB 1.
7   *Swart and Nicol v de Kock and Garner* 1951 (3) SA 589 at 621.
8   A V Dicey *Introduction to the Study of the Law of the Constitution* (10th edn, 1959) E C S Wade chs IV and XIII.
9   Or even *both* Houses, since the Commons and Lords are not in themselves Parliament. In the United States it is easier for the Senate and the House of Representatives to think of themselves as the Congress of the United States, since that is what Article One of the Constitution says they are.

ministers, accordingly, are of no more consequence than those of individual members. This is what gives force to Lord Simonds's objection to Lord Denning's assertion that 'we sit here to find out the intention of Parliament and of ministers and carry it out'.[10] This, Lord Simonds said, was 'a grave misconception':

> The general proposition that it is the duty of the court to find out the intention of Parliament – and not only of Parliament but of ministers also – cannot by any means be supported. The duty of the court is to interpret the words that the legislature has used.[11]

Discussion of the practical utility of the rule against admission of parliamentary debates and proceedings has tended to focus on the potential burden of time and expense imported into litigation, and on the possibilities of abuse by legislators and committees who may be tempted deliberately or tendentiously to create legislative history favouring particular interests and insert it into the record. The report of the English and Scottish Law Commissions in 1969, which refrained from recommending a relaxation of the rule, cited the critical comment of an American author on the unreliability of much of the material resorted to by courts that are seen to be 'fumbling about in the ashcans of the legislative process for the shoddiest unenacted expressions of intention'.[12] The report also remarked on the difficulties faced by those to whom the law is addressed.

> The citizen or the practitioner whom he consults may have a heavy burden placed on him if the context in which a statute is to be understood requires reference to materials which are not readily available without unreasonable inconvenience or expense.

That principle has been judicially noted even in relation to legislation giving effect to international conventions where the rule against admission of *travaux préparatoires* is relaxed. In *Fothergill v Monarch Airlines Ltd*[13] the meaning of 'damage to baggage' under art 26 of the Warsaw Convention on carriage by air was in issue and it was sought to introduce, as an aid to construction, the minutes of the working meetings in 1955 at which the Hague Protocol was negotiated. The House of Lords did not find it necessary to rely on these convention materials. Lord Wilberforce thought they should be admitted only if such material was public and accessible. Lord Diplock said that it would be 'a confidence trick by Parliament and destructive of all legal certainty' if citizens could not rely on the words of an enactment, but had to 'search through all that had happened before and in the course of the legislative process'. 'The source to which Parliament must have intended the citizen to refer',

---

10 *Magor and St Mellons RDC v Newport Corpn* [1950] 2 All ER 1226 at 1236.
11 *Magor and St Mellons RDC v Newport Corpn* [1952] AC 189 at 191. Lord Simonds's sentiment might be compared with that once expressed by Holmes J: 'We do not inquire what the legislature meant; we ask only what the statute means': 'The Theory of Legal Interpretation' (1899) 12 Harv LR 417.
12 C P Curtis 'A Better Theory of Legal Interpretation' (1949) Record of the Association of the Bar of the City of New York 321. It is noticeable that in recent years the US Supreme Court has been less favourably inclined towards the use of legislative materials in statutory interpretation. See eg *Immigration and Naturalisation Service v Cardoza-Fonseca* 480 US 421 (1987); *Thompson v Thompson* 484 US 174 (1988); *Mackey v Lanier Collection Agency and Serv* 486 US 825 (1988).
13 [1981] AC 251.

he added, 'is the language of the Act itself. These are the words which Parliament has itself approved as accurately expressing its intention'.[14]

To some degree, criticism of the rule against *travaux préparatoires* between the wars and after 1945 tended to be part of a wider attack on judicial practice in the United Kingdom which liberal critics tended to see as conservative in its implications because 'formal' or 'literal' or 'mechanical' or 'restrictive' in its technique. It was argued that such techniques often frustrated the true intention of the legislature and that less formal or restrictive rules of interpretation would promote progress and the general welfare. After several decades of conservative legislation, liberals may have become less eager to see the actual intentions of conservative policy-makers given full expression, and perhaps less ready to equate 'literalism' with illiberalism or the search for legislative intention with the avoidance of absurdity and the furtherance of justice. In any event, the British judiciary over the same period has adapted its techniques and cannot now be said to be universally formal or literal in its approach to statutory interpretation.

The decision in *Pepper v Hart*

On 26 November 1992 the rule that what has been said in Parliament may not be cited as direct evidence of the meaning of a statute was modified and greatly relaxed. In *Pepper v Hart*[15] the House of Lords showed itself prepared to treat as authoritative the words of at least some legislators, namely ministers or promoters of Bills. Their views, it was said, could now be cited as an aid to statutory construction where legislation is ambiguous or obscure, or leads to absurdity, and provided that the legislative pronouncements in question are clear.

The issue in *Pepper v Hart* was the monetary value to be attached to the benefits in kind resulting from a concessionary scheme under which members of the staff of a fee-paying school were allowed to have their children educated at one-fifth of the fees charged to parents of other pupils. Similar benefits are available to the employees of many service industries such as airlines, railways and hotels, which supply their employees with concessionary tickets or facilities. An amount equal to the cash equivalent of the benefit is treated by s 63 of the Finance Act 1976 as a taxable emolument. One obvious assessment of the amount of the notional advantage enjoyed by the beneficiaries of the concessionary fees scheme or by concessionary ticket users might perhaps seem to be the difference between the fees or fares paid by them and the amount paid by ordinary passengers or full fee-paying users of the school or service. However, the Act stipulates that the cash equivalent is to be an amount equal to the cost of the benefit, and the cost of the benefit is deemed to be the amount of any expense incurred in or in connection with its provision.

This statutory language could be interpreted in a number of ways. If, as in *Pepper v Hart*, the places filled under the concessionary scheme were surplus places that would not otherwise have been filled at all (or in an airlines case, tickets that would not otherwise have been used – though presumably not every concessionary facility is of this character), the cost of supplying the benefit could be said to be the additional

14   Ibid at 279, 280.
15   [1993] AC 593. See also *Melluish v BMI (No 3) Ltd* [1996] AC 454.

cost of supplying the extra places. This was the view taken by Lord Griffiths and the Lord Chancellor without benefit of Hansard. In the Lord Chancellor's opinion, the expense incurred in providing the benefits was nil. Lord Oliver, Lord Bridge and Lord Browne-Wilkinson, on the other hand, took the view that the cost of the services provided was not the minimal cost of the extra places, but the total cost of supplying the service, divided by the total number of persons using them. What dissuaded them from this opinion, however, was the discovery that, during the parliamentary consideration of the clauses in question at the committee stage of the Finance Bill, the Financial Secretary to the Treasury had said in reply to a question about school fees that, since a clause proposing to tax concessionary benefits at the open market price charged to the public had been withdrawn, so-called in-house benefits would be taxed on the basis of the cost to the employer of providing the benefit. That in itself did not resolve the ambiguity of the phrase 'cost to the employer'. But the minister added that the cost would either be nil or very small. In effect, he was offering to the committee his own interpretation of the meaning of s 63 of the 1976 Act and offering it to members who wished to have that particular view affirmed. (Members who put questions of this kind to ministers in Committee proceedings are not, it must be remembered, putting them with the disinterested objective of clarifying the meaning of legislation. They are generally moved by constituency or pressure group interests and wish to urge the minister in a direction favourable to those interests.)

All of their Lordships, except for the Lord Chancellor, took the view that the rule excluding reference to parliamentary materials should be relaxed. All of them also rejected the view that parliamentary privilege might bar the scrutiny and citation of Hansard when this was done for the purpose of discovering legislative intention. That point, it might indeed be thought, ought not to be in doubt. What parliamentary privilege and art 9 of the 1689 Bill of Rights do is to protect members of Parliament from the imposition of criminal or civil penalties that might arise from what is said by them in the legislature. In this sense, their words are absolutely privileged and it is in this sense that what they say may not be 'questioned or impeached in any court or place out of Parliament'. Such fears might – however implausibly – be relevant where actions are being pursued against members or Ministers. In *Church of Scientology of California v Johnson-Smith*[16] the plaintiff in a libel action was refused leave to introduce evidence of what the defendant had said in the House of Commons; and in *R v Secretary of State for Trade, ex p Anderson Strathclyde plc*[17] an applicant for judicial review unsuccessfully sought to use parliamentary materials to support a factual point. But no conceivable threat, or questioning of any member's speech, is entailed in a scrutiny of legislative procedures for the purpose of interpreting the words of a statute, where no proceedings against members or ministers are in question. The words in the Bill of Rights 1689 that ban questioning or impeaching legislative speech are repeated in art 1 of the Constitution of the United States, where citation of legislative materials is permissible, and no one has ever thought that this freedom of debate clause had any bearing on their admissibility. No one, indeed, might have thought that it had any relevance here had not the Attorney General suggested that any citation of Hansard for the purpose of construing an Act would

---

16 [1972] 1 QB 522.
17 [1983] 2 All ER 233.

constitute a questioning of proceedings in the House, since it would involve an investigation of what the minister or member intended by the words used, and might thus intimidate him in what he might say by attributing legislative effect to his words.[18]   This seems to imply a peculiarly wide notion of questioning and an implausible view of the psychology of members of Parliament, who are more likely to be stimulated than deterred by the thought that their utterances might be treated as important or possessed of legislative significance. Fear of having their words quoted is not one of the major characteristics of the average legislator. 'Questioning', obviously, cannot be given so broad a meaning. As Lord Browne-Wilkinson pointed out, art 9 of the Bill of Rights forbids questioning not only 'in any court' but 'in any place out of Parliament' and it can hardly be supposed that all questioning of the words of members of Parliament by citizens or political commentators is prohibited. (That, indeed, is confirmed by decisions of the Commons Privileges Committee, which has treated only a narrowly defined category of words that tend to obstruct the working of the house as constructive contempts.) In relation to statutory construction, the purpose of citation, if it is allowed, is not to obstruct the House but to further the purposes of the legislature and not to question its independence but to give effect to what has been done.

So the notion that parliamentary privilege provides no obstacle to citation of parliamentary proceedings is plainly right. But whether other constitutional principles ought to rule it out raises wider issues.

The consequences of *Pepper v Hart*

Pepper v Hart posed not only practical questions about what goes on in Parliament and in the courts and the legal profession, but also issues of principle and constitutional theory about the relations between legislature and judiciary. It might be said that philosophical questions come into it as well, since the interpretation of statutes (like the interpretation of anything) invites differences of view about the nature of meaning, intention and rule-governed behaviour. Some particular queries that obviously arise are:

1. *What brought it on?* What were the immediate and less immediate predisposing causes that led to so profound a change of attitude? Some may not think it so profound, but it is.
2. *What exactly did the case decide?* Are the *Pepper v Hart* rules themselves ambiguous, obscure or productive of absurdity?
3. *What has happened since in the courts?* What has been the consequence of the partial exclusion of the exclusionary rule for parliamentary material?
4. *What has happened in Parliament and government?* How has the behaviour of ministers, members of parliament and parliamentary draftsmen been affected by the new régime?
5. *What has happened in the legal profession outside Parliament?*
6. *Who has benefited?* Which of the above are better off? Are judges? Are MPs? Are ministers? Are draftsmen? Are counsel and solicitors? Are litigants?

18   [1992] 3 WLR 1032 at 1059.

We might add:

7. *Has it affected the constitution for better or for worse?*

Antecedents

The jettisoning of the existing rule came on, like many other things, in two ways: gradually and then suddenly. When the Interpretation of Legislation Bill was debated in 1981 there was strong opposition to the admission of parliamentary materials. In 1989 in the House of Lords debate[19] there was a division of opinion, but opposition to the abolition of the exclusionary rule was expressed by Lord Renton, Lord Donaldson and the Lord Chancellor amongst others. The cases immediately preceding *Pepper v Hart* were of a rather special kind. In *Pickstone v Freemans plc*[20] the recourse to Hansard came about because it was relevant to show that a particular provision had been introduced to give effect to community legislation and so it was perhaps peculiarly relevant as evidence of legislative purpose. Many commentators have pointed out that the adoption of a purposive style of interpretation had been acknowledged for some time, and this has in some people's minds been associated with an opposition to supposedly rigid exclusionary rules affecting the derivation of parliamentary intention. Lord Lester, for example, has linked the exclusionary rule with the 'arid wasteland' in which the Victorian law lords and their successors held fast to binding rules of precedent and literal rules of interpretation.[1] He may not have blamed it all on Dicey, but others have. This association of the exclusionary rule with literalism, or semanticism (or even positivism) rests on a confusion of thought of massive proportions, but if it is a confusion that can attack Lord Lester, it can affect the judicial members of the House of Lords and it would seem that it may have. At any rate, it is suggested that, with *Pepper v Hart*, we have seen what Lord Lester describes as the breaking of the ice – the post-Victorian Dicey ice, that is. He also suggested that there has been a powerful European legal influence and that familiarity with the decisions of the European Court of Justice and the European Court of Human Rights has made British judges increasingly aware of the advantages of considering the object and purpose of legislation 'in place of a literal interpretation' (though 'purposive' interpretation is not inconsistent with deriving the meaning of a statutory provision from the statute itself, and considering the words of the statute does not necessarily involve the use of narrow or literal construction).

In the end, *Pepper v Hart* may have been too readily prompted, in part at least – as some judicial departures are – by an attempt to achieve justice in a particular case, and also by a suspicion that the Inland Revenue were defeating the legitimate expectations of the deserving but impoverished middle classes. It may even be true that the House of Lords were prepared to hear argument on the admissibility of parliamentary material because some Law Lords suspected that Revenue officials

---

19   513 HL Deb 18 January 1989, cols 278-307.
20   [1989] AC 66.
 1   'Pepper v Hart Revisited' 15 Statute Law Review 10 at 12 and 'English Judges as Lawmakers' [1993] PL 269 at 272.

were prone to resile from ministerial statements as to the effect of tax provisions[2] and had done so in the instant case.

The Pepper v Hart *rules*

What *Pepper v Hart* has decided could be put in the form of a series of negative propositions as to when parliamentary materials must still be excluded. They must be excluded:

(a) When there is no ambiguity or obscurity or absurdity entailed in giving the words of the statute a meaning that can be convincingly derived from considering the terms of the provision in question in the light both of its immediate context and of the whole statute.

(b) When, although consideration in the light of the statute as a whole fails to resolve an ambiguity or obscurity, the only relevant statements in the course of legislative proceedings are those of persons other than a minister in charge of the Bill in question or of a promoter of the Bill.

(c) When relevant statements have been made by a minister or promoter of the Bill but they are unclear or do not unambiguously clarify the point at issue, or are not directly related to it.

(d) When relevant statements have been made by a minister or promoter but they have been rendered inapplicable by subsequent changes in the terms of the legislation or have been subsequently withdrawn.

Thus, it is clear that in principle the régime of *Pepper v Hart* is a fairly severe one. The rules have a lexical order. Parliamentary materials should not be brought to bear on the question at issue until it has been determined that an ambiguity or obscurity exists. An ambiguity or obscurity does not exist merely because a provision is capable of bearing two meanings or because different courts have reached different conclusions. Nor should parliamentary material be admitted to suggest or create an ambiguity or obscurity. Otherwise, it would be legitimate and necessary to consider such materials in every case. The rules are not directed to the purpose of assessing the evidentiary weight of parliamentary materials, but to the question of their admissibility.

Moreover, the rules imply that counsel must not merely (when permitted to do so) cite the relevant statements, but be in a position to aver that they have not been modified or affected by any subsequent changes in either House at any stage of the legislative proceedings or on other relevant occasions such as parliamentary questions. This duty to demonstrate a negative proposition is an obligation of a fairly high order. Will it do to say 'I looked wherever I thought it might be necessary to look but I found nothing'?

Decisions since Pepper v Hart

Since *Pepper v Hart*, references to Hansard have been made in a large number of cases, many not reported. Attempts to use parliamentary material to persuade a court

---

2   See T St J Bates 'The Contemporary Use of Legislative History in the United Kingdom' (1995) 54(1) CLJ 127 at 129 (quoting Moses QC, one of the Revenue counsel in *Pepper v Hart*).

to depart from an earlier binding precedent have in at least one case been rebuffed,[3] but in three cases in the House of Lords in 1993 reference to Hansard was permitted and seems to have been thought decisive. In *Stubbings v Webb*[4] the material was used to demonstrate that a statute had been passed to give effect to earlier committee recommendations. In that case Lord Griffiths said:

> Lord Denning MR in *Letang v Cooper* . . . was not prepared to assume that Parliament did give effect to the Tucker Committee's recommendations, but we can now look at Hansard and see that it was the express intention of Parliament to do so.

(The result in this case was to overturn a decision of the Court of Appeal and to deprive a plaintiff of a remedy there obtained.) In *R v Warwickshire County Council*[5] it was said that the conclusion arrived at could have been reached without recourse to the relevant ministerial speech. This implies that the provision at issue was not ambiguous and raises the question why the material was admitted at all. In *Chief Adjudication Officer v Foster*[6] the material was used rather oddly to support the view that a regulation was intra vires because it had been used in a way that Parliament had authorised having had the matter explained to it. This seems a dangerous inference from acquiescence. Members of Parliament may or may not have accepted the minister's account of his intentions. Perhaps they wanted to disagree but could not get into the debate to say so. Perhaps they were not there at all when the minister made his statement and never heard it. This, of course, is a general point about inferring the intentions of 650 members (let alone of both Houses and the Crown) from the opinion of one governmental promoter. Similar scepticism might be provoked by the assertion in *Monckton v Lord Advocate*[7] that it might be appropriate to refer to a statement by the Attorney General even if he were not promoting a Bill before the House but putting forward objections to it.

---

3   See eg *Re Bishopgate Investment Management Ltd* [1993] Ch 452. *Pepper v Hart* materials have also been excluded on the ground of absence of ambiguity (*R v Secretary of State for the Home Department, ex p Okello* [1993] Imm AR 531; *DPP v Bull* [1995] QB 88); on the ground that a minister's speech was lacking in clarity (*Doncaster Borough Council v Secretary of State for the Environment* (1992) 91 LGR 459, CA); and on the ground that the materials sought to be introduced were not directed to the specific statutory provision in issue, so that the ministerial statements required interpretation (*Melluish v BMI (No 3) Ltd* [1996] AC 454) (Lord Browne-Wilkinson said in this case that such improper use of the *Pepper v Hart* rules should be checked by orders for costs against the offending party).

4   [1993] AC 498. Courts in Scotland appear to have accepted the *Pepper v Hart* principle. See eg *Short's Trustee v Keeper of the Registers of Scotland* 1994 SLT 65, where extensive reference was made to the reports of two legislative committees which had made recommendations prior to the enactment of the Land Registration (Scotland) Act 1979. In another Scottish case, *AIB Finance v Bank of Scotland* 1995 SLT 2 at 7, Lord Ross said: 'I am doubtful whether in this instance it is legitimate to consider the Hansard Report because I do not think that there is ambiguity or obscurity in the statute.'

5   [1993] AC 583.

6   [1993] AC 754. Cf *Three Rivers District Council v Governor and Company of the Bank of England* (1996) Times, 8 January, where it was suggested that the strict criteria for admissibility laid down in *Pepper v Hart* do not apply when the court is considering the purpose or object of a statute for some reason other than the construction of a particular statutory provision, eg to discover why an Act has been passed or why a particular section has been added to it. (See *Holden & Co v Crown Prosecution Service (No 2)* [1994] 1 AC 22 at 37.)

7   (1994) Times, 12 May.

R v Secretary of State for Foreign and Commonwealth Affairs, ex p Rees-Mogg[8] also raised an issue about the significance of ministerial pronouncements and what they can be used to show. Two ministerial statements were introduced and it was said that they would have been resorted to if necessary if the provisions in question had been ambiguous (so why were they admitted?). David Pannick QC argued that a ministerial statement relied upon by the Crown was based on the advice of the Attorney General, which was wrong. The court said that to allow him to argue that would undermine the use of *Pepper v Hart*. It did not matter if the minister was wrong, or what the source of his advice was, since the point of the citation was to show what the House intended. But perhaps contradiction of a minister's statement and advice might go to the House's intention, since it would presumably not wish to act on mistaken ministerial advice. It is unclear in the *Rees-Mogg* case at what point the court thought that there might be *Pepper v Hart* ambiguity. It was said that there was no ambiguity, but counsel for the Crown 'invited us to look at Hansard in order to resolve the ambiguity'. What exactly did he invite them to do? To look and see if there was an ambiguity? Or, in case there might be an ambiguity, to look? Or did they decide, after he invited them, and after they accepted his invitation, that there was no ambiguity? Or did they know that already? If so, why look?

The Practice Note issued in 1995[9] states that any party intending to refer to any extract from Hansard in support of any such argument as is permitted by the decisions in *Pepper v Hart* and *Pickstone v Freemans plc* must, unless the judge otherwise decides, serve upon all other parties and the court, copies of any such extracts together with a brief summary of the argument intended to be based upon such extract – this to be done not less than five clear working days before the first day of the hearing. But how is any party to know before the court is seized of the case whether the argument is permitted by the decision in *Pepper v Hart* or not, since that cannot be determined until the court has reached the conclusion that a relevant provision is ambiguous or obscure? When the extracts are served on the court, should the judge keep them under lock and key until he has heard arguments based on the statute and not permit reference by the parties to the proceedings until he has concluded that irremovable ambiguity exists?

Parliamentary and governmental reactions

The decision in *Pepper v Hart* provoked Lord Renton in the House of Lords to ask Her Majesty's Government in December 1993 'whether they would confirm that speeches made by ministers of the Crown do not amplify, amend or interpret legislation'. He added that he thought the use of ministerial statements in order to supplement Acts of Parliament was a dangerous practice.[10] In reply, the Lord Advocate said that it was necessary at all times for parliamentary draftsmen to continue to strive as far as possible to encapsulate the desired policy in the words of the statute. He did not say whether he agreed with Lord Renton's assessment of the situation in which the draftsman's strivings had failed and the policy had not

8   [1994] 1 All ER 457.
9   [1995] 1 All ER 234.
10   HL Deb vol 550, 8 December 1953, cols 942, 943.

been encapsulated with complete clarity. Lord Bruce of Donington thought that that situation would prevail more frequently in future because of 'the growing ambiguities, preambles and recitals ad infinitum of European legislation'.

In March 1994, it was announced in the House of Commons[11] that the implications of the decision in *Pepper v Hart* had been considered by an inter-departmental committee and that a number of practical steps for the avoidance or correction of mistakes or ambiguities arising out of ministerial statements during the passage of legislation had been put into practice by guidance to departments on legislative procedures. Issues concerning the cost of litigation were being taken up with legal practitioners' governing bodies throughout the United Kingdom. The costs in question involved the availability of Hansard and thought had been given to the expense that might be incurred by those outside government in tracing the relevant legislative proceedings and the ways in which this might be kept to a minimum. One obvious way of lowering the cost of consulting Hansard would be to lower its now exorbitant price, but no moves in that direction have been detectable. The reported conclusions of the inter-departmental committee seem to be largely directed towards correcting ministerial misstatements during the passage of a Bill. If it proved necessary to correct any ambiguity or error in such statements, the aim, it was said, was to do this as promptly as possible at an appropriate point during the further consideration of the bill. It would be interesting to know what the conclusions of the committee were as to the procedures to be adopted for avoiding ministerial errors in the first place and for advising ministers on the extent to which they should respond to invitations in the House from representatives of particular interest groups to make statements about particular provisions in Bills, and whether they should do so by stating the government's intention or policy in general terms or by seeking to draw conclusions about the ambit or application of particular provisions in the legislation, or offering opinions about whether particular factual situations would be covered by them.

It seems likely, therefore, that one effect of *Pepper v Hart* is that more effort will be put into checking of ministers' briefing materials when they are introducing legislation and also into reviewing related material such as ministers' written replies to members' questions and press releases made on ministerial authority, particularly by the Inland Revenue and Customs and Excise on income tax and VAT. Such documents and explanatory leaflets are always accompanied by disclaimers as to their intended legal effect, but one consequence of *Pepper v Hart* is precisely to give potential legal effect to ministerial and departmental intentions and understandings about the legislative provisions that they are promoting and sponsoring.

Some dangers are as yet not apparent but might be imagined. It could be supposed that the opportunity offered to the Executive to fill out the purposes of legislative provisions by statements in the House could lead to less precisely drafted legislation or to a looser or more simplified form of enactment being adopted.

American debaters on the use of congressional materials have often complained about the possibility of interested parties devoting themselves to stuffing the legislative record with statements that may later be cited as evidence of legislative

---

11   HC Deb vol 239, 7 March 1994, written answers col 70 and 17 March 1994, written answers col 762.

purpose ('raking through the ashcans of the legislative process'). This is limited by the *Pepper v Hart* rules, since only the governmental or private promoters of legislation are treated as authoritative sources. But it is possible for ministers to be urged or pressed into making statements in the heat of debate that can serve the purposes of those who wish to see a particular emphasis or slant put upon an enactment.

Now that the ice has been broken, or the floodgates forced ajar, possible extensions of the *Pepper v Hart* régime seem not beyond the bounds of possibility. The supposition inherent in it that the effect of unclear legislative provisions can properly be assessed by looking to what ministers say they intended to do in introducing legislation raises the question why that intention should not be worthy of citation after the legislation has been introduced and after litigation on it has begun. It would seem absurd to propose that ministers should be able to be called to give expert evidence as to what they intended to do when the effect of the legislation is in dispute in a legal proceeding (especially if the legal proceeding involves some branch of government itself). But if the basic philosophy of *Pepper v Hart* is correct (why guess when you can read the book? why speculate about intention when you can discover it directly, etc?) then why is it absurd to look backwards as well as forwards or to reopen the book after the last page has been turned?

Extra-parliamentary consequences

The difficulty of consulting the relevant materials, particularly the standing committee proceedings, in all parts of the United Kingdom, is obvious. It may be that electronic searching will alleviate a part of this difficulty, but there remains a problem about the indeterminate scope of the research needed to discharge the duty of assuring the court that any relevant material that the search uncovers has not been modified or affected by subsequent statements or changes made at any later stage in the legislative process. As far as debate on the floor of both Houses goes, the relevant Hansard references could be more widely published in reference publications as they are in Current Law Statutes. The perusal of standing committee references is at present a laborious and awkward process, since the numbering of the clauses which end up as a particular section of a Bill is liable to change at various stages as amendments are introduced and there is no present shortcut that will avoid, in the case of recent legislation, lengthy searching through unbound and sometimes disintegrating cardboard boxes in search of what may turn out to be a speck of false gold rather than a crock of the genuine article.

When it comes to subordinate legislation there is, first of all, the difficulty of discovering whether the instrument has been the subject of any parliamentary proceedings at all. The large number of instruments now issued to give effect to community directives, regulations or court decisions for the most part will not have been. But does the task of looking to promoters' intentions then lead to the scrutiny of *travaux préparatoires* in Brussels (in which British representatives may have participated) in order to resolve ambiguities or obscurities in the instruments designed to give effect to their purposes?

Cost benefit

Perhaps the answers to the question who is better off as the result of *Pepper v Hart* are: judges – possibly; MPs – yes; ministers – yes (well, perhaps); draftsmen – no; counsel and solicitors – no; litigants – no; the Constitution – no. The last point deserves to be enlarged upon, since the case against the use of legislative history is simple, well-known and based on fundamental constitutional principles. Ironically, the Supreme Court of the United States is moving in the direction of recognising those principles at the very same time that the House of Lords, under the pretence of removing blinkers, is short-sightedly closing its eyes to them.

Pepper v Hart and the constitution

In *Pepper v Hart* Lord Bridge remarked that the courts should not 'continue to wear blinkers when the points which the courts were called upon to resolve had been addressed in the House. The applicant's case should not be rejected on a technical rule of construction'.

This short statement of the case perhaps does not squarely confront the objections, both practical and of constitutional principle, that have been advanced against the use of legislative materials in the United Kingdom (and increasingly in recent times in the United States). The exclusory rule is something more than a mere technical rule of construction. In *Pepper v Hart*, relaxation of the rule may have worked in favour of the citizen, but its abandonment will not always work in favour of individuals who are in conflict with government. Indeed, the interests of litigants and citizens in general may well be better served by the principle that the meaning of the legislative rules by which their conduct is governed should not depend on the carrying out of investigations into materials that are generally inaccessible to them and relatively inaccessible to their legal advisers.

This consideration was adverted to by Lord Oliver, who thought that the door should not readily be opened to the admission of material not available to the citizen. He added that 'Language – and particularly language adopted or concurred in under the pressure of a tight parliamentary timetable – is not always a reliable vehicle for the complete or accurate translation of parliamentary intention.' This seems to imply that the legislators, or some of them, may have intentions that are not fully embodied in the language of the statute at all, because they have been urged or rushed into the job too quickly, or deprived by the parliamentary timetable of opportunities to perform their legislative duties properly. But if this consideration is taken seriously, it is not clear why these imperfectly translated manifestations of intention should be implemented. Nor is it obviously the case that the particular promoter of a Bill, whether official or unofficial, ought to be treated as having authoritative insight into what the intentions of all or a majority of members of Parliament are. Bills are not enacted into law by their promoters, or by ministers. They are not, for that matter, enacted into law by the legislative majorities in the Commons who vote for them, but by the joint tripartite action of the Queen in Parliament. That is why there is an important question begged by the query posed by Lord Griffiths: 'Why . . . cut ourselves off from the one source in which may be found an authoritative statement of the intention with which the legislation is placed before Parliament?' As to what are such statements of intention authoritative? At best, they merely state what a minister or promoter of a Bill intended to bring about. They do not necessarily state the intentions of those who enacted the legislation. Nor do they conclude the question whether what was intended by some or all members of the legislature has been enacted in words that are appropriate to bringing about that result. The reality of the parliamentary process is that ministers are frequently pressed to state what they think will be the effect of the language used in particular provisions. Sometimes they reply that that is a question that must be left to the courts. The future application of the language of legislation is, indeed, a matter for the courts. Once the language has been given legislative form, there is no reason to treat those who are responsible for initiating its enactment as being more expert as to its meaning than anyone else. Considering the meaning of the language is not, of course, a matter of contemplating grammar, semantics or the literal meaning of isolated words. In the judgment of Lord Griffiths, however, there is a supposition that consulting Hansard is the only alternative to a strict constructionist approach or the adoption of a literal use of language. But a repudiation of the use of legislative materials as evidence of meaning does not entail the adoption of a narrowly literalist approach, or a rejection of the idea that the purposes of legislation that can be derived from a consideration of the statute as a whole may condition the meaning given to particular provisions.

In so far as the majority of the House of Lords founded their conclusion on principle, they merely related it to the duty to give effect to the intention of Parliament and they equated this with a purposive (as contrasted with a literalist) approach to interpretation – though no one in recent times has proposed a literal approach to interpretation.[12] They argue that reference should only be permitted to the words of a minister or promoter of a Bill, and not to those of other members of the legislature; that such reference should only take place when there is ambiguity or obscurity, and when the answer derived from the legislative materials is clear. But, as Lord Oliver conceded, the last consideration is particularly problematical. The clear answer may not be the same as the answer that a minister gives when pressed to say something that will satisfy special interests or particular sections of his own party. This point was acknowledged in the Attorney General's submission – namely, that ministerial explanations are often made to satisfy the political requirements of persuasion and debate. For that reason they are not always made in a judicious manner or in an atmosphere of careful ratiocination. A party political debate with the Whips on is not an ideal forum for the impartial consideration of legislative implications. Complex questions may be raised without notice and answers sometimes given without forethought.

The dissenting view of the Lord Chancellor on the constitutional point was motivated by the practicalities of relaxing the restrictive rule. It would, he thought, involve the possibility of an enormous increase in the cost of litigation. Both the English and the Scottish Law Commission's Report in 1969 and that of the Renton

---

12 Nor is it clear what a literal approach would be. See G Williams 'The Meaning of Literal Interpretation' (1981) 131 NLJ 1128; R S Summers and G Marshall 'The Argument from Ordinary Meaning in Statutory Interpretation' (1992) 43 NILQ 213, 215. Cf F Schauer 'Statutory Construction and the Co-ordinating Function of Plain Meaning' (1990) Supreme Court Rev 231.

Committee in 1975 had advised against changing the rule on those grounds, and nothing had been laid before the court to justify the view that their advice was incorrect. Though the majority had restricted the relaxation of the rule to certain specified cases, practically every question of statutory construction could, he said, be brought under at least one of the heads. Certainly, if the head of obscurity can be invoked by using Hansard to support the view that what appears clear in the language of the statute is unclear or problematical, then the restriction is not a genuine one. The opinion of Lord Bridge reveals, in fact, that it was only the admission of the legislative materials that persuaded him to think that an alternative construction was possible. Reference to parliamentary material is also permissible only when a clear statement by a member or promoter exists. But it is not possible to establish whether that condition is fulfilled without first examining all the legislative proceedings to discover what statements have been made and then conducting an argument as to whether these statements are clear. If, therefore, the rules are ineffective in preventing attempts to introduce reference to the legislative materials in virtually every case, no legal adviser will be able to avoid the obligation to examine the parliamentary proceedings or *travaux préparatoires* – whatever the difficulties – in order to discover somewhere some statement that may assist his argument. Moreover, once publicity is given to this possibility, there is likely to be a multiplication of parliamentary attempts to place on the record statements of intention that will serve particular viewpoints and to obtain favourable ministerial answers that can later be cited in litigation.

The reiteration in *Pepper v Hart* of the proposition that it is the duty of the courts to ascertain the intention of Parliament is not conclusive of the issue, since it leaves open the question how that intention is to be ascertained. The traditional rule rests on the supposition that the intention of Parliament is crystallised in and properly derivable from the terms in which it has been enacted. It is possible for legislators, as for anyone else, to intend what they do not say. 'The beliefs or assumptions of those who frame legislation', as the House of Lords said on a former occasion, 'cannot make law'.[13]

Laws are rules that are binding on citizens, and both justice and legal certainly demand that the rules should be ascertainable. Since legislation may now have its origins in legislative proceedings that are ever more voluminous and extended in time and place (including the committee deliberations of European rule-making bodies and international conventions), both expediency and principle unite to support the view that the exclusory rule ought to be maintained.

It rests on the constitutional and rule-of-law proposition that statutory interpretation is not the discovery and implementation of the intentions of legislators. There is no reason why citizens should defer to, or care about, what particular legislators, or for that matter ministers or governments, intended to do in passing legislation; or what they would have done in unforeseen circumstances if they had managed to foresee them. Citizens are governed by laws and not by the wishes of legislators. Once legislators have formalised their policies in the shape of statutory rules, they must be taken to have enacted and intended whatever it is that the language they have adopted means to those who are competent in its use. All statutes have the purpose of giving

---

13 *Kirkness v John Hudson & Co Ltd* [1955] AC 696 at 714.

proper effect to the language used in them, whatever other general purposes may be embodied in them. Citizens and judges should be able to decide what it is that has been enacted from the statutory words, considered in the light of the statute as a whole and the purposes declared on its face. They should not be compelled to trawl, or pay others to trawl, through 'the ashcans of the legislative process' to discover what their rights and obligations are. Nor should constitutionalism and the separation of powers permit members of the executive and legislative branches to interpret the law as well as make it.

Chapter X

Lawyers in Parliament

Michael Rush and Nicholas Baldwin[1]

> There are more entries in the Journals concerning lawyers than concerning all other classes of men combined.[2]

Introduction

In most, if not all, modern legislatures, the largest single occupational group is the legal profession. Until 1992, this was true of the British House of Commons when, for the first time, members of the education profession outnumbered lawyers.[3] Apart from the obvious explanation that lawyers have a professional interest in the making of the law, two types of explanation are usually advanced. The first is that practising the law can easily be combined with being a member of a legislature in terms of time and effort, since historically most legislatures have been part-time rather than full-time institutions and legal practice is similarly flexible. Furthermore, when legislative salaries were either non-existent or low, the law could provide the necessary income to sustain a political career. The second explanation is that the skills required of a lawyer – collating information, preparing and presenting a case – were equally useful in a legislative role. Lastly, but by no means least, lawyers were invariably prominent in the subsequent development of legislatures.

The British Parliament is no exception, although the extensive involvement of lawyers in the House of Lords is, relatively speaking, a more recent development; lawyers have been present in the House of Commons in significant numbers almost from the outset. Indeed, as early as 1330, an attempt was made to exclude lawyers from membership of the House of Commons and in 1372 a statute was passed

---

1   The authors wish to express their grateful thanks to Janet Seaton of the House of Commons Library, who supplied factual data on which the analysis of the parliamentary activity of lawyer-parliamentarians in the 1994-95 parliamentary session is based. The number of lawyer-MPs and lawyer-peers is based on lists kindly supplied by the Bar Council and the Law Society. There were some discrepancies between these lists, both of which included barristers and solicitors, and systematic information on practising and non-practising lawyers was not available. An inclusive list was adopted, but it should be noted that one or two individuals qualified as lawyers, such as Lady Thatcher, were not included.
2   Edward Porritt *The Unreformed House of Commons: Parliamentary Representation Before 1832* (1909) vol I, p 512.
3   The proportion of lawyer-MPs in 1992 was 14.1%, compared with 15.7% teachers – ranging from primary to higher education. The figures for 1997 were 10.9% and 19.1% respectively. If only schoolteachers are counted, however, the proportions were 8.6% in 1992 and 9.9% in 1997.

preventing lawyers from being returned as members.   It was never properly enforced, but the reason for passing it remained – the strong resentment of lawyer-MPs who used their membership of the Commons to advance their professional careers, often to the neglect of their parliamentary duties.[4] The dislike of lawyers-MPs was also voiced by James I when he issued a proclamation urging electors 'not to choose curious and wrangling lawyers, who may seek reputations by stirring needless questions'.[5] None the less, a legal career came to provide an important route to Parliament, acting as an alternative to the most common route of landed wealth, or to other routes, such as securing a wealthy patron or, increasingly during the late eighteenth and the nineteenth century, first- and second-generation industrial wealth. As John Brooke noted in surveying the background of MPs between 1754 and 1790:

> The law was a hard way to social preferment; it required abilities, constant application, and a measure of good luck. But success at the bar made a man's name known and pointed the way to a seat in the House, and it was a line of life where hard work could overcome the disadvantage of humble origins.[6]

Lawyers in the House of Commons

In medieval Parliaments, lawyers always constituted a significant proportion of MPs: data available on known members of Parliament between 1386 and 1407 shows that the average proportion of lawyer-MPs in the 18 Parliaments summoned was 10.6%, and in the 14 Parliaments called between 1410 and 1421, the average was nearly double: 19.7%.[7] Three centuries later, at the end of the seventeenth century, the proportion had declined to 14%.[8] Between 1715 and 1754 about 10% of MPs were practising lawyers, but as many as 25% were legally qualified.[9] However, from 1754 to 1790 the average proportion of lawyer-MPs was 12.5%, rising to 15.9% between 1802 and 1831.[10] In 1832, however, the proportion fell below 10%, but then rose steadily during the rest of the nineteenth century.

---

4   See *Porritt* vol I, pp 512-513 and J S Roskell *The History of Parliament: The House of Commons, 1386-1421* (1992) pp 56-57.
5   D Barrington *On the Statutes* (1768) quoted by *Porritt* p 513.
6   J Brooke 'The Members' in Sir Lewis Namier and J Brooke (eds) *The History of Parliament: The House of Commons, 1754-1790* (1964) p 105.
7   *Roskell* p 171.
8   B D Henry *The History of Parliament: The House of Commons, 1660-1690* (1983) p 10.
9   R Sedgewick *History of Parliament: The House of Commons, 1715-1754*, vol 1 (1970) pp 145 and 155.
10 G P Judd *Members of Parliament, 1734-1832* (1955) pp 51-52 and 88, Appendix 12.

Table X.1: Percentage (and number) of lawyer-MPs 1832-December 1910

Election	Conservative[a]	Liberal	Irish Nat	Total
1832	4.6 (8)	12.0 (53)	–	9.3 (61)
1835	7.7 (21)	10.9 (42)	–	9.6 (63)
1837	10.2 (32)	11.9 (41)	–	11.1 (73)
1841	9.8 (36)	12.9 (35)	–	10.8 (71)
1847	10.8 (35)	14.0 (41)	–	14.6 (96)
1852	13.0 (43)	17.9 (58)	–	15.4 (101)
1857	15.1 (40)	15.6 (59)	–	15.1 (99)
1859	13.8 (41)	16.8 (60)	–	15.4 (101)
1865	11.4 (33)	16.5 (61)	–	14.3 (94)
1868	10.7 (29)	18.1 (70)	–	15.0 (99)
1874	15.1 (53)	25.2 (61)	–	17.5 (114)
1880	13.9 (33)	22.2 (78)	3.2 (2)	17.3 (113)
1885	15.7 (39)	20.1 (64)	13.9 (12)	17.2 (115)
1886	20.6 (81)	26.0 (50)	15.3 (13)	21.5 (144)
1892	22.4 (70)	26.5 (72)	19.7 (16)	23.6 (158)
1895	22.6 (93)	28.2 (50)	14.6 (12)	23.1 (155)
1900	18.9 (76)	24.0 (44)	20.7 (17)	20.4 (137)
1906	17.2 (27)	22.0 (88)	19.3 (16)	19.7 (132)[b]
1910(J)	21.6 (59)	22.9 (63)	24.4 (20)	21.2 (142)
1910(D)	24.3 (66)	22.8 (62)	23.8 (20)	22.1 (148)

Notes: a Including Liberal Unionists 1886-1910.
   b Including one Labour MP.
Source: J A Thomas *The House of Commons, 1832-1901. A Study of its Economic and Functional Character* (1939) pp 14-17 and J A Thomas *The House of Commons, 1906-1911. An Analysis of it Economic and Social Character* (1958) p 44.

As the membership of the House of Commons became more diversified, the proportion of lawyer-MPs settled at about 20%. Until the second of the two elections of 1910, there were always proportionately more lawyers among the Liberals than the Conservatives and this was reflected in the *number* of lawyers in each of the two parties until 1886, when the defection of the Liberal Unionists deprived the Liberals of a significant number of lawyers. It is not surprising, however, that more lawyers should make their political careers in the Liberal Party, since many were self-made men, the beneficiaries of economic expansion and industrialisation.

Table X.2: Percentage (and number) of lawyer-MPs 1918-35

Election	% lawyers	Average 1918-35		
1918	19.7 (150)	Cons	26.5	
1922	22.9 (141)	Lab	7.0	23.0
1923	21.6 (133)	Lib	35.5	
1924	22.4 (138)			
1929	18.5 (114)			
1931	26.8 (165)			
1935	19.3 (119)			

Source: J F S Ross *Parliamentary Representation* (1948).

Comparable data for the period 1918-35 is, unfortunately, not available, but it is clear from the data shown in Table X.2 that the pattern established towards the end of the nineteenth century continued throughout the inter-war period, with about 20% of MPs being lawyers, mostly Conservatives or Liberals. However, what is not clear from the table are the changes resulting from the displacement of the Liberals by Labour as one of the two major parties. The high average proportion of Liberal lawyers rests on a severely declining base – 163 Liberal MPs were elected in 1918, a mere 21 in 1935. Conversely, from 57 seats in 1918 and becoming the official opposition in 1922, Labour peaked at 287 seats in 1929 and had 154 in 1935. The proportion of Labour lawyers was small, but it was a sign of an important change in the Parliamentary Labour Party (PLP): before 1922, Labour MPs were almost exclusively working class; from 1922, there was a growing middle class element in the PLP.[11] However, the proportion of Labour lawyers never matched that of the Liberals, resulting in an overall decline in the number of lawyer-MPs, as shown in Table X.3.

Table X.3: Percentage (and number) of lawyer-MPs 1945-97

Election	Cons	Lab	Lib/LD (nos)	Other (nos)	Total
1945	19.2 (41)	11.7 (46)	4	1	14.4 (92)
1950	20.5 (61)	14.6 (46)	6	1	18.2 (114)
1951	20.6 (66)	13.2 (39)	5	1	17.8 (111)
1955	20.6 (71)	13.3 (37)	5	–	18.1 (114)
1959	21.4 (78)	13.2 (34)	5	–	18.6 (117)
1964	23.4 (71)	12.9 (41)	4	–	18.4 (116)
1966	24.1 (61)	14.1 (51)	3	–	18.2 (115)
1970	19.1 (63)	15.7 (45)	3	–	17.6 (111)
1974(F)	20.5 (61)	12.3 (37)	3	6	16.9 (107)
1974(O)	20.2 (56)	11.9 (38)	3	5	16.1 (102)
1979	20.6 (70)	9.3 (25)	1	–	15.1 (96)
1983	20.6 (82)	8.1 (17)	4	1	16.0 (104)
1987	17.0 (64)	7.9 (18)	5	1	13.5 (88)
1992	19.3 (65)	7.4 (20)	5	2	14.1 (92)
1997	17.0 (28)	8.1 (34)	5	5	10.9 (72)

Sources: C Mellors *The British MP, 1945-74* (1974) and the Nuffield Election (Macmillan) studies.

From 1945 to 1992, the number of lawyer-MPs remained remarkably stable, but there was a sharp fall in 1997, though this probably has more to do with the scale of the Conservative defeat. However, there has been a slow but steady decline in the proportion, from less 20% to the 10.9% elected in 1997. This decline has affected both major parties, but it has been greater in the Labour Party, falling below 10% in

11 See M Rush 'The Members of Parliament' in S A Walkland *The House of Commons in the Twentieth Century* (1979) pp 69-123.

the last five elections. The increase in the *number* of Labour lawyers from 20 to 34 in 1997 needs to be set against that fact that 16 of the newcomers sit for marginal or semi-marginal seats. The reasons for the decline are not clear, but a major factor is probably changes in political career patterns, which will be discussed below.

Table X.4: Percentage (and number) of barristers and solicitors 1945-97

Election	Cons		Lab		Total[a]	
	Bar	*Sol*	*Bar*	*Sol*	*Bar*	*Sol*
1945	17.4 (37)	1.9 (4)	8.7 (34)	3.0 (12)	11.7 (75)	2.7 (17)
1950	17.1 (51)	3.4 (10)	10.8 (34)	3.8 (12)	14.4 (90)	3.8 (24)
1951	17.1 (55)	3.4 (11)	9.8 (29)	3.4 (10)	14.2 (89)	3.5 (22)
1955	17.4 (60)	3.2 (11)	10.1 (28)	3.2 (9)	14.8 (93)	3.3 (21)
1959	18.1 (66)	3.3 (12)	9.7 (25)	3.5 (9)	15.1 (95)	3.5 (22)
1964	19.1 (58)	4.3 (13)	8.5 (27)	4.4 (14)	14.1 (89)	4.3 (27)
1966	19.0 (48)	5.1 (13)	9.1 (33)	5.0 (18)	13.3 (84)	4.9 (31)
1970	15.2 (50)	3.9 (13)	11.5 (33)	4.2 (12)	13.6 (86)	4.0 (25)
1974(F)	16.8 (50)	3.7 (11)	9.0 (27)	3.3 (10)	13.1 (83)	3.8 (24)
1974(O)	17.0 (47)	3.2 (9)	8.8 (28)	3.1 (10)	12.6 (80)	3.5 (22)
1979	15.0 (51)	5.6 (19)	5.6 (15)	3.7 (10)	10.5 (67)	4.6 (29)
1983	14.1 (56)	6.5 (26)	4.3 (9)	3.8 (8)	10.6 (69)	5.4 (35)
1987	11.4 (43)	5.6 (21)	3.9 (9)	3.9 (9)	8.8 (57)	4.8 (31)
1992	12.5 (42)	6.8 (23)	5.5 (15)	1.8 (5)	9.5 (62)	4.6 (30)
1997	10.9 (18)	6.1 (10)	5.0 (21)	3.1 (13)	7.0 (46)	3.9 (26)

Note: a Including parties other than Conservative and Labour.

Sources: C Mellors (op cit) and the Nuffield Election studies.

Systematic data on the number of barristers, as distinct from solicitors, in the House of Commons is not available before 1945, but there is little reason to doubt that barristers have always been the more numerous. Again, the reason is not clear, but it is likely that it reflects the greater flexibility of work and earning power of barristers. Another reason may be that a greater proportion of barristers' work is centred on London than that of solicitors. The distinction between barristers and solicitors may be becoming less important, however, in that there has been a steady fall in the number and proportion of barristers in the House of Commons and a smaller increase in the proportion of solicitors. Moreover, the decline of barristers has been greater in the Labour Party and the increase in solicitors greater among Conservatives. These developments also probably reflect changing career patterns, among both lawyers and politicians. It should also be noted that the lawyer-MP is a largely male preserve: in 1992 only 4.3% (4) of lawyer-MPs were women (three barristers and one solicitor), compared with 9.2% women in the House as a whole. In 1997, however, the proportion of female lawyer-MPs rose to 12.5%, but this was still well below the 18.2% of women MPs as a whole.[12]

12 One other MP, Claire Ward (Labour, Watford) was a trainee solicitor.

The parliamentary activity of lawyer-MPs

The dominance of party in the House of Commons is invariably taken for granted, notwithstanding the growth of back-bench dissent since the late 1960s. Comparisons of the socio-economic backgrounds of back-bench MPs with their parliamentary behaviour have found only limited correlations,[13] although another study found a stronger correlation between when MPs were first elected and their attitudes towards parliamentary reform.[14] Although David Judge found that back-bench MPs specialise to a significant extent, he also found that they vary over time and type of parliamentary activity.[15] Lawyers might be seen as an exception to the general rule, not in the sense that they would be more likely to defy the party whips, but that, as lawyers, they might engage more frequently in business of particular interest to the legal profession or to which they could contribute particular knowledge and experience.

What follows is based on an analysis of the 1994-95 parliamentary session. The figures resulting from this analysis need to be treated with some caution for a number of reasons. First, the number of lawyer-MPs in 1994-95 is relatively small – 91 (one fewer than the number elected in 1992, following the death in February 1995 of Sir Nicholas Fairbairn, Conservative MP for Perth and Kinross) and when this figure is broken down into smaller groups, such as party or barristers and solicitors, the numbers involved are even smaller. Second, 16 of the 91 were ministers and a further 11 were Labour opposition front-benchers, most of whose parliamentary activity is governed by the positions they hold. This reduced the number of members whose activity was analysed to 64, but this figure also includes Liberal Democrat and Plaid Cymru MPs, all of whom performed both front-bench and back-bench roles, but were treated as back-benchers. Third, back-bench MPs do not have control over all their activities. Leaving aside party pressures, they are free agents in tabling motions, amendments to Bills, and questions for written answer, and in their attendance at standing and select committees, although most standing committees are normally whipped. However, they have no control over whether questions for oral answer they table are answered, and only limited control over their membership of committees or whether they will be called to speak in the Chamber. Fourth, the lack of systematic information about who were and who were not practising lawyers makes it impossible to investigate that particular dimension.

Table X.5: Parliamentary activity by back-bench lawyer and non-lawyer MPs, 1994-95

| Category of MP | Activity (mean no of times/sittings per MP) | | | | |
	OPQs	WPQs	Speeches etc[a]	Standing Comm[b]	Select Comm[c]
Non-lawyers	10.5	68.7	18.7	10.9	23.2
Lawyers	9.3	51.1	17.2	10.4	22.1
Barristers	9.5	40.2	16.8	11.3	18.9
Solicitors	8.8	72.1	19.2	8.8	25.9

13 See S E Finer, H B Berrington and D J Bartholomew *Backbench Opinion in the House of Commons, 1955-59* (1961); H B Berrington *Backbench Opinion in the House of Commons, 1945-55* (1973).
14 A Barker and M Rush *The Member of Parliament and his Information* (1970) pp 378-386.
15 D Judge *Backbench Specialisation in the House of Commons* (1981).

Notes: a Including interventions and points of order recorded in Hansard.

     b Including all standing committees on the committee stage of bills, on statutory instruments, European standing committees, second reading committees, and the Scottish and Welsh Grand Committees.

     c Including Privileges, Procedure, Members' Interests, and Standards in Public Life, but excluding 'domestic' committees dealing with services and facilities.

With the exception of questions for written answer, the figures shown in Table X.5 do not show a marked difference between the parliamentary activities of lawyers and non-lawyers in the Commons. In the case of oral questions and speeches and interventions this is hardly surprising, since members have only limited control over their input in these areas. Similarly, attendance at standing committees is subject to whipping and attendance at select committees to a significant degree is likely to reflect interest. In the case of questions for written answer, however, the significant difference is between barristers and solicitors rather than lawyers and non-lawyers. Indeed, there are a number of differences between barristers and solicitors which may be related to whether barristers are practising or non-practising, notably attendance at select committees and speeches and interventions in the Chamber, in both of which barristers score lower. On the other hand, there is no obvious explanation of why solicitors should table so many more questions for written answer.

Table X.6: Parliamentary activity by back-bench lawyers by party, 1994-95

A. *All activities*

               Activity (mean no of times/sittings per lawyer-MP)

Party	OPQs	WPQs	Speeches etc[a]	Standing Comm[b]	Select Comm[c]
Conservative	8.4	24.7	14.5	10.7	22.0
Labour	10.1	79.4	13.4	6.2	41.2
Lib Dem	17.2	153.8	23.2	8.0	17.2
Plaid Cymru	12.5	163.0	13.5	4.0	21.5

Notes: a Including interventions and points of order recorded in Hansard.

     b Including all standing committees on the committee stage of bills, on statutory instruments, European standing committees, second reading committees, and the Scottish and Welsh Grand Committees.

     c Including Privileges, Procedure, Members' Interests, and Standards in Public Life, but excluding 'domestic' committees dealing with services and facilities.

B. *Select committee attendance*

               Activity (mean no of sittings per lawyer-MP)

Party	Departmental	Legislative[a]	PAC	All scrutiny	All Select Comms
Conservative	22.0	23.4	–	22.4	22.0
Labour	37.2	–	2.0	33.8	41.2
Lib Dem	16.5	–	11.0	8.8	17.2
Plaid Cymru	21.5	–	–	21.5	21.5
All	22.9	23.4	15.5	22.6	22.1

Note: a Ie Channel Tunnel Rail Link Bill, Consolidation, Deregulation, European Legislation, and Statutory Instruments. No lawyer-MPs served on the Select Committee on the Parliamentary Commissioner for Administration.

Table X.6 shows that there are much greater differences between parties than between lawyer and non-lawyer MPs, and these differences extend to different types of select committee. They are, however, probably more a reflection of the roles of government and opposition, with Labour MPs tabling more questions for written answer and being more active on select committees, and Conservatives more assiduous in their attendance at standing committees, with little difference in activities in the Chamber. The activities of the Liberal Democrats and Plaid Cymru members similarly reflect their position in the House, not least their need to fulfil the dual roles of front-bencher and back-bencher.

None of this suggests major differences in parliamentary activity by lawyers and non-lawyers in the House of Commons, but more detailed analysis of committee activity and of speeches and interventions suggests that there is a relationship between lawyer-MPs and the matters in which they are active in Parliament. For example, in 1994-95 lawyers constituted an above-average membership of standing committees on eight Bills: the Charities (Amendment) Bill; the Civil Evidence Bill; the Criminal Appeal Bill; the Criminal Compensation Bill; the Family Homes and Domestic Violence Bill; the Law Reform (Succession) Bill; the Private International Law (Miscellaneous Provisions) Bill; and the Proceeds of Crime Bill – all law reform measures and all government Bills, except the first. Four of these bills were also referred to second reading committees, whose members, as is normal practice, were also members of the standing committee which took the committee stage. In addition, four of the seven Commons members of the Select Committee on Statutory Instruments and two of the 18 members of the Select Committee on Deregulation were lawyers. Seven of the 17 departmental select committees also had above average numbers of lawyers, but of these only the Home Affairs Committee, with five out of 11 lawyer-MPs – including the chair – could be said to have a remit of direct interest to lawyers.

Table X.7: Speeches and interventions[a] by backbench lawyer-MPs on legal matters, 1994-95

Party	Barristers %	Solicitors %	Total %
Conservative	19.5	14.7	17.8
Labour	20.0	14.9	18.4
Lib Dem	21.8	–	21.8
Plaid Cymru	–	3.3	3.3
Total	19.9	13.8	17.8

Note: a The figures represent speeches and interventions by lawyer-MPs on legal matters as a percentages of all speeches by lawyers. Legal matters are defined broadly to include all matters relating to civil and criminal law, the criminal justice system, and related policy matters, and the making of legal points on other matters, including procedural points.

Further analysis of speeches and interventions also shows lawyer-MPs contributing to matters of interest to lawyers or drawing upon their legal expertise and experience. The clearest case is that of Sir Ivan Lawrence (Con), then Chair of the Home Affairs

Committee, who made 19 contributions, of which nine reflected legal interests. These were two on prison security, two on the private security industry, two on the Criminal Appeal Bill, and one on each of the following – the Home Secretary's responsibility for the Prison Service, the disclosure of evidence in criminal cases, and draft statutory instruments on conditional fee arrangements. Barbara Roche (Lab) made 15 contributions, of which five reflected legal interests – two on the Proceeds of Crime Bill, two in an adjournment debate on the policing of London, and one on the Disability Discrimination Bill. Similarly, Sir Anthony Grant (Con) made 18 contributions, of which five were of legal concern, and Mike O'Brien (Lab) 35 contributions, of which seven were of legal concern.

This should not be seen as surprising, but it needs to be placed in context. There were some lawyers-MPs who made no contributions which reflected their professional interests or expertise, whilst some contributions which did reflect such interests, also reflected others. Barbara Roche, for example, is a London member and therefore likely to have an interest in the policing of the capital. Indeed, constituency-related matters are, of course, commonly reflected in most areas of parliamentary activity, but so are other interests which do not stem from the occupational background and experience of MPs and the data presented here accords with the much more extensive and sophisticated research conducted by Judge. In short, there is evidence enough to support the view that the parliamentary activity of lawyer-MPs reflects their legal interests, but none is confined by, or to, those interests. It is crucial to remember that they are members of Parliament not because they are lawyers, but career politicians who happen to be lawyers.

Lawyers in the House of Lords

The House of Lords is the final Court of Appeal for the United Kingdom in civil cases and for England, Wales and Northern Ireland in criminal cases.[16] Although theoretically there is no distinction between the House of Lords in its judicial role and the House of Lords engaged in its other activities, in practice the judicial proceedings are quite separate from all other proceedings. Consequently, only those who are appointed as Lords of Appeal in Ordinary (more commonly referred to as Law Lords) with the specific task of hearing and determining judicial appeals, plus the Lord Chancellor and former Lord Chancellors, normally participate in the House's judicial function. Lord Cooke of Thorndon, formerly President of the Court of Appeal of New Zealand, is an exception. He sits on the Appellate Committee but is not a Lord of Appeal in Ordinary. Legal sittings are quite separate and appeals may be heard when the House has been prorogued or Parliament dissolved.

As in so many things, the judicial function of the House of Lords was a product of evolutionary development, not deliberate creation, it being possible to trace it back to medieval times and even earlier, when kings consulted the great men of the realm to secure support, to discover and declare the law and to dispense justice. At one time, and for a long time, there was 'an entire confidence in the honour and conscience of the noble persons who compose this important assembly, that they

---

16 See L Blom-Cooper and G Drewry *Final Appeal: A Study of the House of Lords in its Judicial Capacity* (1972).

will make themselves masters of those questions upon which they undertake to decide'.[17]   However, with the expansion of the statute book as a result of the agricultural and industrial revolutions, it had become apparent by the mid-nineteenth century that there was a scarcity of members with an adequate knowledge of the law and of legal procedure:

> In order that our judicial duties may be properly discharged, [the House of Lords] ought to be well- provided with Peers who are perfectly acquainted with the common law ... with Chancery Law, with criminal law, with the Scotch law, and with civil law.[18]

In 1856, in an attempt to alleviate the problem, the government sought to introduce the concept of life peerages. The intention was to ennoble a number of eminent judges, thereby adding to the judicial strength of the membership of the House of Lords without causing any permanent increase in the peerage. This move was thwarted by the Committee for Privileges and the situation remained problematical for another 20 years. Then, in 1876, the dearth of judicial talent in the House of Lords was remedied by the passage of the Appellate Jurisdiction Act, which provided for the appointment of a number of Lords of Appeal in Ordinary holding office for life. Such individuals had to have previously held high judicial office for at least two years or to have practised at the Bar for at least 15 years. The maximum number of such Lords of Appeal was set at four. This was increased to six in 1913, seven in 1929, nine in 1947, 11 in 1968 and 12 in 1994. Since the passage of the Judicial Pensions and Retirement Act 1993, Lords of Appeal in Ordinary who have attained the age of 75 are no longer eligible to hear appeals, but they continue as members of the House of Lords, holding as they do peerages for life. In 1997 the number of judicially qualified Lords was 39, including two former Lord Chancellors, retired Lords of Appeal in Ordinary and other peers who were, or had been, holders of high judicial office. In contrast to their fellow-peers, including those qualified as barristers and solicitors, who may not participate in the judicial proceedings of the House of Lords, Law Lords and former Law Lords may participate in all other aspects of the work of the House of Lords.
In 1958 Peter Bromhead noted:

> In the Commons there are, apart from the Law Officers of the Crown, many barristers who are private members, and who are very ready to take part in discussion of the technical legal points in bills. In the Lords ... legal learning is represented mainly by the judges and by the Lord Chancellor and his predecessors still living.[19]

Bromhead produced data which showed that of the 381 new peers created between 1916 and 1956, excluding Law Lords, only 15 (3.9%) were lawyers or, more accurately, received their peerage as a result of their activities as lawyers.
   This situation was changed somewhat by the additions to the membership following the passage of the Life Peerages Act 1958. Although not fundamentally altering the nature of the composition of the House (as, for example, direct elections

---

17   Cited in Lord Longford *A History of the House of Lords* (1988) p 130.
18   Earl Granville, Lord President of the Council and Leader of the House of Lords (HL Deb (3rd series), vol 140, 7 February 1856, col 281).
19   P Bromhead *The House of Lords and Contemporary Politics, 1911-1957* (1958) p 70.

would have done), it enriched it by bringing in members of more varied backgrounds and experiences and by doing so in greater numbers than before – 544 individuals in the first 30 years for example, an average of 18 a year. Of these, 24 (4.4%) received their peerage by virtue of their careers as lawyers. In 1981 the proportion of lawyers among the membership as a whole was 10.2%.[20]

Table X.8: Number of lawyers in the House of Lords, 1994-95

	Law Lords[a]	Other Judges	Barristers	Solicitors	Total
			%		
Hereditary (succ)	–	1	13	10	24 (23.3)
Hereditary (cr)	–	–	1	–	1 (1.0)
Life peers	36	–	34	8	78 (75.7)
Total	36 (34.9)	1 (1)	48 (46.6)	18 (17.5)	103(100.0)[b]
% total members	2.9	0.1	3.9	1.4	8.3

Notes: a Comprising the Lord Chancellor, 12 Lords of Appeal, 14 retired Lords of Appeal, two former Lord Chancellors, and seven other Lords of Appeal.

b Comprising 100 at the beginning of the session and 99 at the end, with four having died during the session and three becoming members during the session.

Table X.8 shows that, at its greatest, there were 103 lawyers (8.3% of the total membership) in the House of Lords during the 1994-95 session. There is, however, a marked contrast between the types of peerages held by lawyers and non-lawyers: 75% of the lawyer-peers in 1994-95 were life peers, whereas as many as 63.2% of the total membership were hereditary peers by succession. All the Law Lords were life peers, which reflects their career paths and mode of appointment. None the less, 63.6% of other lawyer-peers were life peers, although this applies more to barristers (70.8%) than solicitors (44.4%). This, too, almost certainly reflects their respective career paths, in that solicitors are more likely to be peers who qualified as solicitors, whereas barristers are more likely to be barristers who were awarded peerages. Given the presence of the Law Lords, the House of Lords inevitably includes eminent members of the legal profession, such as Lords Scarman, Browne-Wilkinson, Slynn, Nolan, the late Lord Denning, and Lord Wilberforce – but there are also other eminent members of the profession among lawyer-peers – solicitors, such as Lords Mishcon, Prys-Davies, and the late Lord Goodman, and barristers, such as Lord Shawcross (chief prosecutor for the United Kingdom at the Nuremberg war crimes trial and a former member of the international court at The Hague) and Lord Lester, the prominent human rights lawyer.

In comparison with the House of Commons, there were numerically more lawyers in the Lords in 1994-95 – 91 lawyer-MPs and 103 lawyer-peers, although, because of the much larger membership of the upper House, the proportions were reversed –

20 N Baldwin, unpublished PhD thesis *The Contemporary House of Lords* University of Exeter (1985) p 33, table 8. It was between 9% and 10% through the 1970s.

14.0% compared with 8.3%. However, if Law Lords are excluded, the number of lawyer-peers falls to 66 (5.3%). As in the Commons, there were also markedly more barristers than solicitors – the ratio in the Commons of barristers to solicitors in 1994-95 was 2:1, in the Lords it was 2.7:1. Women accounted for only 6.6% of the total membership of the House of Lords and among lawyer-peers 5% were women, a little higher than the proportion of women lawyer-MPs in 1992, but significantly fewer than the 12.5% elected in 1997.

Table X.9: Lawyers in the House of Lords by political grouping, 1994-95

	Law Lord/judge	Category Barrister	Solicitor	Total	All peers
		per cent (no)			
Conservative	5.4 (2)	50.0 (24)	38.9 (7)	32.0 (33)	39.9
Labour	–	12.5 (6)	27.8 (5)	10.7 (11)	9.1
Lib Dem	–	14.6 (7)	11.1 (2)	8.7 (9)	4.5
Cross-bench	94.6(35)	16.7 (8)	22.2 (4)	45.6 (47)	24.5
None	–	6.2 (3)	–	2.9 (3)	19.7
Bishops	–	–	–	–	2.2
Total	100.0(37)	100.0 (48)	100.0(18)	100.0(103)	100.0

As Table X.9 shows, the Law Lords were almost entirely cross-benchers, but, as in the Commons, barristers were more likely to be Conservatives. However, compared with the total membership of the Lords, lawyers were somewhat under-represented among the Conservatives, over-represented among the Liberal Democrats, and about the same for Labour, but these proportions do not differ markedly from the party affiliations in the Lords as a whole.

The parliamentary activity of lawyer-peers

Table X.10: Attendance at sittings[a] of the House of Lords by lawyer and non-lawyer-peers, 1994-95

Attendance per cent (no)	Lawyers	Non-lawyers	All peers
None[b]	10.6 (11)	31.5 (359)	29.8 (370)
Non-regular[c]	36.9 (38)	33.0 (376)	33.3 (414)
Regular[d]	52.4 (54)	35.5 (404)	36.9 (458)

Notes: a The total number of sitting days in 1994-95 was 142.

b Including peers without writs (including minors) and peers with leave of absence.

c Attending less than two-thirds of the total number of sittings.

d Attending two-thirds or more of the total number of sittings.

The figures for attendance by lawyers and non-lawyers in the House of Lords, seen in Table X.10, demonstrate clearly that lawyer-peers are more likely to attend than non-lawyers. Overall, 89.3% of lawyer-peers attended in 1994-95, compared with 68.5% of non-lawyers. In addition, lawyer-peers are likely to be more frequent in their attendance than non-lawyers. Regular attenders, defined as those who attended two-thirds or more of the sittings, constituted 52.4% of lawyers and 35.5% of non-lawyers and the proportions for those who attended at least three quarters of the sittings were 35.9% and 27.9%, respectively. Because of the marked difference between the overall membership of the House and day-to-day attendance, it is helpful to look at attendance on what can be termed the 'average' day. This is calculated by adding the total number of attendances throughout the session and dividing this by the number of sitting days during the session. This process is then repeated for each category subdivision. Doing this for the 1994-95 session shows that lawyer-peers accounted for 11.4% of the membership of the House on the average day, compared with 8.3% of the total sessional membership and the 10.5% of the membership which attended.

Table X.11: Parliamentary activity by lawyer and non-lawyer peers, 1994-95

Activity (mean no of times/sittings per peer)

Category	Oral PQs Tabled	Supp	Written PQs	Speeches and interventions	Select committee membership
Lawyers	0.8	4.3	1.8	8.3	0.6
Non-lawyers	0.6	2.7	2.6	4.8	0.4

The data presented in Table X.11 reinforces the analysis of attendance, with lawyers being more active than non-lawyers in all aspects of parliamentary activity, except that of written parliamentary questions. This latter finding parallels that for lawyer and non-lawyer-MPs. Thus, compared with their overall membership of 8.3%, lawyer-peers tabled 14.2% of the questions for oral answer and asked 15.7% of the supplementaries, made 16.8% of the speeches and interventions, and accounted for 16.5% of the membership of select committees. Within these figures, however, there were significant concentrations of activity by a minority of lawyer-peers. For example, excluding ministers and other office-holders from the calculations (ie those who answer rather than ask questions), the total of 73 oral questions tabled by lawyers were asked by as few as 15.1% of the lawyer-peers. Similarly, the 398 supplementary questions were asked by 35.3% of the lawyers; 169 written questions were tabled by a mere 7.8%. Speeches and interventions, however, involved 68.0% of lawyer-peers.

More importantly, of the speeches and interventions by back-bench lawyers, 38.1% were on legal, law-related or procedural matters. On the one hand, this might seem a less focused concentration than expected, given the presence of the Law Lords, but it was more than twice the proportion found for lawyer-MPs, which places the matter in a clearer perspective – there is indeed a stronger 'lawyerly' contribution in the Lords compared with the Commons.

It is also of interest to examine the particular contribution made by the Law Lords to the non-judicial work of the House. Although serving – and in some respects retired – Lords of Appeal in Ordinary (though not serving or retired Lord Chancellors) are governed by a convention preventing them from participating in party political controversy, they are nevertheless able to participate in the parliamentary activity of the House of Lords. The convention does not prevent them from contributing on legal points during the passage of Bills involving controversy, both party-political and other kinds, and they do get involved in the general work of the House such as questions, debates and committee work. For example, Lord Bingham, the Lord Chief Justice, made his maiden speech in July 1996 during a debate on the United Kingdom's existing constitutional settlement and of the implications of proposals for change, focusing his remarks on the constitutional relationship between the British courts, the European Court of Human Rights in Strasbourg and the status of the European Convention in British courts. During this debate, the retired Lord of Appeal, Lord Donaldson, also spoke. Another example would be that of Lord Ackner, who served as a Lord of Appeal in Ordinary from 1986 until 1992 and who was a member of the House of Lords Select Committee on Murder and Life Imprisonment in 1988-89. Similarly, the Law Lords were vigorous participants in the debates on the various proposals for law reform brought forward by Lord Mackay of Clashfern, when he was Lord Chancellor. As Lord Mackay, pointed out in 1996:

> [t]he presence of the most senior members of the judiciary in this House enables the legislative process to draw on a tremendous concentration of legal expertise and judicial experience with benefits going far beyond consideration of what is usually called 'lawyers' law'.[1]

Career patterns

For the most part, the House of Lords lies outside the mainstream of the political career pattern in Britain, with the important proviso that it affords a locus for the latter days of a significant proportion of career politicians, almost all of whom attain the peak of their careers as MPs. The major exception is, of course, some holders of the post of Lord Chancellor, such as Lord Elwyn-Jones or Lord Hailsham, for whom the Lords offers the culmination as well as the twilight of their political careers. There are some other exceptions, such as former MPs who achieve a higher ministerial office in the Lords than they do in the Commons. Lord Richard, a Minister of State as an MP, but Lord Privy Seal, Leader of the House of Lords and a member of the Cabinet in the Labour government formed in 1997, is a case in point. Others never achieve office as MPs, but do so as peers, Lord Hoyle, former chair of the Parliamentary Labour Party, for instance. These are, of course, all career politicians. Yet others have previously accepted life peerages and are subsequently appointed to ministerial office and most Prime Ministers use the House of Lords to draft in individuals they wish to appoint ministers. Thus, the House of Commons is the principal locus of career politicians, but the House of Lords plays a limited but significant role.

---

1   HL Deb vol 573, 3 July 1996, col 1450.

What, then, of the career patterns of lawyers-MPs? In the nineteenth century it was fairly common for lawyer-MPs to secure judicial appointments. Thus, Harold Laski found that of 139 judges appointed between 1832 and 1906 no fewer than 80 (57.6%) had been MPs, although it should be noted that 33 of the 80 (41.3%) had served as Attorney General or Solicitor General.[2] Later studies have produced much lower figures – 23% of judges in 1956 had been either MPs or parliamentary candidates[3] and, in 1970, Henry Cecil found only ten former MPs among 117 judges (8.5%).[4] And John Griffith notes that no MP has been appointed to the High Court or to Court of Appeal since 1977.[5] Similarly, until relatively recently, lawyer-MPs were quite commonly appointed recorders or assistant recorders which, unlike judgeships, are compatible with continued membership of the House of Commons, but such appointments are now uncommon, usually numbering only a handful.[6]

The major reason for the decline in the number of lawyer-MPs securing judicial appointments is undoubtedly the regularisation of recruitment to such positions, with part-time judicial experience now being a prerequisite for a full-time judicial appointment. But it has also become increasingly difficult to combine part-time legal and judicial work with membership of Parliament. As noted in ch VII, above, as long ago as 1971 the review body on MPs' pay argued that '. . . by any reasonable standard . . . most Members must be considered as working on a full-time basis'[7] and subsequent surveys of MPs have shown that the trend has been reinforced.[8] Moreover, once elected, the overwhelming majority of MPs continue their political careers until retirement, death or electoral defeat intervene. Added to this, most MPs are first elected to Parliament between the ages of 30 and 50 – a substantial proportion between 35 and 45 – most retire at or near normal retirement age, and the average length of service is 18 years. The rise of the full-time MP has been accompanied by a process of professionalisation – improvements in the level of pay and the provision of services and facilities. And last, but by no means least, the opportunities of achieving ministerial office have also increased significantly from 60 ministers in 1900 to 113 in 1997. This expansion in ministerial posts has been mostly to the benefit of MPs, with only about 20 peers now holding office. As many as 40% of MPs are now likely to hold ministerial office at some time during their political career.[9]

2   H Laski 'The Technique of Judicial Appointment' in H Laski *Studies in Law and Politics* (1932) p 168.
3   (1956) Economist, 15 December, p 946. No distinction was drawn between MPs and candidates.
4   H Cecil *The English Judge* (1970) p 26.
5   J A G Griffith *The Politics of the Judiciary* (5th edn, 1997) p 20.
6   For example, John Morris (Attorney General from May 1997 and former Secretary of State for Wales) served as a recorder from 1982 to 1997 and Humfrey Malins (Conservative MP for Croydon NW 1983-92 and Woking 1997-) as an assistant recorder from 1991 to 1996 and as a recorder since 1996. Two peers, Lord Archer of Sandwell (Solicitor-General 1974-79 and Labour MP 1966-92) and Lord Meston were also recorders.
7   Review Body on Top Salaries (TSRB), *First Report: Ministers of the Crown and Members of Parliament*, 1971 (Cmnd 4836) para 25.
8   See TSRB, *Report No 8*, 1976 (Cmnd 6574) Appendix A; TSRB, *Report No 12*, (Cmnd 7958) Appendix C; TSRB, *Report No 20,* 1983 (Cmnd 8881-II) s 1; and Review Body on Senior Salaries, *Report No 38*, 1996 (Cm 3330-II) s 2.
9   For an account of these developments see M Rush, 'Career Patterns in British Politics: First Choose Your Party . . .' in F F Ridley and M Rush (eds) *British Government and Politics since 1945: Changes in Perspective* (1995) pp 68-84.

One office which might be thought particularly appropriate for lawyer-MPs is that of Speaker. As Philip Laundy has pointed out: 'Of the twenty-two Speakers who by 1974 had held office since Arthur Onslow [1728] all but seven have been lawyers.'[10] However, as he acknowledges in a footnote, the balance between 1900 and 1974 was only five to four in favour of lawyers and, since 1976, when Selwyn Lloyd retired, every Speaker has been a non-lawyer. Put another way, for 57 of the years since 1900, non-lawyers rather than lawyers have occupied the Speaker's Chair. It is also worth noting that in the 1994-95 session not one of the 22 members of the Chairmen's Panel was a lawyer, nor were either of the Deputy Speakers.

Table X.12: The English and Scottish Law officers 1900-97: parliamentary experience

Office	MP on appt	MP after appt	Never MP	MP after holding office	Total
Attorney Gen	28	–	–	–	28[a]
Solicitor Gen	38	2	1	1	42[b]
Lord Adv	21	1	9	1	32[c]
S-G Scot	12	8	16	7	43[d]

Notes: a 28 individuals, of whom two held office twice.
   b 39 individuals, of whom one held office three times and one twice.
   c 31 individuals, of whom one held office twice.
   d 41 individuals, of whom two held office twice.

More importantly for lawyer-MPs, there are particular career paths which are closed to other parliamentarians, though, ironically, not necessarily to non-parliamentarians. These are the English and Scottish law offices – the Attorney General, the Solicitor General, the Lord Advocate, and the Solicitor General for Scotland, plus the Lord Chancellor. The holders of all these offices must be barristers, those appointed English law officers, members of the English Bar, and those as Scottish law officers, members of the Scottish Bar.[11]

The office of Attorney General has always been held by a lawyer-MP since 1900 and that of Solicitor General almost always so. Indeed, Tony Blair's appointment of Charles Falconer as Solicitor General, with a seat in the House of Lords, is without parallel this century and only one holder, Sir Walter Monckton, Solicitor General in the short-lived 1945 caretaker government, held the office entirely as a non-parliamentarian, not becoming an MP until 1951. There is thus little or no problem in finding suitable lawyer-MPs to fill these two posts. However, the Scottish law offices present a different picture: 11 of the 31 individuals appointed Lord Advocate

10 P Laundy 'The Speaker and His Office' in S A Walkland (ed) *The House of Commons in the Twentieth Century* (1979) p 129.
11 Historically, the posts of Lord Chancellor of Ireland and the Attorney General and Solicitor General for Ireland should be added for the period 1900-21, but they have been excluded from the discussion that follows.

and no fewer than 31 of those appointed Solicitor General for Scotland were not MPs on appointment. Furthermore, nine of the Lord Advocates and 16 of the Solicitor Generals were never MPs. One solution to this problem has been to award peerages to non-MPs, a solution adopted in the case of the last five Lord Advocates, including the present holder, but for only one Solicitor General for Scotland. The reason for the frequent appointment of non-parliamentarians is simple – a lack of suitable lawyer-MPs who are also members of the Scottish Bar. And lest this be thought to be a problem arising from the small number of Scottish Conservatives before their total obliteration in 1997, it is not so – it has been a problem for much of this century and earlier and for all parties.

Table X.13: The law officers 1900-97: ministerial careers[a]

Office	Appt as A-G	Appt as Lord Adv	Appt as Lord Chan	Appt as other minister
Attorney Gen	–	–	9	14
Solicitor Gen	18	–	10	17
Lord Adv	–	–	1	4
S-G Scot	–	17	–	2

Note: a Excluding present law officers and the Lord Chancellor.

The two Scottish law offices largely provide career patterns of their own. As can be seen from Tables X.12 and X.13, 17 of the 41 individuals appointed Solicitor General for Scotland between 1900 and 1997, excluding the present holder, subsequently became Lord Advocate, but only two later held other ministerial offices and none became Lord Chancellor. Similarly, of the 31 individuals appointed Lord Advocate, only one, Lord Mackay of Clashfern, became Lord Chancellor (1987-97) and only four held other ministerial offices. Indeed, this pattern can be taken a stage further: no fewer than 37 of the 53 individuals who held the offices of either Solicitor General for Scotland or Lord Advocate (or both) between 1900 and 1997 were subsequently appointed judges in Scotland. In summary, then, the career patterns of holders of the Scottish law offices tend to be semi-detached from Parliament, often not being filled by an MP and often not part of a clearly-defined political career.

Considerable similarities are found with the English law offices, but the holders of these are much more in the mainstream of politics: almost without exception MPs are appointed as Solicitor General and Attorney General and 22 of the 46 individuals who held either or both offices between 1900 and 1997 also served in other ministerial posts, 16 after having served as a law officer. Eighteen of the holders also became Attorney General after serving as Solicitor General, 15 moving directly from the latter to the former, and only one, Sir William Jowett, unusually, served as Attorney General in the second Labour government (1929-32) before serving as Solicitor General (1940-42).[12]

---

12 Jowett's appointment as Solicitor General in 1940 is explained by the fact that he was a Labour nominee and the Labour Party was the junior partner in the wartime coalition.

Twelve went on to become Lord Chancellor, of whom all but two had previously held both law offices and a further 12 later became judges, although none has been appointed a judge since 1962. In addition, one holder of the post of Solicitor General, Sir Harry Hylton-Foster, went on to become Speaker of the House of Commons. The career patterns of Lord Chancellors is more varied, some being mainstream politicians, the culmination of their career being appointment as Lord Chancellor, others being drafted in from outside the mainstream. Thus, of the 21 individuals appointed Lord Chancellor since 1900,[13] 15 have previously served as MPs, but of the rest, three had held peerages as Law Lords, one had been a member of the Lords since being appointed Lord Advocate, one was made a peer on appointment, and two were made peers before being made Lord Chancellor. One of the latter is the present Lord Chancellor, Lord Irvine of Lairg, who was awarded a peerage in 1987 and served as Shadow Lord Chancellor from 1992 to 1997.

Table X.14: Lawyer-MPs[a] in the Major and Blair governments, 1997

	Major	% Cons lawyer-MPs	Blair	% Lab lawyer-MPs
		Per cent (no)		
Barristers	17.4 (15)	12.5	14.8 (13)	5.0
Solicitors	8.1 (7)	6.8	3.4 (3)	3.1
Total	25.5 (22)	19.3	18.2 (16)	8.1

Note: a   Expressed as a percentage of the number of MPs holding ministerial office.

The five legal appointments in the government provide career opportunities for lawyer-politicians, but are not always filled by career politicians, nor are they filled by politicians whose ministerial careers are confined to legal appointments. On the wider front, however, lawyer-politicians tend to achieve an above-average proportion of ministerial posts, as Table X.1 illustrates. In John Major's government, more than 25% of ministerial posts were held by lawyers, substantially above the nearly one in five Conservative lawyer-MPs, while the government formed by Tony Blair in May 1997 had more than twice the proportion of lawyer-MPs than the PLP. In both governments, however, barristers were numerically and proportionately better represented than solicitors. This pattern of lawyers being likely to achieve ministerial office, and barristers more so than solicitors, is reaffirmed by analysing the proportion of lawyers holding the four major offices of state this century – Prime Minister, Chancellor of the Exchequer, Foreign Secretary, and Home Secretary, as Table X.15 clearly shows

---

13   This excludes Lord Halsbury, who was Lord Chancellor in 1900, since he had held office since 1895, having previously been Lord Chancellor in 1885-86 and 1886-92. He left office on the resignation of the Conservative government in 1905. He was made a peer on first taking office in 1885.

Table X.15: Lawyer-MPs holding the four major offices of state, 1900-97

Period	Barristers	Solicitors	Total
	Per cent (no)		
1900-97	29.2 (26)	3.4 (3)	32.6 (29)
1945-97	36.5 (19)	–	36.5 (19)

Conclusion

Lawyer-politicians have always played, and continue to play, an important and prominent part in Parliament and in government, often greater than their numbers would suggest. However, it is crucial to bear in mind that in both Houses, especially the House of Commons, they are neither limited to, nor do they necessarily specialise in, essentially 'lawyerly' matters, with, of course, the important exceptions of filling the five legal offices of state and fulfilling the judicial function of the House of Lords. Indeed, lawyers could be said to be most prominent, relative to their numbers, in holding ministerial office, particularly the four major offices of state. None the less, the numbers and proportions of lawyers in politics appears to be in decline, and this is almost certainly a reflection of changing career paths, especially the advent of the full-time MP. How far this pattern will change further in the event of an elected or partly-elected House of Lords remains to be seen. A more profound impact, on the House of Lords in particular, would result from the total hiving off of its judicial function, if it were to involve the Law Lords no longer being members, given the contribution they currently make to it non-judicial work. However, notwithstanding the decline in the number of lawyer-politicians, the skills and expertise acquired by lawyers will likely continue to attract them to politics and continue to make them attractive to those who select parliamentary candidates and those who advise on and choose members of the House of Lords, so long as it retains a significant nominated element. In short, lawyers will continue to play a significant role in Parliament.

Chapter XI

Parliament and human rights

Robert Blackburn

Introduction

With the successful passage of the Human Rights Act 1998, the United Kingdom is now set to embark on a revolution in its legal and parliamentary methods for protecting the individual rights and freedoms of its citizens. This statute of major constitutional importance incorporates into our judicial, parliamentary and governmental systems express recognition of the fundamental rights and freedoms as contained in the European Convention on Human Rights (ECHR), an international treaty of the Council of Europe to which the United Kingdom was a founding father in 1950.

The Human Rights Act is thereby ushering into our legal system a whole new field of jurisprudence to which, previously, our courts could only allude without taking direct notice. Under s 3 of the Human Rights Act, the human rights principles of the ECHR will become mandatory relevant considerations in the exercise of public discretionary power affecting the individual, enforceable by way of judicial review proceedings. Section 6 makes it unlawful for a public authority to act in any way which is incompatible with a convention right. The full range of existing forms of relief or remedies will be available to the courts at their discretion to enforce these new positive rights of the individual, including damages under s 8. And, what is unique and unprecedented in our constitutional law, the superior courts are to be empowered to pass judgment on the legitimacy of provisions in primary parliamentary legislation itself. Under s 4, the court may make a formal 'declaration of incompatibility' between the legislation in dispute and the human rights articles of the ECHR. Whilst these declarations will not affect the continuing validity of the relevant sections in the offending legislation, this process of judicial scrutiny of primary parliamentary Acts is nevertheless of great significance for the future potential and development of a homegrown constitutional Bill of Rights.

Within Whitehall, it will become a mandatory legal requirement for government ministers and their civil servants to examine and draw up a written report on the human rights implications of all legislation that is being prepared. Section 19 provides that the minister in charge of a Bill in either House of Parliament must either make and publish a written statement to the effect that, in his or her view, the provisions of the Bill are compatible with the convention rights, or, if he or she is unable to make such a statement, the minister must certify that the government nevertheless wishes the House to proceed with the Bill. In the latter case, MPs and peers will be on express notice of the implications of the legislation that is being proposed. This internal audit procedure is just part of the Labour government's declared intention to create a new awareness – or 'culture' – of human rights within and across official bureaucracies generally.

The net effect of the Human Rights Act will be to extend considerably the role of parliamentary scrutiny in the field of human rights affairs. For not only are the human rights articles of the ECHR bound to figure much larger in the minds of MPs and peers as a result of incorporation into the judicial system and by being specially referred to in human rights impact statements accompanying each Bill, but under s 10 a new legislative process is created whereby fast-track remedial orders may be enacted to respond swiftly to human rights violations in our existing body of primary parliamentary legislation, as determined either by a decision of the European Court of Human Rights at Strasbourg or by a declaration of incompatibility by the High Court or appellate bodies. These remedial orders will be affirmative statutory instruments (subject to a single stage of approval in each House) yet they will be authorised under the terms of the Human Rights Act to amend measures of primary legislation where considered appropriate (s 10(3)). The wider future significance of the remedial order procedure under the Act, therefore, being an extraordinary process in itself coupled with this 'Henry VIII' clause, may well be to galvanise pressures at Westminster towards the establishment of a parliamentary committee on human rights. Furthermore, of particular poignance at this time, when the long-term function of a reformed Second Chamber is being focused on as an inevitable concomitant to Labour's plans to extract the hereditary element from the House of Lords, a more distinctive role for the House of Lords in the context of human rights is becoming ever more probable.

This chapter offers some reflections on the implications of the Human Rights Act which impinge upon the future functions, practices and procedures of Parliament. It is written on the threshold of what promises to be a major readjustment in our legal and parliamentary traditions – what one peer, during the lengthy debates on the passage of the Human Rights Bill, rightly described as 'a defining moment in the life of our constitution'.[1]

Towards a constitutional Bill of Rights

The election of the new Labour government in May 1997, supported by a clear mandate and a 179-seat majority in the House of Commons, has heralded a new attitude to human rights in this country. As Baroness Helena Kennedy QC has put it, just as democratic rights were the dominant idea at the beginning of the twentieth century, so human rights are now starting to play the same key role as we approach its end.[2] The 1992 general election, lost by Labour, proved a watershed in the party's

---

1   Lord Kingsland, HL Deb, 3 November 1997, col 1234. This chapter draws on and reproduces some of the author's earlier writings: see especially 'A Bill of Rights for the 21st Century' in R Blackburn and J Busuttil (eds) *Human Rights for the 21st Century* (1997); 'A Parliamentary Committee on Human Rights' and 'The House of Lords' in R Blackburn and Lord Plant (eds) *Constitutional Reform Now* (1998); R Blackburn *Towards a Constitutional Bill of Rights for the United Kingdom* (1998).

2   Back cover of Blackburn *Towards a Constitutional Bill of Rights* (n 1 above).

ideology concerning constitutional 'rights'. Against a long-standing historical tradition which was distrustful of any measure that would promote greater involvement of the judiciary in the protection of individual liberties, Labour undertook a major review of its constitutional reform programme under its then leader, John Smith, and its home affairs spokesman at the time, Tony Blair. The resulting report was published in 1993.[3] This comprehensive programme of proposals, dealing with both short- and long-terms objectives, at last unequivocally committed the party to incorporation of the ECHR, a target now accomplished by the Human Rights Act. But the same document proposed further reforms which should be borne carefully in mind when considering the parliamentary implications of the Human Rights Act.

For the Human Rights Act is just the beginning, not the end, of a process of human rights reform that will have major ramifications for parliamentary procedures in both Houses. Labour's 1993 report, subsequently endorsed by the party conference, concluded that:

> the incorporation of the European Convention on Human Rights is a necessary first step, but it is not a substitute for our own written Bill of Rights ... There is a good case for drafting our own Bill of Rights.[4]

In other words, it was believed the Human Rights Act would lead to the later development of a separate constitutional Bill of Rights, with a more up-to-date drafting of human rights articles for indigenous purposes in the United Kingdom and some measure of entrenchment. Labour's proposal was for 'the establishment of an all-party commission that will be charged with drafting the Bill of Rights and considering a suitable method of entrenchment'. The party's pre-election literature in 1996-97 made no mention of a home-grown Bill of Rights, concentrating instead on what was desirable and achievable in its first term of office.[5]

None the less, parliamentarians must clearly keep in mind the probability of a home-grown Bill of Rights in the foreseeable future – possibly by the year 2020. Whatever the Blair administration's current views on the matter may be (or be presented as being), there is already substantial existing support for a home-grown Bill of Rights, and this will almost certainly increase as the successful implementation of the Human Rights Act acclimatises our traditions and processes of government to the notion of a positive legal statement of human rights. Some influential think-tanks on the centre-Left, such as the Institute for Public Policy Research, and pressure groups such as Liberty have published policy analyses on the subject, giving their full support to a British Bill of Rights and even offering their own legislative blueprints on the subject.[6] On the centre-Right, the Conservative leadership in its present early phase of opposition may oppose a Bill of Rights for the time being, but we should

---

3   *A New Agenda for Democracy: Labour's Proposals for Constitutional Reform* (1993).
4   Ibid, pp 29-32.
5   See in particular *New Labour New Britain: Labour's Contract for a New Britain* (1996); *Bringing Rights Home: Labour's Plans to Incorporate the European Convention on Human Rights into UK Law* (1996); *Because Britain Deserves Better: Labour Election Manifesto* (1997).
6   Institute for Public Policy Research *A British Bill of Rights* (revised edn, 1996) and *A Written Constitution for the United Kingdom* (revised edn, 1993); Liberty *A People's Charter* (1991) and *Bill of Rights* (1995).

recall that it was members of the Conservative front-bench team in the years prior to taking office in 1979 who were among the leading early advocates of a Bill of Rights.[7] Indeed, the 1979 Conservative election manifesto contained a specific promise to hold all-party talks on a Bill of Rights (a pledge which was subsequently dropped once the party was in office).

Potentially even more significant is the fact that the Liberal Democrats have adopted a detailed, comprehensive programme of reform including a written constitution and entrenched Bill of Rights.[8] As a source of influence upon government policy in the future, Liberal Democrat objectives may become far more significant if, as seems likely, changes to the electoral system are made (following the Jenkins Commission Report on the Voting System which is due to appear in 1998 and the promised referendum on the matter) which result in their level of support in the country being translated into a greater number of Liberal Democrat MPs in the Commons. Already the Labour Party and Liberal Democrats are actively co-operating in the field of constitutional reform, as evidenced by the two parties' Joint Consultative Committee Report on Constitutional Reform in March 1997 and by Tony Blair's creation of a special Cabinet Committee with Liberal Democrat membership, whose terms of reference are 'to consider policy issues of joint interest to the Government and Liberal Democrats'.

Bills of Rights generally have a number of distinguishing characteristics.[9] The first, of course, is the type of rights and freedoms which are included within the document. A second is the degree of special legal status and priority which is afforded to the document. In both these respects the Human Rights Act is not equivalent to a Bill of Rights in a proper constitutional sense, though it is an important step in that direction. The Human Rights Act seeks to give legal recognition in United Kingdom law to an international treaty – the European Convention on Human Rights, as negotiated and agreed between member states to the Council of Europe in 1950. As stated in the opening sentence of the Explanatory Memorandum accompanying the Human Rights Bill, its purpose is 'to give further effect in domestic law' to the ECHR. Rulings on the application of the human rights articles of the convention will ultimately be determined by an international court at Strasbourg, the European Court of Human Rights. The Strasbourg Court will hear appeals from petitioners who lose their cases about human rights violations in the United Kingdom courts. A home-grown constitutional Bill of Rights, by contrast, would be the basis for a self-contained judicial and legal process operating within this country.

This represents one of the strongest arguments in favour of the enactment of a home-grown Bill of Rights in the longer term. As time goes on, the flaws in the drafting of the ECHR for contemporary British purposes will become increasingly apparent. It is unsurprising that the convention drafted in 1950 is not an entirely accurate reflection of prevailing perceptions of individual or minority rights and freedoms in the more advanced state of British society today. Most obviously, over the past 50 years, major social and moral developments have been taking place in the

---

7   See eg Lord Hailsham *Elective Dictatorship* (Dimbleby Lecture, 1976) and Sir Keith Joseph *Freedom Under Law* (1975).

8   Liberal Democrats *Here We Stand: Proposals for Modernising Britain's Democracy* (1993) and *Constitutional Declaration* (1996).

9   See Blackburn *Towards a Constitutional Bill of Rights* (note 1 above) ch 3.

field of equality and non-discrimination. The revolution in information technology has thrown up major new difficulties affecting the protection of privacy. John Wadham, Director of the National Council for Civil Liberties (Liberty), has identified a range of key 'missing rights' in the convention – and therefore the Human Rights Act itself.[10] These include provisions covering: the right to information; the rights of immigrants, asylum seekers and those being extradited; anti-discrimination measures; the absence of any specific rights for children; gaps in standards guaranteed for the criminal justice system and procedures for detention; and a weak provision on personal privacy not even extending to basic procedural matters covering intrusion into homes and surveillance of individuals. Once we have accommodated the idea of positive human rights in our legal and parliamentary systems, a growing need will be perceived for a more soundly-drafted and up-to-date legal statement of citizens' fundamental rights and freedoms. This is so not simply to preserve the credibility of the law and the judicial process which seeks to apply those positive human rights in cases brought before the courts, but because whatever document we regard as laying down our basic rights – and currently the Human Rights Act is the nearest document we possess – will acquire an immense authority as an official point of reference and set of principles permeating the work of Parliament in all its business, both in chamber and in committee. No doubt, in the drafting of a home-grown Bill of Rights, the articles of the ECHR (and of the International Covenant on Civil and Political Rights) will form a starting point for whatever elaboration is thought appropriate and necessary, because our national Bill of Rights will need to be consistent with our wider international obligations.

The second characteristic of Bills of Rights mentioned above – that of their special legal status and priority – means that any Bill of Rights worthy of that name must constitute a higher body of legal principle to which ordinary administrative and legislative measures should conform. In other words, constitutional Bills of Rights are generally 'entrenched' in some way, with some superior status being conferred upon the document and some special legislative process being established for the making of future amendments or derogations from its provisions.[11] The future development of a Bill of Rights for the United Kingdom, therefore, is likely to entail a legal and parliamentary distinction being drawn between human rights law (perhaps encompassed within a wider notion of constitutional law) and ordinary legislative enactments. By reference to parliamentary practice elsewhere, it would be normal for amendments and derogations to require the consent of both Houses and possibly some special majority. The Human Rights Act, by contrast, is not formally entrenched in this way. Instead, its legal effect is interpretative. Under the terms of the Act, the role of the courts, whenever it is alleged in legal proceedings that a citizen's rights and freedoms have been unlawfully infringed, is to interpret the law or administrative power in question by reference to the articles of the ECHR and jurisprudence on the subject. The convention's principles will themselves become grounds for challenging the exercise of statutory

---

10 'Why Incorporation is Not Enough' in R Gordon and R Wilmot-Smith (eds) *Human Rights in the United Kingdom* (1996) pp 26ff.
11 See F Klug 'The Role of a Bill of Rights in a Democratic Constitution' in A Barnett, C Ellis and P Hirst (eds) *Debating the Constitution* (1993) pp 44ff. Some countries have enacted interpretative legal measures calling themselves 'Bill of Rights' (most notably the New Zealand Bill of Rights Act 1990) but these are not constitutional Bills in the generally accepted sense.

discretionary powers and administrative decisions. But if the power or regulation in question is clearly incompatible, then the offending legislative measure prevails. As expressed in s 3: 'So far as it is possible to do so, primary legislation and subordinate legislation must be read and given effect in a way which is compatible with the Convention rights.' While this approach adopted by the Labour administration (the 'British model of incorporation', as its spokesmen termed it) is entirely appropriate to a legal measure seeking to give further effect in United Kingdom domestic law to an international treaty, it does not meet the normal criteria for a Bill of Rights.

None the less, there is no doubt that the Human Rights Act contains the seeds of a major, growing distinction emerging in our judicial and parliamentary systems between human rights law and ordinary legislation. In at least three interconnected respects, the Act requires human rights matters to be dealt with by the courts and by Parliament in a manner that is distinct and constitutionally different from ordinary law. First, the new rule of judicial interpretation in s 3 makes the status of the convention's principles substantially stronger than any normal interpretation Act would do. The White Paper accompanying the Human Rights Bill made it clear that the intention behind the Act was for the judiciary to go –

> far beyond the present rule which enables the courts to take the Convention into account in resolving any ambiguity in a legislative provision. The courts will be required to interpret legislation so as to uphold the Convention rights unless the legislation itself is *so clearly incompatible with the Convention that it is impossible to do so.*[12]

This is the most powerful rule of interpretation possible, requiring a very clear and emphatic contradiction to the articles and jurisprudence of the ECHR before they can be overridden.

Secondly, wherever the High Court, Court of Appeal or House of Lords finds itself unable to reconcile a provision of primary legislation with our obligations under the ECHR, the courts may issue a 'declaration of incompatibility'. The net effect of a declaration of incompatibility under s 4 of the Human Rights Act will be to require the government to remedy the violation and present legislative proposals to Parliament to bring the law into conformity with the judicial ruling. This is analogous to the international obligation already owed by the United Kingdom (and member states of the Council of Europe) whereby it must take positive action in response to adverse rulings before the European Court of Human Rights. What is so interesting about this power under s 4, in the context of the development of a constitutional Bill of Rights, is that its practice will serve to familiarise our legal and parliamentary traditions with the concept of a domestic court adjudicating upon the validity of an Act of Parliament upon expressly stated human rights principles. In other words, it will help to smooth the transition towards a constitutional Bill of Rights by facilitating general acceptance of its practice and desirability.

Thirdly, the Human Rights Act lays down a special legislative process for dealing with human rights legislation. Under s 10, a 'fast-track' procedure has been approved by Parliament, whereby the government may respond promptly to declarations of incompatibility in our domestic courts or an adverse ruling in

---

12 Home Office *Rights Brought Home: The Human Rights Bill* 1997 (Cm 3782) p 9 (author's italics).

Strasbourg. In suitable situations, where swift action is necessary to redress a human rights injustice and a Bill procedure would be politically impracticable that session, the government may present a draft order to Parliament with a one-stop method of approval in each House similar to an affirmative statutory instrument. Since such orders fall outside the scope of the Parliament Acts 1911-49, the House of Lords retains its original power of legislative veto.[13] Therefore, its approval to such remedial orders will always be necessary before they can take permanent legal effect.

The wider parliamentary significance of this is considerable. It is, in effect, serving to elevate the role of the House of Lords as a parliamentary mechanism and to safeguard against any possible future misuse of the remedial order procedure – for such safeguards in this new legislative arrangement there must be. Human rights law is concerned with striking an appropriate balance between conflicting individual rights and between particular rights and the national interest. In practice, this sometimes involves the imposition of restrictions and the 'levelling-down' of individual rights. Furthermore, emergency or urgent legislation in the past has not infrequently been concerned specifically with implementing such restrictions upon individual rights. It is therefore particularly important that parliamentary scrutiny procedures are effective in safeguarding against rushed remedial orders which may have wider implications for human rights beyond the different kinds of 'urgency' which might exist.[14] If – as is the intention of the Human Rights Act – the courts are to refer matters of human rights violation to Parliament for legislative action, then both the Commons and the Lords should have, separately, adequate procedures providing for their in-depth consideration of the matter (see below) and the necessary powers to enforce that scrutiny and reject any measures not commanding general consent. The only legislative veto the House of Lords possesses with respect to primary legislation concerns another species of constitutional legislation, being Bills to prolong the life of Parliament beyond five years (in other words, to suspend general elections and perpetuate the government in office). The veto the House of Lords currently possesses over statutory instruments generally is a historical accident, arising from the fact that delegated legislation was a rare phenomenon at the beginning of this century prior to the Parliament Act 1911, and therefore it was not thought necessary to include it within the terms of the Parliament Act. So today, between the nonsense of the House of Lords possessing only a one-year power over Bills of first-class constitutional importance, whilst having an absolute power of veto over the smallest minutiae of administrative regulation in delegated statutory orders, there exists this special legislative procedure for human rights remedial orders – an end result which is soundly based on good constitutional logic. Its significance for the role and power of the House of Lords, however (see further below), was a fact largely unnoticed during the parliamentary debates on the Human Rights Bill.

13 On the legislative effect of the Parliament Acts, see J A G Griffith and M Ryle *Parliament: Functions, Practice and Procedures* (1989) pp 503ff.
14 In response to parliamentary and other pressures, the original form of the Human Rights Bill was amended to include an extended consultation period of 60 days in the Act (in contrast to the 40 days normally applicable to statutory instruments).

Parliamentary human rights scrutiny procedures

Human rights are now poised to become a major reference point for parliamentary scrutiny procedures generally. Both in the short term and in the long term, there are major implications for parliamentary scrutiny mechanisms consequential upon the adoption of a human rights code in our law, both by way of the Human Rights Act and as a result of later developments with regard to a home-grown Bill of Rights.

Until the Human Rights Act 1998, no serious thought had been given at Westminster to the creation of a parliamentary committee on human rights.[15] No parliamentary committee had ever earlier been set up with a specific scrutiny function relating to civil liberties and human rights. Neither had any existing select committee ever incorporated any statement of human rights into its terms of reference, either of a domestic or an international nature. Traditionally, this rested on the belief that Parliament always conducted its legislative and administrative scrutiny functions having regard to the implications of government business for the rights and freedoms of the individual, and consequently no special mechanism in either House of Parliament was necessary. In 1977 a House of Lords inquiry on incorporation of the ECHR declared itself sceptical about the utility of a special committee on human rights, believing that such a committee was no more likely to detect a breach of human rights standards than the House as a whole would be in its general conduct of scrutinising government bills and administrative practices.[16]

Over the past 20 years, however, it has become increasingly evident that the United Kingdom government and Westminster Parliament are capable of carrying out administrative practices and enacting legislative measures that contradict internationally accepted standards of human rights. As is well known, since granting the right of individual petition to its citizens in 1965, the United Kingdom government has often been held to be in violation of the ECHR by the European Court of Human Rights. Political and legal recognition of this fact was a major contributory factor in bringing about the shift in opinion in favour of incorporating the ECHR into our own domestic affairs. But few people wish to rely upon the courts and litigation alone to protect our human rights. Today, more than ever, with a positive statement of human rights being implanted in our law for the first time under the Human Rights Act, it will be essential for Parliament to perform its proper role of scrutinising the conduct of government and legislative proposals for conformity with individual rights and freedoms.

The new Labour government has publicly stated that, in principle, it supports the idea of a parliamentary committee on human rights, but believes that the pressure and initiative behind any specific proposals should come from within Parliament itself.[17] Thus, in its White Paper on the Human Rights Bill, the government said that such a committee and what its role and powers might be 'is a matter for Parliament itself to decide'. But even if such a committee is set up within the near future, its functions

---

15 For earlier discussions and proposals, see D Kinley *The European Convention on Human Rights: Compliance without Incorporation* (1993); M Ryle 'Pre-legislative Scrutiny: A Prophylactic Approach to Protection of Human Rights' [1994] PL 192; R Blackburn 'A Parliamentary Committee on Human Rights' (n 1 above).

16 *Report of the Select Committee on a Bill of Rights* (HL 176, 1977-78) p 38.

17 See White Paper (n 2 above p 14; also HL Deb, 27 November 1997, col 1150 and HC Deb, 16 February 1998, col 857.

will be limited and are most unlikely to extend to the full range of possibilities for human rights scrutiny procedures which have been canvassed in the context of the Human Rights Act and beyond. In other words, the introduction of human rights scrutiny functions at Westminster will be incremental, a building-block exercise, probably commencing with pre-legislative scrutiny. Parliamentary institutions in the United Kingdom prefer a process of experiment and evolution before setting up for themselves any permanent major innovation.

The most important function for any new procedures will be the scrutiny of legislative proposals for their compliance with the articles and jurisprudence of the ECHR. This is likely to be regarded as the highest priority for implementation, and will also be the most significant factor shaping the overall parliamentary scheme which emerges with respect to its new human rights work generally. The work involved will be in the nature of a technical exercise, comparing and predicting the compatibility of the law proposed with the prospect of litigation under the ECHR, both in our domestic courts and before the European Court of Human Rights at Strasbourg. The type of scrutiny would not extend into the merits of whether the legislation in question was desirable or not in itself, upon which diverse interpretations and ideological points of view might be adopted. Only the two Chambers of Parliament as a whole, assisted in the normal way through their existing committees, would be equipped to conduct policy debates and decision-making of that kind.

Several significantly different forms and processes of legislation will have to be accommodated by whatever committee scheme of parliamentary scrutiny is devised. First, government primary legislation, which consists of about 40 public Bills each year, will need to be considered for compliance with human rights standards. Secondly, private members Bills and private Bills will need to be scrutinised separately, as the internal government audit procedures and the published ministerial human rights impact statement accompanying government Bills – as required under s 19 of the Human Rights Act – will not apply to these types of legislation. Thirdly, the very large quantity of secondary legislation, which consists of at least 1,500 statutory instruments every year will need to be examined. Fourthly, of special importance will be the new legislative category of remedial orders, which may be enacted under s 10 of the Human Rights Act as a fast-track process when the government wishes to respond swiftly to a declaration of incompatibility in our domestic courts or an adverse ruling in the European Court of Human Rights. Fifthly, some consideration of human rights implications might be thought necessary with regard to European law-making. Any scrutiny arrangements deemed necessary under this head, however, will be of a very different nature from the scrutiny of domestic legislation, since the Westminster Parliament's role with respect to European legislation is limited to the expression of an opinion on Commission proposals in advance of the meeting of the Council of Ministers – the body that decides to adopt the legislation or not.

A policy consultation paper issued by the Labour Party whilst still in opposition in 1996[18] proposed that any new human rights scrutiny body at Westminster could have 'a continuing responsibility to monitor the operation of the Human Rights Act'. The scope of a continuing function of this kind is not clear, and could be drawn very

---

18   Labour Party *Bringing Rights Home* (1996).

widely. Such a function might include periodic general reviews of the Act, gauging the cumulative impact of incorporation of the ECHR upon the substance of British domestic law, as well as upon the administration of the courts and litigation before the Court of Human Rights at Strasbourg. The scrutiny committee in question might consider it worthwhile to initiate separate special inquiries into aspects of particular importance or significance to the working of the Act, such as the courts' use of their powers under s 4 to make 'declarations of incompatibility' between statutory provisions and human rights, and questions of citizens' access to justice in the enforcement of their human rights. The committee would no doubt seek to identify areas for improvement, where the Act was perceived by members as working less effectively than it might, and to bring forward recommendations for action.

A major area in which Parliament may wish to extend its functions of scrutiny over the coming years lies in the field of international human rights treaties. The focus of this work would be twofold. The first function would be to scrutinise whether the present obligations of the United Kingdom government under the terms of the international instruments to which it was a party were being properly carried out to the satisfaction of the Westminster Parliament. This would have a wider remit than simply the ECHR and would most certainly include the International Covenant on Civil and Political Rights (ICCPR) and the International Covenant on Economic, Social and Cultural Rights (both treaty enactments of the United Nations). One issue of recent controversy has been the failure of the United Kingdom government to consult Parliament prior to carrying out its reporting obligations to the United Nations Human Rights Committee, as required under the terms of the ICCPR.[19] Similar reporting obligations are owed under a number of other international agreements to which the United Kingdom is a member, such as the International Labour Organisation and the Committee on the Elimination of Discrimination against Women. Any new human rights scrutiny procedures, therefore, might be expected to involve these draft reports being submitted to Parliament for debate, preceded by the examination and preparation of a memorandum by a specialist committee on the subject.

An important second task in the field of scrutiny of treaty matters raises more fundamental issues governing the relationship between the Executive and Parliament. To what extent should Parliament be consulted about, and possibly control, the treaty-making powers in general which the government possesses under the royal prerogative? For the purpose of this chapter, it is a sufficient illustration to mention that in 1951 when the United Kingdom government agreed and ratified the ECHR itself, no parliamentary approval was sought or required, and no consultation or debate on the subject ever took place. This was similarly the case when the United Kingdom government ratified the ICCPR in 1976. More recently, Protocol 11 to the ECHR, reforming litigation procedures at Strasbourg and creating an enlarged Court of Human Rights, was ratified by the United Kingdom government in 1994 without any parliamentary scrutiny at all. There is now widespread agreement that Parliament should be involved in the process of human rights treaty-making and amendment, and any new scrutiny arrangements that emerge as a result are likely to involve a specialist committee for the purpose. Amendments to the articles of the European Convention

---

19   Lord Lester 'Taking Human Rights Seriously' in R Blackburn and J Busuttil (eds) *Human Rights for the 21st Century* (1997).

on Human Rights will assume even greater significance after 1998, following our incorporation of the convention under the terms of the Human Rights Act.

A different, more wide-ranging human rights function for some new or pre-existing committee would be the undertaking of inquiries and preparation of advisory reports. A Labour government White Paper in October 1997[20] said that a new parliamentary human rights committee 'might conduct enquiries on a range of human rights issues relating to the Convention, and produce reports so as to assist the Government and Parliament in deciding what action to take'. The following month, when presenting the Human Rights Bill to the House of Lords for second reading debate, the Lord Chancellor, Lord Irvine, further stated that:[1]

> It would be a natural focus for the increased interest in human rights issues which Parliament will inevitably take when we have brought rights home. It could, for example, not only keep the protection of human rights under review, but could also be in the forefront of public education and consultation on human rights. It could receive written submissions and hold public hearings at a number of locations across the country. It could be in the van [sic] of the promotion of a human rights culture across the country.

As elaborated upon here by the Lord Chancellor, such a function would be unprecedented in Westminster terms. The workload involved would be potentially vast, and the notion of a Westminster select committee travelling around the country holding public hearings seems rather unrealistic. These political utterances may be explicable in terms of the government trying to combat any disappointment that it failed to provide for an independent Human Rights Commission in the Human Rights Act. For it was widely believed that a Human Rights Commission should have been established concomitant with incorporation of the ECHR in order to help facilitate the workings of the new Act, and that among the most important functions of the Commission would be the promotion of greater public awareness and education about human rights matters, the undertaking of inquiries into subjects of special concern, and the constitution of an expert independent advisory body for subjects referred to it by government and parliamentary bodies.[2]

None the less, with or without a Human Rights Commission, there would be advantages in including inquiries and advisory reports on human rights affairs within the terms of reference of a suitable parliamentary body. To some extent, this would overlap with the work of the House of Commons Home Affairs Committee, particularly as, following the Human Rights Act, that committee is likely to refer to the human rights principles of the ECHR as a de facto set of guidelines, affecting aspects of its work and the criteria to be applied to government administration and policy – not only in relation to the Home Office, but also to the responsibilities covered by the Lord Chancellor's department. Whatever new human rights committee might be entrusted with this wide-ranging role, however, it could be relied upon to proceed by way of complementing rather than duplicating existing forms of parliamentary inquiry and

20 White Paper *Rights Brought Home* (1997).
1 HL Deb, 3 November 1997, col 1234.
2 See generally S Spencer 'A Human Rights Commission' in R Blackburn and Lord Plant (eds) *Constitutional Reform Now* (1998).

to undertake inquiries only where it felt that other forms of parliamentary attention to some human rights issues either did not exist or had failed.

There are a number of ways in which these scrutiny, deliberative and advisory functions might be introduced into the workings of Westminster, most of which would work satisfactorily for immediate purposes. Three general approaches might be identified. First, the new human rights functions could be allocated among existing parliamentary committees. This would be particularly feasible if, at least initially, the innovation concentrated on pre-legislative scrutiny for compliance with the ECHR. The chief contenders for taking on these new legislative responsibilities would be the Joint Select Committee on Statutory Instruments and the House of Lords Select Committee on Delegated Powers and Deregulation.[3] Both already sift through secondary and primary legislation, respectively, and their terms of reference could be extended to include questions of human rights compliance. The enlarged workload for these committees would almost certainly involve the creation of one or more subcommittees to either or both of them.

A second, more ambitious, option would be to conduct a wider reorganisation of pre-legislative select committees, integrating human rights into whatever new scheme of arrangements is adopted. The existing bodies affected would, again, be the Joint Select Committee on Statutory Instruments and the House of Lords Select Committee on Delegated Powers and Deregulation. The most likely rationale for any such reorganisation would be a streamlining of the special pre-legislative scrutiny processes, distinguishing between primary and secondary legislation. So, for example: the Committee on Delegated Powers and Deregulation might be wound up; a new joint committee on primary legislation could be created to deal with human rights and delegated powers; and the existing Joint Committee on Statutory Instruments could have its terms of reference extended to include human rights and deregulation orders. The resulting two new joint committees would need to establish a subcommittee structure to cope with their large overall workload.

But perhaps a more straightforward approach would be simply to establish a new Select Committee on Human Rights to discharge most or all of the functions currently being proposed by Labour. This could be in the form of: (a) a single joint committee of both Houses; (b) two committees established in the Commons and Lords respectively; or (c) some structure combining both joint and independent elements for the purposes of carrying out functions of a different nature. Thus, if each House contributed seven members to a joint committee, they could deliberate jointly for the purposes of reporting on technical matters (notably in offering expert advice on legislative compliance with the jurisprudence of the ECHR) and meet separately on matters of a political or policy-orientated nature (such as in offering opinions on the merits of government policy at home or internationally).

How other countries organise their parliamentary scrutiny arrangements with respect to human rights will be influential in shaping the eventual outcome of the new committee work at Westminster. A wide number of foreign legislatures now possess human rights committees of their own. A recent survey by the Inter-Parliamentary Union found that 52 countries have a committee or subcommittee expressly devoted

---

3   For an account of these two committees, see R Blackburn 'A Parliamentary Committee on Human Rights' in *Blackburn and Plant* (n 2 above).

to some aspect of human rights, with a further 44 addressing the subject within a committee with broader remit, such as constitutional or foreign affairs.[4] However, any clear lessons for the United Kingdom are obscured by the very wide diversity of arrangements to be found operating across these countries, with special human rights audit and scrutiny functions traversing the whole range of public institutions. Most pre-legislative scrutiny arrangements are undertaken by bodies operating outside Parliament, for example: by the Attorney General's office, as in New Zealand; within government department human rights units, particularly justice ministries as in Canada and the Netherlands; by some form of constitutional council, as in France; or by a government-funded human rights commission or institute, as in Australia, Norway and Denmark. The majority of countries also have significantly different indigenous political characteristics, rendering their own forms of scrutiny process less persuasive or compatible with Westminster traditions.

So far as parliamentary committees on human rights are concerned, however, it is the Australian Parliament which is recognised as having pioneered scrutiny procedures and which provides us with the most advanced model for the United Kingdom. Australia has two important committees which address pre-legislative scrutiny on human rights grounds: the Senate's Standing Committee for the Scrutiny of Bills (scrutiny of primary legislation) and its Standing Committee on Regulation and Ordinances (scrutiny of secondary legislation). The terms of reference of both committees are of a wider constitutional nature than human rights alone. In the case of the Australian Committee for the Scrutiny of Bills, its responsibility is to report on any provision in a Bill which affects any of the following principles: violation of personal rights and liberties; undue dependency on ill-defined administrative powers, or non-reviewable administrative decision; and inappropriately delegated legislative powers or removal of parliamentary scrutiny of such powers. It was this committee, more than any other foreign model, that proved particularly influential in the House of Lords' decision to set up its own Select Committee on the Scrutiny of Delegated Powers in 1992, described above. This experiment having proved successful, the House of Lords might well be encouraged to follow the Australian pattern of this committee one step further, by extending its terms of reference to embrace legislative compliance with the terms of the ECHR.

So far as the Senate's Committee on Regulations and Ordinances is concerned, four criteria exist against which it proceeds to scrutinise delegated legislation. These guiding principles are that orders: (i) must be in accordance with the parent Act; (ii) must not adversely affect personal rights and liberties; (iii) must not oust the jurisdiction of the courts on administrative matters; and (iv) should not contain matter more appropriate for parliamentary enactment. Where any of these principles appear to have been infringed, the committee will present a report to the Senate. The Australian Parliament has one further human rights committee of some importance, the Sub-Committee on Human Rights, which currently operates under the terms of the Joint Standing Committee on Foreign Affairs, Defence and Trade. This subcommittee has the large responsibility for reviewing Australia's entire human rights policy programme both at home and abroad and, not surprisingly, some of the reports it has produced since its establishment in 1991 have been widely publicised and influential.

---

4   Inter-Parliamentary Union *World Directory of Parliamentary Human Rights Bodies* (1993).

Before long it is likely to emerge from out of the shadow of its existing parent committee into a separately organised Joint Committee on Human Rights, a parliamentary development it itself recommended in November 1994.

The establishment of new human rights scrutiny procedures at Westminster over the next decade will be an important future component of Parliament's control of executive action and is to be warmly welcomed. It will help pre-empt administrative practices and help minimise the prospect of poorly-drafted or misguided provisions reaching the statute book. It is generally agreed that the prevention of public activity and legislation likely to offend fundamental rights is preferable to relying alone upon litigation under the Human Rights Act and a judicial ruling on the matter. These new developments will also, particularly in the non-legislative functions to be performed, serve to imbue the working of Parliament with a sharper sense of respect for individual rights and freedoms. Baroness Williams, the former Education Secretary in the Labour government of the 1970s, put this point well during debates in the House of Lords on the Human Rights Bill:

> Involving Parliament more in issues of human rights, giving it clear responsibilities, is not only a way of ensuring that human rights are more generally understood in the country, but also of recognising that Parliament itself could usefully discharge many functions that it is not currently asked to do. There is a great deal of talent and ability in both Houses of Parliament which remain to be tapped in the interest of trying to ensure that human rights are properly upheld.[5]

Human rights and House of Lords reform

Members of the House of Lords have for several years now held themselves out as being able and willing to assume human rights scrutiny functions. Indeed, in July 1994 Lord Irvine himself, whilst in opposition, was a co-signatory to a memorandum prepared by Lord Simon of Glaisdale, Lord Alexander of Weedon, Lord Lester of Herne Hill and himself which proposed to the Liaison Committee of the House of Lords –

> a significant extension of the committee work of the House into an area where, we suggest, Parliament has an important scrutiny function to exercise, and where the House could bring to bear considerable expertise and experience . . . It would be desirable for the House of Commons to devise procedures of its own or to join with our House in undertaking the work. However, it seems to us to be work which is, in any event, well suited to the interests and concerns of the House of Lords and to its constitutional role.[6]

The deeper implication of the Human Rights Act (and any later constitutional Bill of Rights) will be to sharpen perceptions of the functions and powers of the House of Lords with respect to human rights and constitutional law generally. Several factors in this process are already beginning. As discussed above, the House of Lords now possesses a legislative veto over remedial orders under the Human Rights Act. These

5   HL Deb, 27 November 1997, col 1147.
6   *Scrutiny of Legislation for consistency with obligations under the European Convention on Human Rights* (1994) para 9.

human rights orders will be high-profile parliamentary events on the relatively rare occasions that they occur, and it can confidently be anticipated that the House of Lords will take its responsibilities of scrutinising and approving these human rights laws very seriously. Also, the House of Lords looks certain to be actively involved (possibly as the leading partner) in the new human rights scrutiny procedures. The Labour Party, in its policy papers 1996-97 and in its front-bench speeches during the passage of the Human Rights Bill 1997-98, publicly indicated that if and when a parliamentary committee on human rights is established, it favours a joint committee.[7] Furthermore, in the absence of any initiative on some of the human rights scrutiny reforms discussed above, especially pre-legislative scrutiny for compliance with the ECHR, the House of Lords will almost certainly institute its own independent scrutiny procedures.

If, as predicted above, the prospect of a constitutional Bill of Rights gathers momentum in the early part of the twenty-first century, then the divergence between a wider perception of constitutional law, embracing human rights law, and ordinary legislation will be taken one step further. Furthermore, anticipation of the new legal relationship between the Scottish and Westminster Parliaments is already beginning to foster a wider appreciation of the desirability of a formal written constitution. If support for a written constitution, of which a Bill of Rights formed part, gathered momentum, then this would point still more clearly in the direction of a formal distinction being drawn between a higher body of constitutional law in which the Second Chamber might be expected to perform some special functions, and ordinary parliamentary enactments which were subordinate to that constitutional law. It is worth noting that some Labour policy documents over the past ten years have already proposed that the Second Chamber should have an elevated role with respect to the protection of human rights. A 1989 policy review document[8] specifically included in its constitutional recommendations that the House of Lords should take on a special function in protecting human rights, and be given extended legislative powers of delay over government Bills affecting basic rights and freedoms. The same view was reiterated by the Plant Commission on Electoral Systems in 1993 when considering a suitable method of elections to the Second Chamber (both Plant and the earlier 1989 policy review backed a directly-elected House of Lords).[9]

As Professor Francis Jacobs, advocate-general at the European Court of Justice, has observed: 'By a strange legal anachronism, some States, notably the United Kingdom, still seem to consider that treaties are matters for governments alone.'[10] In the field of treaty-making and international human rights, the pressures towards greater parliamentary involvement in executive decision-making will grow, and in the formulation of what new powers and procedures this will involve, the House of Lords will have a legitimate claim to an equal standing with that of the House of Commons. The United Kingdom is now the only Parliament in the European Union that lacks a formal mechanism for securing parliamentary scrutiny and approval to

---

7   See eg *Bringing Rights Home: Labour's Plans to Incorporate the European Convention on Human Rights into UK Law* (1996) p 12; also *Report of the Joint Consultative Committee on Constitutional Reform* (1997) p 6.

8   Labour Party *Meet the Challenge, Make the Change* (1989).

9   Labour Party *Report of the Working Party on Electoral Systems* (1993) ch 4.

10   Quoted in HL Deb, 28 February 1996, col 1531.

treaties and other major foreign policy decisions. The 1924 Ponsonby 'rule' (which is effectively a Foreign Office circular describing the department's intended practice) is ineffective as a means of establishing Parliament's rights of scrutiny. It involves the voluntary practice of governments laying treaties signed by the United Kingdom before Parliament as Command Papers after their entry into force, and, in the case of treaties requiring legal ratification, a copy being placed on the Table of the House 21 days beforehand.[11] Both Labour and Liberal Democrat policy documents in recent years have proposed policies for extending Parliament's control over a number of foreign policy matters including treaties, which are currently negotiated and ratified by the government under the extra-parliamentary authority of the Crown prerogative. In a 1993 policy paper,[12] the Labour Party argued that treaty-making (along with military involvement of United Kingdom forces overseas) was a matter requiring new formal rules for securing proper parliamentary scrutiny and approval. 'Treaty after treaty is concluded without the formal consent of Parliament',[13] the Labour document concluded, and indeed (as referred to above) the two major international human rights treaties to which the United Kingdom is a party – the ECHR in 1950 and United Nations ICCPR in 1976 – were not subject to any form of parliamentary discussion or scrutiny, and ratification of Protocol 11 to the ECHR in 1994 was a matter not even announced to, let alone debated or approved by, either House of Parliament.

Surely, following incorporation of the ECHR into the domestic law of the United Kingdom, future amendments to the ECHR itself should, as a matter of parliamentary practice, be agreed and ratified by Parliament. And in any new scheme of arrangement for extending its powers, whether by way of statutory reform and/or parliamentary self-regulation through standing orders, it would be natural for the House of Lords to carry out some distinctive role, either independently or jointly with the work of the Commons. More generally, if reform of the Crown prerogative of treaty-making comes to involve a new requirement for an affirmative resolution in Parliament, then it would be consistent with the practice of many other bicameral legislatures that both Houses, not simply the executive-dominated lower House, possess procedures and powers that ensure the effective debate, scrutiny and approval of what has been negotiated and proposed by the government.

Such new directions in the development of parliamentary functions come at an opportune time, because reform of the House of Lords is high on the agenda of the new Labour government. The 'first stage' of removing hereditary peers from membership of the Chamber is likely to take place in the 1998-99 parliamentary session. The 'second stage' of House of Lords reform, according to the Labour government, may involve a joint committee of both Houses examining the question of a permanent basis for reform and bringing forward recommendations. Meanwhile, the Human Rights Act, the prospect of a homegrown Bill of Rights, new committee procedures on human rights, and a desire for parliamentary involvement in international human rights treaties – will all substantially influence perceptions in Whitehall and at Westminster of what the constitutional functions and powers of a reformed Second Chamber should be in a democratised Parliament fit for the twenty-first century.

---

11 See also Foreign Office *Guidelines on Explanatory Memoranda for Treaties* (1996).
12 Labour Party *A New Agenda for Democracy* (1993).
13 Ibid, p 33.

Parliamentarians of all parties should welcome the implications of these changes, which will call for a formal re-statement of the distinctive role and functions of the House of Lords for the future. The political parties should embrace some form of complementary division of business between the two Houses of Parliament, and recognise that some such division already exists or is emerging in practice. This should then be reflected in the theory and practice of Parliament and in the powers and regulation controlling the relationship between the two Houses.

It is worth recalling that the Parliament Act 1911 was enacted as a temporary, interim measure.[14] As a piece of legislation it had the immediate, specific objective of overriding the political opposition in the Tory-dominated House of Lords to the social reform programme of the then Liberal Government. The preamble to the Act made it clear that its purpose was simply to restrict the powers of the Lords for the time being, pending a permanent basis for reform being agreed and implemented. The real question, which the expedient of the 1911 Act deferred and the later 1949 Act compounded, was: in respect of which types of business (apart from those of a financial and purely administrative nature) should the Second Chamber retain its power of veto or possess an extended power of delay? The Parliament Acts ceased some time ago to be a satisfactory basis for relations between the two Houses of Parliament, and the implications of the Human Rights Act together with those of other developments likely to take place in the near future, point to the need for some clear rationalisation of its powers which distinguishes between legislation of different kinds. Thus, public general Bills and other forms of primary legislation fall into one category, over which the Second Chamber should exercise a short delaying power of one year (as at present) or two years (as has been recommended by many). A similar power should exist with respect to ordinary statutory instruments, being subject to a one-stage parliamentary process not capable of amendment. But Bills dealing with major constitutional subject matter and human rights law, including remedial orders under the Human Rights Act, should be placed in a special category for which the House of Lords should have their earlier, pre-1911, right of veto restored or be given some extended power of delay. Recently, reports from the Liberal Democrats and from respected think-tanks, including the Institute for Public Policy Research, have advocated such powers for a reformed House of Lords.[15] Some of the policy documents of the Labour Party have also pointed in this direction. If the Westminster Parliament is to become a bicameral system, structured upon a complementary division of function, with the Second Chamber taking on an extended role in the field of constitutional law and human rights, then it follows that a significant extension of its powers will be involved. Furthermore, if a de facto category of constitutional legislation emerges as a consequence of other reforms, as has been suggested in this chapter, then this will serve to develop further the notion of a body of fundamental law in relation to which the reformed Second Chamber has a special role to play.

A more indirect effect of these implications of human rights reform upon the future of the House of Lords may be to clarify the principles upon which its membership

14   The preamble to the 1911 Act declares that: 'whereas it is intended to substitute for the House of Lords as it at present exists a Second Chamber constituted on a popular instead of hereditary basis, but such substitution cannot be immediately brought into operation . . .'

15   Institute for Public Policy Research *Reforming the Lords* (1993) and *A Written Constitution for the United Kingdom* (revised edn, 1993).

should be determined since one important point on House of Lords reform bears constant re-statement: a pre-condition for settling any permanent basis for reforming the composition of the Second Chamber is the prior determination of the proper role, functions and powers the House should possess. The preparation of a convincing practical rationale for a bicameral legislature at Westminster – involving human rights and constitutional law functions being attributed to a reconstituted House of Lords – would be conducive to the straightforward and perhaps obvious solution of establishing direct popular elections. Over the next few years, the democratic argument in favour of electing members to the House of Lords is likely to prove irresistible; justly so, as the case for the status quo or any other revised system of nomination and appointment is weak. The 'expertise argument' commonly employed by those who defend the status quo – that the House of Lords needs persons of a special level of ability and knowledge, best determined through a system of executive appointment – is misleading at best and an affront to contemporary principle at worst. Few constitutionalists would dare justify the same line of political reasoning with respect to any other parliamentary or regional assembly in the United Kingdom. Under an electoral system, the political process relies upon the parties' recruitment and selection of suitably qualified candidates who will best represent and command the confidence of the electors for the particular parliamentary work involved. There would be no better evidence of the United Kingdom's new commitment to the best practices of democracy and human rights than opening up, to an open and transparent system of popular election, the procedures whereby it chooses its political representatives in the upper house.

Chapter XII

Legal aspects of relations between the United Kingdom and the Scottish Parliament: the evolution of subordinate sovereignty?

John McEldowney

Introduction

The purpose of this chapter is to consider the likely relationship between the United Kingdom and Scottish Parliaments under the proposals in the Scotland Bill.[1] This involves considering the main legislative and financial powers of the Scottish Parliament and the scope of decentralisation provided for in the Bill, and takes experience under devolution in Northern Ireland between 1920 and 1972 as an example of how relations between the two Parliaments might operate.

The description of the United Kingdom as a unitary state emphasises the centrality of a single elected government headed by a Prime Minister and Cabinet under the sovereignty of a single Parliament. This description is likely to require revision in the light of the forthcoming introduction of a Parliament for Scotland with devolved legislative powers and functions. The term 'union state'[2] may be used to describe the new relationship envisaged under the government's proposals for devolution for Scotland and Wales as a way of emphasising the continuation of the sovereignty of the Westminster Parliament and continuity with the past. Within the new constitutional order in the United Kingdom and in Europe, the Scottish Parliament may obtain a greater transfer of legislative authority than was at first realised.

The Scotland Bill 1997 offers a form of decentralisation that will have far-reaching effects on the role of the British Parliament and its future relationship with the new Scottish Parliament. What is on offer through the process of decentralisation begun by the Devolution Bill is home rule for Scotland, with a directly elected Parliament with tax-raising powers. Devolution of this variety is organic and, as the experience of a Scottish Parliament takes root, it is likely that further legal and constitutional authority will be conceded by the English Parliament to the new Scottish Parliament.

---

1   Bill 104 of 1997-98.
2   See S Rokkan and D Urwin *Economy, Territory Identity: Politics of West European Peripheries* (1982) and *Strategies for Self-Government: The Campaigns for a Scottish Parliament* (1996). An illuminating and useful analysis is provided by Vernon Bogdanor in his conference paper 'Devolution: The Constitutional Aspects' University of Cambridge Centre for Public Law (January 1998).

Parliamentary sovereignty, retained by the United Kingdom Parliament under the Scotland Bill, may be transformed by the gradual acquisition of what may be termed 'subordinate sovereignty' by the Scottish Parliament.

This chapter is intended to address three questions which are at the heart of the relationship between the Scottish Parliament and the United Kingdom Parliament. First, what is the legislative competence of the Scottish Parliament and, in its relationship with the United Kingdom Parliament, where does the balance of sovereignty lie? Secondly, how will relations between the Scottish and Westminster Parliaments actually function under the proposals in the Bill? Finally, what is the future role of the courts in adjudicating disputes about the powers of the two Parliaments? It is first necessary to provide a historical analysis which explains how the doctrine of parliamentary sovereignty owes much to the legislative union between Scotland and England and the Union with Ireland.

The Acts of Union: sovereignty and delegation

The Union between England and Scotland in 1707 created the new nation of Great Britain. In constitutional terms, this came about through the assertion of the authority of the new Parliament of Great Britain and the creation of full political and economic union. In fact, this was not a revolutionary break with the past but an attempt to embrace change through continuity with the past.

The strengthening of parliamentary power[3] through the Union with Scotland came at the expense of the former English and Scottish Parliaments, which ceased to exist by virtue of the Union. Legislation was adopted by both the Scottish and English Parliaments to give effect to the Union.[4] The Parliament of Great Britain became sovereign, it is argued, because of the inheritance it gained from the abolition of the English and Scottish Parliaments. The British Parliament acquired further powers after 1707, primarily at the expense of the monarch. The two centuries that followed witnessed the development of constitutional conventions and the democratisation of government through, first, the Great Reform Act in 1832 and further electoral reforms, notably in 1867. Constitutional conventions reflected the centrality of Parliament in the life of the nation.

During this period, the subject matter of legislation expanded to cover public health, sanitation, local government, a wide variety of social problems including the scope of the criminal law, and some responsibility for the protection of the rights of the subject.

The Act of Union with Ireland of 1800 created the United Kingdom of Great Britain and Ireland. The Irish Parliament was abolished and the authority of the Parliament of the United Kingdom of Great Britain and Ireland[5] was secured through Irish representation in the new Parliament of the United Kingdom. Laws in force in Ireland fell under the powers of the United Kingdom Parliament and were thereby

---

3　See J D B Mitchell *Constitutional Law* (1968) pp 69-74.
4　The Scottish Act APS XI, 406; and the corresponding English Act 6 Anne c 11.
5　See Poyning's Law 1495, which extended English legislation to Ireland through various ordinances.

subject to amendment. As with the Anglo Scottish arrangements mentioned above, the Union was reached through the agreement of both Parliaments.[6]

The history of the Government of Ireland Act 1920 falls outside the scope of this chapter. It is sufficient to note here that, originally, the 1920 Act provided for two Parliaments, one in Northern Ireland and the other in Southern Ireland. The creation of the Irish Free State intervened and the Anglo Irish Agreement in 1921 gave rise to an altogether different settlement,[7] leading to the eventual creation of the Irish Republic.

The importance of Northern Ireland for this chapter is in providing a model of devolution that makes for a useful comparison with the proposed devolution for Scotland in the Scotland Bill.[8] The Parliament of Northern Ireland, created by the Government of Ireland Act 1920,[9] had extensive powers to make laws for the 'peace order and good government of Northern Ireland'. This was a familiar formula for conferring wide powers on a colonial legislature, leaving scope for virtually unfettered legislative power. The grant of power to the Northern Ireland Parliament was subject to excepted matters[10] and reserved matters[11] that fell outside the authority of the Northern Ireland Parliament. There were further express limitations on the competence of the Northern Ireland Parliament, such as the prohibition of legislation with an extra-territorial effect. Another limitation was that Acts of the United Kingdom Parliament extending over Northern Ireland could prevail over Northern Ireland Acts even where the subject matter of the United Kingdom Parliament Act was one that fell within the jurisdiction of the Northern Ireland Parliament. A process of certification by the Attorney General was provided for to ensure that Bills of the Northern Ireland Parliament were valid within the terms of the 1920 Act. Gaps were filled by enabling legislation[12] subsequently passed by the United Kingdom Parliament. Restrictions[13] on the powers of the Northern Ireland Parliament contained within the 1920 Act were supplemented by s 75, which unambiguously asserted the sovereignty of the United Kingdom Parliament. This assertion of sovereignty was intended to address Unionist fears of weakness in the Union between Great Britain and Northern Ireland. The 1920 Act was supplemented by the Ireland Act 1949.

Within this framework there was considerable scope for the Northern Ireland Parliament to legislate on a wide variety of subjects. Claire Palley noted:[14]

---

6   Dicey's analysis of the passage of the Act of Union is provided in an important article where he argues that the Act of Union 1800 was obtained through fraud: A V Dicey 'Two Acts of Union: A Contrast' (1881) 36 Fortnightly Review 463-484.

7   Irish Free State (Agreement) Act 1922.

8   See B Hadfield 'Scotland's Parliament: A Northern Ireland perspective on the White Paper' [1997] PL 660.

9   See H Calvert 'Constitutional Law in Northern Ireland' [1968] NILQ; Sir Arthur Quekett *The Constitution of Northern Ireland* (1946). Also see J D B Mitchell *Constitution Law* (2nd edn, 1968).

10 These referred to matters that lay within the exclusive jurisdiction of the Parliament of the United Kingdom; those that fell within the remit of the Northern Ireland Parliament were transferred powers.

11 These were matters that might be at one time transferred to an all Ireland body: see s 9 of the Government of Ireland Act 1920. Also reserved matters were powers to impose income tax and a variety of fiscal matters.

12 Northern Ireland (Miscellaneous Provisions) Act 1932.

13 These included ss 4, 5, 21, 22, which prohibited laws interfering with religious equality, and laws which took property without compensation.

14 C Palley *The Evolution, Disintegration and Possible Reconstruction of the Northern Ireland Constitution* (1972) p 389.

Put positively the Northern Ireland parliament may legislate on matters relating to law and order, to the police, to courts other than the Supreme Court, to civil and criminal law, to local government, to health and social services, to education, to planning and development, to commerce and industrial development and internal trade, to agriculture and to finance.

Newark in 1953 summarised the essence of the constitutional position under the 1920 Act as follows:

> it would be a mistake to read the 1920 Act to see what the Stormont Parliament could do; instead it should be assumed it could do everything, and the Act should be read to see what it cannot do.[15]

Throughout the life of the Northern Ireland Parliament from 1920 until 1972, the United Kingdom Parliament adopted a working convention about how Northern Ireland matters should be dealt with which reflected Newark's approach. Discussion at Westminster of matters with a Northern Ireland dimension was ruled out of order. At first, this formed part of the Speakers Rules[16] of the House of Commons. A parallel convention could be found in the Speakers Rules of the Parliament of Northern Ireland:[17] there the convention was that matters that were reserved matters outside the jurisdiction of the Parliament of Northern Ireland should not be discussed at Stormont. Secondly, it became clear that at Westminster there was great reluctance to engage in passing legislation that might affect the domestic affairs of Northern Ireland. For many years there was a tacit agreement between the government of Northern Ireland and the government of the United Kingdom that no legislation would be passed at Westminster for Northern Ireland without the consent of the government of Northern Ireland.[18]

Conventions were not the only source of the idea that, somehow, Northern Ireland, through the 1920 Act, had gained a degree of 'sovereignty' over its own affairs. The Northern Ireland courts developed a presumption of constitutionality when Northern Ireland Acts of Parliament were in issue. This presumption became a 'saving doctrine' when the Northern Ireland courts were faced with an array of challenges[19] to the validity of Northern Ireland legislation. The doctrine or presumption of constitutionality was also applied on appeals to the House of Lords[20] from the Northern Ireland courts.

It is possible to analyse the example of devolution in Northern Ireland between 1920 and 1972 in the following terms. A certain degree of 'sovereignty' had been devolved to the Northern Ireland Parliament, while the ultimate sovereignty of the United Kingdom Parliament was retained. On this analysis, the actual working of the government of Northern Ireland under the 1920 Act appears to have had an organic quality. Devolution permitted a great deal of distinctive policy development in Northern

---

15   See F Newark 'The Constitution of Northern Ireland' in D G Neill *Devolution of Government* (1953).
16   See HC Deb vol 162, 19 April 1923, cols 2246-2247.
17   See NI Parl vol 8, cols 490-492.
18   A full discussion of this analysis appears in Calvert (n 9 above) pp 94-110. There is an important analysis offered in HC Research Paper 93/3 p 43.
19   See *Belfast Corpn v O D Cars Ltd* [1960] NI 60; *McEldowney v Forde* [1971] AC 632.
20   *Gallagher v Lynn* [1937] AC 863.

Ireland. Sometimes there were frustrations, as in the area of law reform where Northern Ireland was said to lag behind the rest of the United Kingdom. Laws on major issues such as land law (the absence in Northern Ireland of the Law of Property Act 1925), trial by jury in civil cases, and in areas of town and country planning and matrimonial disputes, differed markedly from English law.[1]

The Kilbrandon Commission, of which Professor Newark was a prominent member, appeared not to take account of the extent of the delegation of law making power that Northern Ireland enjoyed. The Kilbrandon definition appears to see devolution as a single event in time. The Northern Ireland example in fact shows that devolution permits continuous change and developments which were not envisaged in the original devolution legislation. Kilbrandon's definition of devolution as the 'delegation of central government powers without the relinquishment of sovereignty',[2] accentuated the importance of reserved sovereignty without paying attention to the permissive nature of 'delegated sovereignty' which is possible within the grant of devolution. In short, the experience under the 1920 Act was that, within delegated sovereignty in its wider sense, Northern Ireland developed its own identity. It is possible to see this development as a useful illustration of the inherent flexibility that may be built into a system of devolution. Even allowing for the special conditions prevalent in Northern Ireland, it is hard not to see that similar developments might occur in Scotland under the form of devolution proposed in the Scotland Bill.

Finally, with respect to Northern Ireland, Hadfield's analysis[3] of the Northern Ireland Constitution Act 1973 is helpful in showing the 1973 Act to be a model of its kind of devolution: an Assembly with legislative powers devolved on an extensive rolling basis, depending on agreement being reached through a power sharing executive. Such 'rolling devolution' gave supervisory powers to the United Kingdom Parliament, including control over various excepted powers[4] which were withheld from the Assembly's legislative competence. It is a moot point whether under such arrangements the excepted powers would be relinquished at some time in the future to a Northern Ireland Assembly. There were incentives to rolling devolution in the design of the 1973 legislation: agreement at a power sharing level might give rise to extended powers – even greater than under the 1920 Act; and within certain reserved matters there was room for the Assembly to legislate with the agreement of the United Kingdom Parliament.

The value of the 1973 Act is that it provides a further illustration of the organic nature of devolved powers. Replacing the 1920 Act with this more 'interactive form' of devolution in 1973 was intended to promote agreement within the Assembly in Northern Ireland and between it and the United Kingdom Parliament and government.

1   This point was often made clear to the students of Northern Ireland law, who were left to the difficult task of learning the distinctive nature of the Northern Ireland legal system without the benefit of suitable material and textbooks. Access to information was limited. See the useful and informative material now provided by the Servicing the Legal System project at the Queen's University of Belfast and the work of the Northern Ireland Legal Quarterly.

2   See *Royal Commission on the Constitution 1969-1973* vol I report (Cmnd 5460) (1973) para 543. Also see the analysis provided in T Jones, 'Scottish Devolution and demarcation disputes' [1997] PL 283-297.

3   B Hadfield 'Scotland's Parliament: A Northern Ireland perspective on the White Paper' [1997] PL 660.

4   The 1973 Act listed excepted matters in Sch 2; Sch 3 contained reserved matters.

This ambition was never realised and the 1973 Act was never tested to its full potential[5] in terms of gaining powers for the Assembly.

The legislative competence of the Scottish Parliament

The lessons of Northern Ireland are useful[6] when evaluating the nature of the devolution proposed in the Scotland Bill. It is first necessary to explain how the present day proposals for Scotland came about. The essentially unitary nature of the United Kingdom with its centralised powers in London under a single Parliament gave rise to pressure in the 1970s to provide some form of decentralised system of government for Scotland. The Kilbrandon Report[7] in 1973 rejected separatism for Scotland and also for Wales. It recommended some form of devolution for Scotland. The Scotland Act 1978 provided for an elected assembly with legislative and executive powers. While a majority of those who voted in favour in a referendum supported devolution, these only formed 32.9% of the electorate and did not satisfy the 40% requirement under the legislation and so the Act was repealed.

The Scotland Act 1978 attempted to list all the powers to be transferred to the proposed Scottish Parliament. This approach may have been an attempt to avoid the permissive quality of the 1920 Act and avoid the possibility of devolution for Scotland achieving a life of its own. There was also a degree of deliberate vagueness in the 1978 Act, intended to leave room for doubt as to precisely what Scotland might end up with.[8]

The Scotland Bill 1997[9] grants legislative competence to the proposed Scottish Parliament in cl 27, which provides that 'the [Scottish] Parliament may make laws, to be known as Acts of the Scottish Parliament'. This follows some of the familiar wording of the Northern Ireland Constitution Act 1973, relating to the power of the Northern Ireland Assembly to make measures.[10]

The procedures and extent of legislative competence of the Scottish Parliament may be found in cll 28-35. These clauses cover the general legislative competence and jurisdiction of the Scottish Parliament. They must be read in conjunction with Sch 5 to the Bill, which details the reserved matters upon which the Scottish Parliament cannot legislate.

There is in the Scotland Bill no express assertion of the continuing sovereignty of the Westminster Parliament set out in the same way as in s 75 of the Government of Ireland Act 1920. However, in cl 35 there is provision that the Act of Union with Scotland 1706 and the Union with England Act 1707 should have effect. This is calculated to provide a 'technical' protection[11] of the United Kingdom Parliament's sovereignty.

---

5   The Assembly and power sharing executive had limited powers from January to May in 1974.
6   This point is forcefully made by Hadfield n 3 above. There is an additional point that devolution provides in the form of a written constitution a different perspective on the role of constitutional law. A new Northern Ireland Assembly was elected on 24 June 1998. There is to be a transitional period before it becomes fully operational.
7   *Report on the Royal Commission on the Constitution* 1969-1973 (Cmnd 5460).
8   See V Bogdanor *Devolution* (1979); Constitution Unit *Scotland's Parliament* (1996).
9   See the White Paper on Scottish Devolution *Scotland's Parliament* 1997 (Cm 3658).
10 The 1973 Act stipulated that such measures had the same force and effect as Acts of the United Kingdom Parliament once agreed by the Secretary of State for Northern Ireland.
11 *Scottish Office The Scotland Bill: A Guide* (December 1997) Annex A.

It is also clear that the Scotland Act will not be entrenched or protected against repeal or amendment. The principle that Parliament cannot bind its successors leaves open the possibility that the Parliament of Scotland may be abolished or its powers amended by a United Kingdom Act of Parliament. Of course, such a theoretical possibility has to be considered in the light of the wishes of the people of Scotland who are unlikely to wish to see removal of the legislative powers of the Scottish Parliament.

The legislative competence of the Scottish Parliament is limited under an extensive list of reserved matters falling under Sch 5. The details of Sch 5 include the Constitution, Foreign Affairs, the European Union, Defence and the Public Service. There is, in addition, a long list of financial and economic matters, including firearms, entertainment, immigration and nationality, intellectual property, and consumer protection, including matters falling within the public utility or newly privatised sector, which are all reserved.

The above list includes a wide range of activities which the Scottish Parliament might, foreseeably, at some time in the future, find desirable to bring within their competence. There is specific power under cl 29 to make modifications to the Schedule by subordinate legislation. It is thereby envisaged as a possibility for the future that a United Kingdom Parliament will want to devolve further powers to the Scottish Parliament.

There is provision for testing the legality or *vires* of any proposed Scottish Bill to ensure that no Bill can be introduced, should the Presiding Officer of the Scottish Parliament determine that it is outside the legislative competence of that Parliament. Issues as to the competence of such a Bill may be referred to the Judicial Committee of the Privy Council.[12] This may be regarded as a constitutional court for Scottish matters.

The question arises as to whether, within the fundamental doctrine of sovereignty of the United Kingdom Parliament, there is scope for the Scottish Parliament to have any 'delegated sovereignty'. The view that the government intended to devolve considerable powers to the Scottish Parliament is supported in the White Paper when it underlines the idea of 'devolving wide ranging legislative powers to the Scottish Parliament'.[13]

Notwithstanding the continuing ultimate sovereignty of the United Kingdom Parliament, it is unlikely that it would be used to abolish the Scottish Parliament, for obvious political reasons; within the restrictions of a subordinate legislature there is considerable scope for development and the acquisition of more extensive powers.

The example of Northern Ireland shows how considerable practical devolution in addition to that outlined in the enabling legislation can take place through the development of conventions. The courts may find the presumptions of constitutionality such as applied in Northern Ireland to be useful means to safeguard the process of constitution building. Thus, the courts may seek to uphold legislation of the Scottish Parliament in preference to any 'implied repeal' by Acts of the United Kingdom.

---

12   Clause 34 enables the Secretary of State to prohibit the submission of a Bill for Royal Assent within four weeks of its passing all its stages if he believes that it contains provisions incompatible with international obligations.
13   White Paper (n 9 above) para 4.2.

Finance

There is also scope for the financial provisions of the Scotland Bill to encourage some independence for policy makers on fiscal matters within Scotland. Major powers of taxation were specifically withheld[14] from the Northern Ireland Parliament[15] under the 1920 Act. So also in the proposals for Scotland the general responsibility for fiscal, economic and monetary policy, including taxation, rests with the United Kingdom government. This includes the general responsibility to administer the European Union's Structural Funds, which remains a reserved matter outside the competence of the Scottish Parliament under Sch 5.

Within these general constraints, however, some important powers on financial matters are devolved to the Scottish Parliament. Clause 61 establishes a Scottish Consolidated Fund and provides for the Secretary of State to make payments into the fund. Borrowing powers are included, as is the power for the Treasury to issue to the Secretary of State out of the National Loans Fund moneys required for ministers. Audit and financial powers are also included within the powers of the Scottish Parliament. An important tax varying power is found in cll 69-75 of the Scotland Bill. The basic rate of income tax may be varied 'by not more than 3%' for Scottish taxpayers. A widely drafted power under cl 75 permits the Treasury to modify enactments to take account of the Scottish Parliament's tax raising powers. These fiscal matters will ultimately provide an important opportunity for the Scottish Parliament to develop strategies affecting a whole range of financial matters including pensions and investments.

Local government in Scotland is an important part of the legislative authority of the Scottish Parliament. It may be possible, within the general limitations on the Scottish Parliament and the financial limitations on the local authorities in Scotland, for the Scottish Parliament to legislate to alter the existing arrangements for local government finance. This is particularly important given Scotland's history with respect to the poll tax. In that context there is to be an Independent Commission for Scotland to consider local government finances. This is likely to prove an important and controversial role. In the area of local government it is likely that the first work of the new Scottish Parliament will be to review the workings of the new 32 unitary or single-tier local government authorities under the Local Government (Scotland) Act 1994.

Conclusions

The first conclusion is that judicial review will heavily impact on the Scottish Parliament. Its relations with the Westminster Parliament will be subject to judicial scrutiny as questions are raised as to the competences of each. Here the Northern Ireland experience may be useful as an illustration of how the courts may develop constitutional presumptions to uphold the validity of legislation passed by the – subordinate – Scottish Parliament.

---

14 This did not prevent the Northern Ireland Exchequer from having limited taxation powers in relation to death duties, licence fees, property levies etc.
15 See ss 21 and 22 of the Government of Ireland Act 1920.

The second conclusion relates to the legislative authority of the new Scottish Parliament. Devolution demerges the two legislatures. It appears to do so without the advantages of a federal or confederal solution whereby the powers of both Parliaments are addressed in the constitutional structures that are created. Devolution provides for the decentralisation of power without the relinquishment of sovereignty. In strict constitutional theory, the Westminster Parliament maintains its own sovereignty, gained through the Acts of Union that created the Parliament of the United Kingdom of Great Britain and Ireland. But, as outlined in this chapter, devolution has an organic quality. An elected subordinate body is likely to gain legitimacy during its political life. This adds to the authority of politics less removed from the lives of the people that it affects than London. Powerful forces of nationalism and patriotism are at work in Scotland. Mixed together with these emotions are the twin attractions of self-reliance and a desire to discard any English inheritance. These are potent forces that will ebb and flow in the political life-cycles of the Scottish Parliament. There are also inherent dangers.   Nationalism may claim primacy over liberal tendencies. Homogeneity may be preferred to difference, and conformity accepted as part of an inward looking style of politics. Vested interests may triumph and factionalism prevail.

There is equally enormous beneficial potential. Scotland may forge a different kind of Union with the United Kingdom through the Scottish Parliament than was possible through a United Kingdom Parliament. The Scottish Parliament's subordinate sovereignty may strengthen under the pressures of subsidiarity from the European Union. Eventually, Scotland may pull together the civil law tradition with the common law to leave an enduring legacy. The relationship between the two legislatures is difficult to predict, but the diversity of two Parliaments rather than one may enhance the political and constitutional culture of the United Kingdom as a whole.

Further Reading

Chapter II

Bagehot, W *The English Constitution* (1993) Fontana.

Barker, A and Rush, M *The Member of Parliament and his Information* (1970) Allen and Unwin.

Biffen, J *Inside Westminster* (1996) Andre Deutsch.

Bradshaw, K and Pring, D *Parliament and Congress* (1981) Quartet.

Butt, R *The Power of Parliament* (2nd edn, 1969) Constable.

Code of Conduct, The (HC 688, 1995-96).

Compton, Sir E *Review of the administrative services of the House of Commons* (HC 254, 1974).

Crossman, R *The Diaries of a Cabinet Minister* (1976) Hamish Hamilton.

Griffith, J A G and Ryle, M *Parliament: Functions, Practice and Procedures* (1989) Sweet and Maxwell.

Home Office *Clarification of the law relating to the bribery of Members of Parliament* (1996).

Home Office *The prevention of corruption* (1997).

House of Commons (Accommodation) Report of the Select Committee (HC 184, 1953-54).

House of Commons (Administration) Report to the Speaker (HC 624, 1974-75) (Bottomley Report).

Ibbs, Sir R et al *House of Commons Services* Report to the House of Commons Commission (HC 38, 1990-91).

Irvine of Lairg, Lord *Keynote address to a conference on a UK Bill of Rights* (4 July 1997) transcript.

Joint Committee on Parliamentary Privilege, Minutes of Evidence (HC 401, 1997-98).

Lawrence, M 'The administrative organisation of the House of Commons' (1980) 48 Table 68.

Leopold, P M 'The publication of controversial Parliamentary papers' (1993) 56 MLR 690.

Limon, D and McKay, W (eds) *Erskine May: Parliamentary Practice* (22nd edn, 1997) Butterworths.

Morrison of Lambeth, Lord *Government and Parliament* (3rd edn, 1964) Oxford University Press.

Nolan Committee *Standards in Public Life* (Cm 2850, 1995) (2 vols).

Owen, J B *The rise of the Pelhams* (1957) Methuen.

Proctor, W 'Implementing Ibbs' (1992) 60 Table 66.

Rush, M and Shaw, M (eds) *The House of Commons: services and facilities* (1974) Allen and Unwin.

Seaton, J and Winetrobe, B 'Confidence motions in the UK Parliament' (1995) 64 Table 34.

Chapter III

JUSTICE *The Administration of the Courts* (1986).

Oliver, D and Drewry, G *Public Service Reform: Issues of Accountability and Public Law* (1996) Mansell.

Paterson, A and Bates, St J *The Legal System of Scotland* (2nd edn, 1986) Green.

Piper, R (ed) *Aspects of Accountability in the British System of Government* (1996) Tudor.

Shetreet, S *Judges on Trial* (1976) North Holland Publishing.

Spencer, J R *Jackson's Machinery of Justice* (8th edn, 1989) Cambridge University Press.

Stephens, R *The Independence of the Judiciary: The View from the Lord Chancellor's Office* (1993) Clarendon Press.

Woodhouse, D *The Pursuit of Good Administration: Ministers, Civil Servants and Judges* (1997) Clarendon Press.

Chapter IV

Bradley, A W and Ewing, K D *Constitutional and Administrative Law* (12th edn, 1997) Longman.

de Smith, S and Brazier, R *Constitutional and Administrative Law* (7th edn, 1994) Penguin.

Griffith, J A G and Ryle, M *Parliament: Functions, Practice and Procedures* (1989) Sweet and Maxwell.

Leopold, P M in O Hood Phillips and P Jackson *Constitutional and Administrative Law* (7th edn, 1987) Sweet and Maxwell, pp 129-252.

Limon, D and McKay, W (eds) *Erskine May: Parliamentary Practice* (22nd edn, 1997) Butterworths.

Loveland, I *Constitutional Law: A Critical Introduction* (1996) Butterworths, chs 5, 6, 8 and 15 (part).

Marshall, G in M Ryle and P G Richards (eds) *The Commons Under Scrutiny* (3rd edn, 1988) Routledge, pp 212-228.

Marshall, G in S Walkland (ed) *The House of Commons in the Twentieth Century* (1979) Clarendon Press, pp 204-246.

Chapter V

Barnett, H *Constitutional and Administrative Law* (1995) Cavendish.

Bradley, A W and Ewing, K D *Constitutional and Administrative Law* (12th edn, 1997) Longman.
Griffiths, J A G and Ryle, M *Parliament: Functions, Practice and Procedures* (1989) Sweet and Maxwell.
Joint Committee on Parliamentary Privilege Report (HL 50, HC 40, 1997-98).
Leopold, P M 'Parliamentary Free Speech, Court Orders and European Law' (1998) 4 Journal of Legislative Studies 58-69.
Limon, D and McKay, W (eds) *Erskine May: Parliamentary Practice* (22nd edn, 1997) Butterworths.
Sharland, A and Loveland, I 'The Defamation Act 1996 and Political Libels' [1997] PL 113.
Zellick, G 'Bribery of Members of Parliament and the Criminal Law' [1979] PL 31.

Chapter VI

Edwards, J *The Attorney General, Politics and the Public Interest* (1984) Sweet and Maxwell.
Edwards, J *The Law Officers of the Crown* (1964) Sweet and Maxwell.
Home Office *Rights brought home: the Human Rights Bill*, Cm 3782, October 1997.
House of Commons (Accommodation) Report of the Select Committee, HC 184, 1953-54, May 1954.
Limon, D and McKay, W (eds) *Erskine May: Parliamentary Practice* (22nd edn, 1997) Butterworths.
Lock, G F 'The application of the general law to Parliament' [1985] PL 376.
McGee, D 'Parliament and caucus' [1997] NZLJ 137.
Miers, D and Page, A *Legislation* (2nd edn, 1990) Sweet and Maxwell.
Redlich, J *The Procedure of the House of Commons* (1908) Archibald Constable.
Speed, Sir R 'Speaker's Counsel' (1982) LXIII Parliamentarian 15.
Williams, O C *The historical development of private bill procedure and standing orders in the House of Commons* (1948) HMSO.
Woodhouse, D 'The Attorney General' (1997) 50 Parliamentary Affairs 97.
Woodhouse, D 'The Parliamentary Commissioner for Standards: lessons from the "cash for questions" inquiry' (1998) 51 Parliamentary Affairs 51.

Chapter VII

Brazier, R 'It *is* a constitutional issue: fitness for ministerial office' [1994] PL 431-451.
Cabinet Office *Ministerial Code* (July 1997).
Committee of Privileges *First Report* (HC 118, 1946-47).
Committee on Standards and Privileges *First Special Report* (HC 34, 1996-97).
Committee on Standards and Privileges *Third Report: The Code of Conduct and the Guide to the Rules relating to the Conduct of MPs* (HC 604, 1995-96).
Committee on Standards in Public Life (the Nolan Committee) *First Report* (Cm 2850-I, 1995).

Government's Response to the First Report from the Committee on Standards in Public Life (Cm 2931, 1995).

Harrison, M *Trade Unions and the Labour Party since 1945* (1960) Allen and Unwin.

House of Commons *The Code of Conduct together with the Guide to the Rules Relating to the Conduct of Members* (HC 688, 1995-96).

Inquiry into the Export of Defence Equipment and Dual-Use Goods to Iraq and Related Prosecutions (HC 115, 1995-96) (The Scott Report).

Law Commission *Legislating the Criminal Law: Corruption* (Law Com no 248; HC 524, 1997-98).

Limon, D and McKay, W (eds) *Erskine May: Parliamentary Practice* (22nd edn, 1997) Butterworths.

Marshall, G 'Parliamentary Privilege' in M Ryle and P G Richards (eds) *The Commons Under Scrutiny* (1988) Fontana, pp 212-228.

Marshall, G 'Parliamentary Privilege' in S A Walkland (ed) *The House of Commons in the Twentieth Century* (1979) Oxford University Press, pp 204-246.

Muller, W D *The Kept Men? The First Century of Trade Union Representation in the British House of Commons, 1874-1975* (1977) Harvester.

Register of Members' Interests (October 1997 edn [New Parliament]; HC 291, 1997-98).

Ridley, F F and Doig, A (eds) '"Sleaze": Politics, Private Interests and Public Reaction' (1995) 48 Parliamentary Affairs 551-749 (special edition).

Rush, M 'The Professionalisation of the British Member of Parliament' *Papers in Political Science: 1* (1989) Department of Politics, University of Exeter.

Rush, M *The Selection of Parliamentary Candidates* (1969) Nelson.

Select Committee on Members' Interests *First Report* (HC 326, 1991-92).

Select Committee on Standards in Public Life *First Report* (HC 637, 1994-95).

Shaw, M 'Members of Parliament' in M Rush (ed) *Parliament and Pressure Politics* (1990) Oxford University Press, pp 92-107.

Top Salaries Review Body (TSRB) *Ministers of the Crown and Members of Parliament* (Cmnd 4836).

Woodhouse, D *Ministers and Parliament: Accountability in Theory and Practice* (1994) Oxford University Press.

Chapter VIII

Administrative Justice – Some Necessary Reforms Report of the Justice–All Souls Review of Administrative Law (1998) Clarendon Press.

Giddings, P (ed) *Parliamentary Accountability: A Study of Parliament and Executive Agencies* (1995) Macmillan, pp 139-152.

Giddings, P *The Ombudsman in Britain: a qualified success in government reform* (1982) 60 Public Admin 177-195.

Gregory, R and Drewry, G *Barlow Clowes and the Ombudsman* [1991] PL 192, 408.

Gregory, R, Giddings, P, Moore, V and Pearson, J *Practice and Prospects of the Ombudsman in the United Kingdom* (1995) Edwin Mellen Press.

Gregory, R and Hutchinson, P *The Parliamentary Ombudsman: A Study in the Control of Administrative Action* (1975) Allen and Unwin.

Gwyn, W B *The British PCA: Ombudsman or Ombudsmouse?* (1973) 35 Journal of Politics 45-69.

Lord Chancellor's Department *Access to Justice: Interim Report of the Lord Chancellor on the Civil Justice System in England and Wales* (June 1995).

Seniviratne, M *Ombudsmen in the Public Sector* (1994) Open University Press.

Stacey, F *The British Ombudsman* (1971) Clarendon Press.

White Paper *Open Government* (Cm 2290, 1993).

Chapter IX

Bates, T St J 'Judicial Applications of Pepper v. Hart' (1993) J Law Soc Scotland 251.

Bell, J and Engle, Sir G *Cross; Statutory Interpretation* (2nd edn, 1987) Butterworths chs 2 and 6.

Bennion, F A R *Statutory Interpretation* (2nd edn, 1992) Second Supplement (1995) at B.58.

Clifford, D J and Salter, J *How to Understand an Act of Parliament* (1996) Cavendish, ch 26.

Corry, J A 'The Use of Legislative History in the Interpretation of Statutes' (1954) 32 Can Bar Rev 624.

Eskridge, W N Jr 'The New Textualism' (1990) 37 UCLA LR 621.

Evans, J *Statutory Interpretation: Problems of Communication* (1989) Oxford University Press, ch 12.

Lyell, Sir N 'Pepper v. Hart: The Government Perspective' (1994) 15 Statute LR 1.

MacCormick, D N and Summers, R S *Interpreting Statutes: A Comparative Study* (1991) Dartmouth.

Mackay, Lord 'Finishers, Repairers and Polishers: The Judicial Rôle in the Interpretation of Statutes' (1989) 10 Statute LR 151.

Miers, D 'Taxing Perks and Interpreting Statutes: Pepper v. Hart' (1993) 56 MLR 695.

Oliver, D 'Pepper v. Hart: A suitable case for reference to Hansard' [1993] PL 5.

Sellar, D P 'The Relevance of Pepper v. Hart to Company Practitioners' (1993) SLT (News) 357.

Walker, N 'Discovering the Intention of Parliament' (1993) SLT (News) 121.

Chapter X

Barker, A and Rush, M *The Member of Parliament and his Information* (1970) Allen and Unwin.

Berrington, H B *Backbench Opinion in the House of Commons, 1945-55* (1973) Pergamon.

Blom-Cooper, L and Drewry, G *Final Appeal: A Study of the House of Lords in its Judicial Capacity* (1972) Oxford University Press.

Bromhead, P *The House of Lords and Contemporary Politics* (1958) Routledge and Kegan Paul.

Brooke, J 'The Members' in Sir L Namier and J Brooke (eds) *The History of Parliament: The House of Commons, 1754-1790* (1964) History of Parliament Trust and HMSO.

Duke Henry, B *The History of Parliament: The House of Commons, 1660-1690* (1983) History of Parliament Trust and HMSO.

Finer, S E, Berrington, H B and Bartholomew, D J *Backbench Opinion in the House of Commons, 1955-59* (1961) Pergamon.

Griffith, J A G *The Politics of the Judiciary* (5th edn, 1997) Fontana.

Judd, G P *Members of Parliament, 1734-1832* (1955) Yale University Press and Oxford University Press.

Judge, D *Backbench Specialisation in the House of Commons* (1981) Heinemann.

Mellors, C *The British MP, 1945-74* (1978) Saxon House.

Porritt, E *The Unreformed House of Commons: Parliamentary Representation Before 1832* (1909) Cambridge University Press, vol I.

Roskell, J S *The History of Parliament: The House of Commons, 1386-1421* (1992) History of Parliament Trust and HMSO.

Ross, J F S *Parliamentary Representation* (1948) Eyre and Spottiswoode.

Rush, M 'Career Patterns in British Politics: First Choose Your Party . . .' in F F Ridley and M Rush (eds) *British Government and Politics since 1945: Changes in Perspective* (1995) Oxford University Press, pp 68-84.

Rush, M 'The Members of Parliament' in S A Walkland *The House of Commons in the Twentieth Century* (1979) Oxford University Press.

Sedgewick, R *History of Parliament: The House of Commons, 1715-1754* (1970) History of Parliament Trust and HMSO, vol 1.

Thomas, J A *The House of Commons, 1832-1901: A Study of its Economic and Functional Character* (1939) University of Wales Press.

Thomas, J A *The House of Commons, 1906-1911: An Analysis of it Economic and Social Character* (1958) University of Wales Press.

Chapter XI

Blackburn, R *Towards a Constitutional Bill of Rights for the United Kingdom* (1998) Pinter.

Blackburn, R and Plant, Lord (eds)*Constitutional Reform Now* (1998) Longman, esp ch 1, Blackburn 'The House of Lords' and ch 18, Blackburn 'A Parliamentary Committee on Human Rights'.

Blackburn, R and Busuttil, J (eds) *Human Rights for the 21st Century* (1997) Pinter, esp ch 2, Blackburn 'A Bill of Rights for the 21st century' and ch 4, Lord Lester 'Taking Human Rights Seriously'.

Gordon, R and Wilmot-Smith, R (eds) *Human Righs in the United Kingdom* (1996) Oxford University Press, esp ch 4, J Wadham 'Why Incorporation is Not Enough'.

Institute for Public Policy Research *A British Bill of Rights* (revised edn, 1996) IPPR.

Institute for Public Policy Research *A Written Constitution for the United Kingdom* (revised edn, 1993) Mansell.

Kinley, D *The European Convention on Human Rights: Compliance without Incorporation* (1993) Dartmouth.

National Council for Civil Liberties *A People's Charter* (1991) Liberty.

National Council for Civil Liberties *Bill of Rights* (1995) Liberty.

Ryle, M 'Pre-legislative Scrutiny: A Prophylactic Approach to Protection of Human Rights' [1994] PL 192.

Chapter XII

Bogdanor, V *Devolution* (1979) Oxford University Press.

Calvert, H *Constitutional Law in Northern Ireland* (1968) Northern Ireland Legal Quarterly.

Constitution Unit *Scotland's Parliament* (1996).

Dicey, A V 'Two Acts of Union: A Contrast' (1881) 36 Fortnightly Review.

Hadfield, B 'Scotland's Parliament: A Northern Ireland perspective on the White Paper' [1997] PL 660.

Jones, T 'Scottish Devolution and demarcation disputes' [1997] PL 283-297.

Mitchell, J D B *Constitutional Law* (1968) Edinburgh University Press.

Newark, F 'The Constitution of Northern Ireland' in D G Neill *Devolution of Government* (1953) Northern Ireland Legal Quarterly.

Palley, C *The Evolution, Disintegration and Possible Reconstruction of the Northern Ireland Constitution* (1972) Barry Rose.

Quekett, Sir A *The Constitution of Northern Ireland* (1946) HMSO.

Rokkan, S and Urwin, D *Economy, Territory Identity, Politics of West European Peripheries* (1982) Sage.

Rokkan, S and Urwin, D *Strategies for Self-Government: The Campaigns for a Scottish Parliament* (1996) Sage.

Royal Commission on the Constitution 1969-1973 (the Kilbrandon Report) (Cmnd 5460, 1973).

Scottish Office *The Scotland Bill: A Guide* (December 1997).

White Paper on Scottish Devolution *Scotland's Parliament* (Cm 3658, 1997).

Appendix 1[1]

Registrable interests for members of the House of Commons (specific categories)

1. Remunerated directorships in public and private companies.
2. Remunerated employment, office, profession etc., including membership of Lloyd's. The annual amount of remuneration in respect of the provision of parliamentary services (e.g. as a parliamentary consultant or adviser) must be declared in bands of up to £1,000, between £1,000 and £5,000, and bands of £5,000 thereafter.
3. Clients for whom parliamentary services are provided.
4. Sponsorship or financial or material support to the Member (this relates particularly to trade union or Co-operative Party sponsorship of Labour MPs, but also to other relevant donations).
5. Gifts, benefits and hospitality in the UK, excluding gifts of less than £125 in value, or benefits of less than £215 in value.
6. Overseas visits by Members or their spouses not wholly borne by the Member or by UK public funds, but excluding visits organised by the Inter-Parliamentary Union, the Commonwealth Parliamentary Association, the Council of Europe, or the European Union.
7. Overseas benefits and gifts, subject to the same conditions as UK benefits and gifts.
8. Land and property of substantial value, other than the residences of the Member or Member's spouse.
9. Shareholdings greater than £25,000 in value or greater than 1 per cent of the issued share capital of the company or body, including holdings held by or on behalf of the Member's spouse or dependent children.

Source: Introduction, *Register of Members' Interests* (October 1997 edn) [New Parliament] (HC 291, 1997-98) pp iv-v.

---

1   See ch VII.

Appendix 2

The meaning of 'maladministration'

1. **The 'Crossman Catalogue':**

   'bias
   neglect
   inattention
   delay
   competence
   inaptitude
   perversity
   turpitude
   arbitrariness
   and so on'

   HC Deb, 734, 1966-67, 18 October 1966, cols 51-52.

2. **The 'Reid Catalogue':**

   'rudeness
   unwillingness to treat the complainant as a person with rights
   refusal to answer reasonable questions
   neglecting to inform a complaint on request of his/her rights or entitlement
   knowingly giving misleading or inadequate advice
   ignoring valid advice or overruling considerations which would produce an
       uncomfortable result for the overruler
   offering no redress or manifestly disproportionate redress
   showing bias re colour, sex, or any other grounds
   omitting to notify those who thereby lose a right of appeal
   refusing to inform adequately of right of appeal
   faulty procedures
   failure by management adequately to monitor compliance with procedures
   cavalier disregard of guidance which is intended to result in equitable treatment
       of service users
   partiality
   failure to mitigate the effects of rigid adherence to the letter of the law where that
       produces manifestly inequitable treatment'

   PCA, 1993 Annual Report (HC 112, 1993-94) para 7.

Index

2 5 5 3 9 7

10
10
19

9 7 5

100 8 9 1 9 7

7 8 1
8

65

635